P9-DXI-699

The Practice of Emotionally Focused Couple Therapy

BASIC PRINCIPLES INTO PRACTICE SERIES
Series Editor: Natalie H. Gilman

The *Brunner-Routledge Basic Principles into Practice Series* is designed to present—in a series of concisely written, easily understandable volumes—the basic theory and clinical principles associated with a variety of disciplines and types of therapy. These volumes will serve not only as "refreshers" for practicing therapists, but also as basic texts for the college and graduate level.

The Practice of Emotionally Focused Couple Therapy
Second Edition: Creating Connection
Susan M. Johnson, Ed.D.

Manual for Clinical Psychology Trainees, Third Edition
James P. Choca, Ph.D. and Eric J. Van Denburg, Ph.D.

Clinical Social Work: Definition, Practice, and Vision
Rachelle A. Dorfman, Ph.D.

The Spectrum of Child Abuse: Assessment, Treatment, and Prevention
Kim R. Oates, M.D.

Psychosomatic Disorders: Theoretical and Clinical Aspects
Ghazi Asaad, M.D.

Therapy with Stepfamilies
Emily B. Vishner, Ph.D. and John S. Vishner, M.D.

Psychotherapeutic Metaphors: A Guide to Theory and Practice
Philip Barker

Essentials of Hypnosis
Michael D. Yapko, Ph.D.

Understanding Mental Disorders Due to Medical Conditions or Substance Abuse: What Every Therapist Should Know
Ghazi Asaad, M.D.

Essentials of Psychoanalysis
Herbert S. Strean, D.S.W.

Family Therapy: Fundamentals of Theory and Practice
William A. Griffin, Ph.D.

The Practice of Emotionally Focused Couple Therapy

Second Edition

Creating Connection

Susan M. Johnson

Brunner-Routledge
Taylor & Francis Group

NEW YORK AND HOVE

Published in 2004 by
Brunner-Routledge
270 Madison Avenue
New York, NY 10016
www.brunner-routledge.com

Published in Great Britain by
Brunner-Routledge
27 Church Road
Hove
East Sussex BN3 2FA U.K.
www.brunner-routledge.co.uk

Copyright © 2004 by Taylor & Francis Books, Inc.
Brunner-Routledge is an imprint of the Taylor & Francis Group.

Cover design: Elise Weinger
Cover image: © Farida Zaman/CORBIS

Printed in the United States of America on acid-free paper.

All rights reserved. No part of this book may be reprinted or reproduced
or utilized in any form or by any electronic, mechanical, or other
means, now known or hereafter invented, including photocopying and
recording, or in any information storage or retrieval system, without
permission in writing from the publishers.

10 9 8 7 6

Library of Congress Cataloging-in-Publication Data

Johnson, Susan M.
   The practice of emotionally focused couple therapy : creating
   connection / Susan M. Johnson.—2nd ed.
      p.: cm.—(Basic principles into practice series)
   Includes bibliographical references and indexes.
   ISBN 0-415-94568-2 (pbk. : alk. paper)
   1. Marital psychotherapy.   2. Focused expressive psychotherapy.
3. Emotions.   I. Title.   II. Series.
   (DNLM: 1. Couples Therapy.   WM 430.5.M3 J69p 2004]

RC488.5.J59   2004
616.89' 1562—dc22   2004002316

Dedication

This book is dedicated, like the first edition, to my generous and loving partner, John Palmer Douglas— the love of my life.

CONTENTS

FOREWORD TO
THE SECOND EDITION

I told you so. Almost ten years ago, I wrote the foreword to the first edition of *The Practice of Emotionally Focused Couple Therapy*, and predicted that this book and the method of therapy it describes would lead the field of couple therapy back to a saner and more human view of treating troubled intimate relationships—and it has.

Not that this was such a brilliant prediction on my part, as all the signs pointed in that direction. Object relations approaches to couple therapy began to be resurrected and refined about a decade and a half ago, and rekindled an interest in the inner lives of intimate partners that had been sorely lacking for the first three decades in the history of family therapy (Gurman & Fraenkel, 2002). But object relations theory, as compelling and powerful as I personally find it to be in helping understand marital problems (Gurman, 2002), had never quite become mainstream in the MFT field, partly because of its unfortunate association with the earlier psychoanalytic thinking that the pioneers of family therapy so completely eschewed, and partly, maybe mostly, because of its cumbersome language and inaccessibility to most clinicians.

During roughly the same period that object relations therapy with couples was staging a comeback, behavioral approaches were in their heyday, and seemed to offer a genuinely teachable, researchable, and rational alternative. Unfortunately for these approaches, the data seemed to indicate that their effects were neither as likely nor as lasting as had been hoped. Researchers tried to explain what was missing from typical behavioral intervention with couples that seemed to put a ceiling on its helpfulness. Alas, while behavioral methods had seemed to be a rational alternative to the murky psychodynamic (pre–object relations) approaches of the preceding several decades of couple therapy, they were, in retrospect, perhaps a bit *too* rational. That is, observability of behavior and attention to cognitive processes were the dominant characteristics of these ways of working with couples, but affect took a backseat. Not that it had to. There was absolutely no reason—and there still is no reason, from a behavioral and social learning theory perspective—not to attend to affect, even highlight it, in couple therapy. As behavior therapists started to recognize the limitations of their methods for bringing about change in couple relationships, they gradually incorporated more "acceptance"-oriented interventions, most of which, in my view, were inching closer and closer to modern psychodynamic styles and, interestingly, to the style of EFT therapists—that is, of Sue Johnson and her colleagues. Behavior therapy with couples had confronted its affect phobia and been desensitized! But behavior therapy no longer merely did not fear affect; it actually embraced affect. Why? Because, as EFT theorists had been saying all along, it is emotion that organizes attachment bonds, and, after all, long-term, committed relationships are about attachment.

There is nothing more fundamental, undeniable, and human about intimate relationships than attachment bonding. Attachment is not some saccharine idea dreamed up by feel-good humanists, as I think some people believe. It is a scientifically substantiated basis for understanding human relatedness, with deep-lying roots in modern neuroscience as well as modern family psychology (Lewis, Amini & Lannon, 2000). Attachment theory allows an appreciation of the inevitable interaction between the inner and outer lives of people that is truly integrative and systemic. Not *systemic* as in the organizational principles of corporations, or the operation of complex technological devices and machines, but *systemic* as in truly humanly systemic. Corporations and machines may interact at different levels of organization, but they do not look forward to seeing each other, they do not miss each other when they are apart, and they do not mourn losing each other. As family therapist Fred Duhl so aptly put it more than twenty years ago, "It is hard to kiss a system."

This second edition of *The Practice of Emotionally Focused Couple Therapy*, in a way, then, is about how partners kiss—that is, how they connect and, when involved in distressing patterns, how they can be helped to reconnect. As good as the original edition was, this one is even better. Sue Johnson provides a much more substantial introduction to the ideas involved in attachment theory, giving the clinician a more grounded sense of why EFT interventions make sense. And there are more refined descriptions of EFT interventions, and their sequencing and pacing. Short of having a videotape, this edition shows about as much of a method of therapy as you can "see" via the printed word.

I will close with yet another prediction: *The Practice of Emotionally Focused Couple Therapy* will have a third edition. I hope I am invited back to write another foreword, so I can see how astute my first prediction was ten years ago!

Alan S. Gurman, Ph.D.
Professor of Psychiatry
University of Wisconsin Medical School

REFERENCES

Gurman, A. S. (2002). Brief integrative marital therapy: A depth-behavioral approach. In A. S. Gurman & N. S. Jacobson (Eds.), *Clinical handbook of couple therapy*, 3rd edition (pp. 180–220). New York: Guilford Press.

Gurman, A. S., & Fraenkel, P. (2002). The history of couple therapy: A millennial review. *Family Process, 41,* 199–260.

Lewis, T., Amini, F., & Lannon, R. (2000). *A general theory of love.* New York: Vintage Books.

FOREWORD FROM THE FIRST EDITION

As I sat down to write this foreword, words came with great difficulty. I asked myself why Susan Johnson had asked me to say anything in the first place. Then, at once, I flashed on an editorial I had written ten years earlier, when I was the editor of the *Journal of Marital and Family Therapy*. The title of that editorial was "A Time for Connections." With that in mind, I instantly knew why she had invited me. We were kindred clinicians, seeking to break down artificial and dangerous boundaries.

There are important boundaries that *The Practice of Emotionally Focused Couple Therapy: Creating Connection* successfully crosses. The first, and most obvious, boundary is whatever separates the members of a couple therapy emotionally. Now, focusing on closing this gap may not seem to constitute a particularly striking breakthrough for clinical practice, but look again. For most of the last two decades, what many of us have considered to be "advances" in couple therapy have involved such therapeutic maneuvers as exhorting mates to trade discrete desirable behaviors, instructing them to pretend to have certain interactional problems, and asking about overnight miracle changes as though doing so would bring about miracles overnight.

Lo and behold, we seem to have forgotten that people usually make long-term intimate commitments because they love each other, need each other, and find their connection to be the most important relationship they think they'll ever have with anyone. Is this mushy nonsense? No, it's real life. And it is in these real-life, real-time terms that Susan Johnson pushes us to work with couples in therapy. This partner–partner connection is ultimately what couple therapy is all about. Sure, some of the above-mentioned techniques can facilitate important changes in couple interaction, but do interactional changes necessarily lead to connection at the gut experiential level? No, not necessarily. Although focusing on the emotions involved in a couple's interactions may seem an obvious thing to do, it is not what many of us have been doing. So Dr. Johnson's clear demonstration of how to reintroduce emotion into the interactional field does, indeed, qualify as a clinical breakthrough.

In a related vein, she asks us to help relationship partners reconnect to themselves. Emotional Focused Therapy addresses the "split off," the anxiety-laden, the unacceptable within ourselves, without the usual psychojargon that so insidiously pathologizes perfectly normal and understandable human behavior. Many family and couple therapists have shown that inner experience can be shifted by behavioral and structural changes in family interactions. Dr. Johnson reminds us persuasively that patterns of interaction can likewise be changed by facilitating change in a couple's inner experience. Some methods of therapy are better at producing external change, but it is probably true that all effective therapies help produce change at multiple levels of human experience. Dr. Johnson reawakens our awareness to the fact that significant change in couple therapy can come about by individually focused, yet contextually sensitive clinical methods that, for too long, have been discounted and demeaned in the field of family and couple therapy.

If *The Practice of Emotionally Focused Couple Therapy: Creating Connection* reflects where the field of couple therapy is going, then perhaps it signals the return to the realm of psychotherapeutic sanity, in which people are dealt with not as cybernetic systems or containers of perverse strivings, but as people. If I am being too optimistic, and this is not where the field is currently headed, then perhaps *The Practice of Emotionally Focused Couple Therapy: Creating Connection* will help to lead us there.

Alan S. Gurman, Ph.D.
Professor of Psychiatry
University of Wisconsin Medical School

ACKNOWLEDGMENTS

First I must acknowledge, as I did in the first edition of this book, all the couples and families who honor me by including me in their struggle to build better relationships and stronger attachment bonds. Every one of them teaches me something new. Every one of them moves me and helps me learn about the hopes, fears, and strengths of my human family.

Second, I would like to thank my professional colleagues, fellow writers, fellow therapists at the Ottawa Couple & Family Institute, for all the incredible stimulation and comradeship that continues to make the field of adult love and couple and family therapy the most fascinating of all. So, we may soon send a man to Mars! This is a minor endeavor compared to finding the secrets of how to create, hold on to, and renew the strong, loving bonds we all depend on to grow, to stay sane, and to stay truly human. In particular, I have appreciated the work of groundbreaking colleagues such as adult attachment theorist Dr. Phil Shaver from Davis University, and marital researcher Dr. John Gottman from the University of Washington. My own School of Psychology colleagues such as Dr. Valerie Whiffen at the University of Ottawa also deserve acknowledgment, as do my wonderful fellow EFT therapists and authors at the Ottawa Couple & Family Institute.

But most important of all, I wish to thank my family and my students. My students for tackling the research projects that keep expanding the horizons of our work, and my family for all the love and support they offer me when I fly off to give yet another talk or pound away at the keyboard in my office. It is their love and support that give me the safe haven and secure base to continue on.

INTRODUCTION

This book is a revision and updating of the 1996 book titled *Emotionally Focused Marital Theory*. It is intended to serve as the basic therapeutic manual for *Emotionally Focused Couple Therapy (EFT)*. As in the first edition, there is also one chapter on Emotionally Focused Family Therapy (EFFT).

EFT has continued to grow and develop as a model of couple therapy. Outcome research has consistently validated the effectiveness of this model and its ability to create lasting change, even with high-risk populations. As in the 1996 edition, the theory of change, the process steps, and the interventions of EFT are described in detail, albeit with new clinical refinements included and improved descriptions.

In contrast to the 1996 book, the following sections have been added: EFT has been placed in the context of the revolution in couple therapy; adult attachment theory is growing astronomically and is described in more detail; a more extensive section has been added on emotion; empathy has also been described in more detail; attachment injuries and the method of working with them are also described; a second example has been added to the EFFT chapter; recent research on EFT–meta-analyses and process research is included; and lastly, a second session of EFT from a second case has been added at the end of the book. The essence of EFT, perhaps clarified in this second edition, remains the same. EFT focuses on the construction of the emotional experience and interpersonal drama of a distressed couple as this construction unfolds in the present moment. The EFT therapist helps the couple shape this construction into the form of a more secure attachment that nourishes and strengthens both partners.

For those who wish to read further about EFT, see the lists of books, recent chapters, and other material in the Additional Readings chapter at the end of the book. A therapist workbook designed to accompany this volume is in press. This workbook and the tapes and resources listed on the EFT Web site—**www.eft.ca**—will assist therapists who are in the process of learning this model.

1

THE FIELD OF COUPLE THERAPY AND EFT

A revolution is occurring in the field of couple therapy (Johnson, 2003). Many different kinds of insights and formal research studies are converging and creating the momentum for this revolution. Recent research that describes marital distress and satisfaction is congruent with research that outlines the impact of negative and positive relationships on people's health and functioning and with research on effective clinical interventions. All this research also ties in with studies on the nature of the bonds of adult love. At last, *many different kinds and levels of thinking and investigation are all pointing in the same direction and forming a cohesive picture.* Our understanding of the importance of close relationships and how they become distressed, our ability to specify effective interventions and outline the process of change, and our ability to explain the processes that define adult love have now reached a critical point where we can truly talk about couple therapy as an art and a science, based on description, prediction, and explanation. EFT has emerged from and contributed to this revolution, and, as a model, it continues to evolve and grow.

The beginning couple therapist no longer has to accept the idea that, to quote the songwriter Lynn Miles, "Love is a warm wind—you can't hold it in your hand" and that the process of the repair of love relationships is therefore a nebulous and random affair. There are now empirically validated patterns of marital distress and road maps of adult bonding to help the therapist journey with a distressed couple toward a more stable and satisfying relationship. This text offers the EFT clinical road map in a format updated from the 1996 first edition.

The goals of this new edition are to:

1. Offer the couple therapist a clear and well-researched conceptualization of adult love and bonding processes.
2. Outline the principles of EFT and the stages and steps in relationship repair and recovery.
3. Describe EFT interventions and key change events.
4. Elaborate on how EFT can be applied to different kinds of partners and couples as well as to families (EFFT).
5. Offer a road map to the resolution of common impasses in the process of relationship repair.

In the 21st century, therapists can be clearer about the nature of marital distress: that it is essentially about being flooded by negative emotions and trapped in narrow, constricting inter-actions (Gottman, 1994). They can find in the couple therapy literature clearly specified technologies for change, in the form of empirically validated treatment interventions (Snyder & Wills, 1989; Johnson, Hunsley, Greenberg & Schindler, 1999; Jacobson, Christensen, Prince, Cordova & Eldridge, 2000). They can read the vast and growing literature that now exists on the nature of adult love (Sternberg & Barnes, 1988; Hazan & Shaver, 1994; Feeney, 1999)—a phenomenon that, until recently, has been very much neglected in the couple therapy field (Roberts, 1992). In addition, new elaborations on impor-tant aspects of couple therapy, such as the role of emotion in the change process (Johnson & Greenberg, 1994; Johnson, 1998) and key interventions in change events (Bradley & Furrow, 2004; JMFT 30, pp. 233–246), are available.

Couple therapy as a discipline seems to be coming of age (Johnson & Lebow, 2000). Its application is also widening; it

is now used to address more and more "individual" symptomatology, such as depression, anxiety disorders, and
chronic illness (Johnson, 2002; Kowal, Johnson & Lee, 2003;
Dessaulles, Johnson & Denton, 2003). This makes sense in
light of recent research that links the quality of intimate relationships and social support to individual physical and psychological health, through mechanisms such as effective
immune system functioning and the amelioration of life
stress and trauma (Burman & Margolin, 1992; Kiecolt-Glaser
& Newton, 2001; Pennebaker, 1990; Whisman, 1999). A
strong loving relationship also potentiates individual growth
and self-actualization and is associated with a coherent
positive sense of self (Ruvolo & Jobson Brennen, 1997;
Mikulincer, 1995).

In fact, there is more and more evidence that the "nurtu-
rant solace" offered by close relationships protects us from
physical and emotional disease and improves resilience
(Taylor, 2002). This research offers both very general conclusions, such as that isolation is more dangerous for human
beings than smoking (House et al., 1988), and very specific
conclusions, such as that confiding in others has a positive
effect on the cardiovascular system, preventing specific adverse
effects of aging (Uchino, Cacioppo & Kiecolt-Glaser, 1996). This
research is also beginning to focus on the neurobiology of close
relationships and identify specific mechanisms, such as levels
of the so-called cuddle hormone oxytocin (Taylor et al., 2000),
that appear to protect us from disease.

Couple therapy is also becoming more and more recognized as a major mental health intervention, perhaps because
of the recognition of the negative impact of divorce on
couples, families (Cummings & Davis, 1994; Hetherington &
Kelley, 2002), and communities, or perhaps because, in North
American societies, other sources of community seem to be
rapidly dwindling (Putnam, 2000). The loss of "social capi-
tal" has been linked to the escalation in levels of depression
and anxiety in these societies (Twenge, 2000). Many of us
have no choice but to depend more and more on our intimate partners for support and connection. Many of us, in

fact, appear to now functionally live in a community of two. In this context, the quality of their closest relationship becomes increasingly significant in people's lives.

The general public is also becoming more and more aware of the value of using consultation and professional advice to help repair distressed couple and family relationships. Adult love is beginning to be seen as a process that can be understood, influenced, and repaired. A marriage partnership is more and more being framed as intentional (Doherty, 2001), rather than something that rests in the hands of romantic whim, chance, and fate. This book is then part of the movement toward a more delineated, scientific, and impactful set of interventions in the expanding field of couple therapy.

THE EMERGENCE AND GROWTH OF EFT

Emotionally Focused Couple Therapy (EFT) was formulated in the early 1980s (Johnson & Greenberg, 1985; Greenberg & Johnson, 1986) as a response to the lack of clearly delineated and validated couple interventions, particularly more humanistic and less behavioral interventions. It was called EFT to draw attention to the crucial significance of emotion and emotional communication in the organization of patterns of interaction and key defining experiences in close relationships. It also focused on emotion as a powerful and often necessary agent of change, rather than as simply part of the problem of marital distress. This focus on the need to address emotion and the power of emotion to create change in marital therapy was not part of the established literature on couple therapy at the time. In fact, the field of couple therapy could be seen then, and even now, as being almost affect phobic. Emotion has often been viewed overall as a secondary complication arising during the course of behavior and/or cognition, as a dangerous disruptive force in therapy, or as simply an inefficient agent of change. On some level, it was always clear to couple therapists that changes in affect were an essential part of relationship repair, but such changes were presumed to arise through cognitive and behavioral means.

In recent years, however, the compelling role of emotion in marital distress and couple therapy has become much more accepted (Gottman, 1994). The study of emotion has continued to advance (Plutchik, 2000; Tomkins, 1991; Lewis & Haviland-Jones, 2000). The key role of emotional regulation and engagement in marital happiness and distress (Johnson & Bradbury, 1999), and the emotional nature of human attachments (Bowlby, 1988, 1991; Johnson, 2003) has become more elaborated. Other approaches besides EFT have also begun to incorporate a focus on emotion (Cordova, Jacobson & Christensen, 1998; Gottman, 1999), although many others do not address this issue at all. In general, in the last decade, the necessity of addressing emotion in the process of relationship repair has been clarified, and specific methods and interventions to address it effectively have become more available.

As a model of intervention, EFT arose from systematic observation of couples in therapy and the process by which they succeeded in repairing their relationships. Recent models of marital distress, such as Gottman's model, also have a grounding in the observation and the coding of specific interactions between intimates, as do models of adult close relationships such as attachment theory. It is perhaps not surprising, then, that there is consonance among EFT as a model of intervention, researched descriptive models of distress, and relational theories such as attachment. Distressed couples taught Les Greenberg and me, the originators of EFT, how to describe the process of change outlined in EFT and the interventions that promoted this change process. The first EFT manual was written as part of the first outcome study, which compared EFT to untreated couples and couples who completed a behavioral communication and skills training intervention (Johnson & Greenberg, 1985). The results of EFT in this first study were impressive enough to spark another two decades of research on EFT.

At this point, there are eight studies in existence examining the impact of EFT on marital distress. The most rigorous of these were integrated into a meta-analysis. There are also two studies examining the impact of EFT on intimacy enhancement and on low sexual desire (Johnson, Hunsley, Greenberg & Schindler, 1999). In general, these studies were rigorous with adherence checks to ensure that therapists were, in fact, following the EFT protocol and checks on factors that can distort results, such as attrition rates. For the clinician, the most significant facts about the research on EFT are:

- The meta-analysis found that EFT demonstrates a very healthy and encouraging effect size. Couples included in this analysis showed a 70 to 73 percent recovery rate from marital distress in 10 to 12 sessions of therapy, and a 90 percent rate of significant improvement. This compares with a 35 percent recovery rate for couples receiving behavioral interventions (Jacobson et al., 1984). In terms of outcome, EFT compares favorably with other tested approaches (Johnson, 2003).

- In general, EFT does not seem to have a problem with relapse after treatment termination. This has been identified as a major problem in the behavioral interventions (Jacobson & Addis, 1993). In perhaps the most at-risk population included in an EFT study, namely the parents of chronically ill children, results were stable after two years (Clothier, Manion, Gordon-Walker & Johnson, 2002).

- There is preliminary evidence that the alliance with the therapist is important in predicting the outcome of EFT, and the female partner's faith in her partner's caring is also very predictive. Initial distress level, usually the most important predictor of outcome in psychotherapy, was not found to be very powerful in predicting couples' levels of satisfaction four months after the end of therapy. Engagement in the tasks of therapy seems to be more linked to outcome than initial distress level. EFT also seems to be effective with traditional couples and

with men who have trouble with withdrawal and difficulty in expressing emotion (Johnson & Talitman, 1997).

• There is considerable research on the process of change
in EFT. The question of how change occurs is particularly important to the practitioner. Key change events
have been studied in EFT and key interventions identified (Bradley & Furrow, 2004; Johnson, 2003). New
tasks and processes, such as the resolution of attachment injuries by a process of forgiveness and reconciliation, have been identified and are being studied
(Johnson, Makinen & Millikin, 2001).

Research on the nature of marital distress (Gottman, 1994)
and adult attachment (Cassidy & Shaver, 1999; Johnson &
Whiffen, 2003) also strongly validates the focus of the EFT
therapy process and the targets of intervention.

There are then more and more answers to the four key
questions for any intervention, namely: does it work; does it
work relative to other approaches; how does it work, that is,
what has to happen in therapy sessions for change to occur;
and, lastly, what precisely does the therapist have to do to
create change?

At the same time as new research into the effects of EFT
interventions was being conducted, the theoretical conceptualization underlying EFT was also expanding and becoming more research based. EFT always focused on the relationship between partners in terms of an emotional bond,
rather than a bargain to be renegotiated. It always focused on
emotional engagement and corrective experience rather than
teaching skill-building sequences or creating insight. However, the relevance of attachment theory (Bowlby, 1969, 1988)
has become more and more apparent, and has dovetailed
with the continuing delineation of EFT interventions and
change process (Johnson, 2003b). Social psychologists have
continued to contribute to the study of adult love, and attachment theory is now clearly the most promising perspective
on adult love relationships (Hazan & Shaver, 1987; Hazan &
Zeifman, 1999; Feeney, 1999). In general, attachment theory

is recognized as "one of the broadest, most profound and most creative lines of research in 20th century psychology" (Cassidy & Shaver, 1999, p. x). Adult attachment theory has grown exponentially and has become a more and more vital part of EFT, offering the therapist a map to the terrain of adult love relationships.

At this point, EFT is the most empirically validated approach to couple therapy, apart from the behavioral approaches, and has 20 years of outcome and process research to draw on. The purpose of this book is to teach clinicians how to implement EFT in as systematic a way as possible, given the uniqueness of every couple and every relationship, and the intricacies of the therapy process.

The strengths of EFT can be summarized as follows:

- Its assumptions, strategies, and interventions are clearly specified and delineated. It is brief, being usually implemented in 8 to 20 sessions; replicable; and has been used to train numerous practicing couple therapists.

- There is substantial empirical support for its effectiveness with general and specific populations, for example, with parents of chronically ill children (Walker et al., 1994), and it is associated with large treatment effects (Johnson, Hunsley, Greenberg & Schindler, 1995). It has also given rise to research on the process of change and the delineation of key change events and client variables associated with treatment success, which allows therapists to begin to match clients to treatment and tailor treatment to particular clients.

- The process of the couple's journey through therapy is clearly outlined in three stages and nine steps.

- This approach is grounded in a clear theoretical base. This base consists of first a theory of change, which arises from a synthesis of humanistic experiential therapy and systems theory, and second a theory of adult love, which is viewed as an attachment process. Both adult attachment theory and experiential interventions have a substantial and growing research base (Cassidy & Shaver, 1999; Elliot, 2002).

- EFT is applicable to many different kinds of clients. It is used for a wide variety of couples and partners, including partners from different cultures and social classes (Denton, Burleson, Clarke, Rodriguez & Hobbs, 2000), gay couples (Josephson, 2003), older couples (Bradley & Palmer, 2003), and couples suffering from chronic illness (Kowal, Johnson & Lee, 2003) or from depression and anxiety disorders such as post-traumatic stress disorder (Johnson, 2002). There is preliminary evidence that EFT reduces depression in partners (Dessaulles, Johnson & Denton, 2003), and a study on EFT with traumatized anxious partners and their spouses is under way.

- EFT interventions are extremely congruent with recent empirical studies on the nature of marital distress, which focus on rigid interactional patterns and compelling negative affect, and studies on the nature of adult attachment.

THE EFT APPROACH

What Is EFT and How Does It Differ From Other Approaches?

EFT is integrative; it looks within and between. It integrates an *intrapsychic* focus on how individuals process their experience, particularly their key attachment-oriented emotional responses, with an *interpersonal* focus on how partners organize their interactions into patterns and cycles. It considers how systemic pattern and inner experience and sense of self evoke and create each other.

The process of experiencing and the process of interaction are touchstones for the therapist as he or she attempts to guide the distressed couple away from negative and rigidly structured internal and external responses, toward the flexibility and sensitive responsiveness that are the bases of a secure bond between intimates. The interactional positions adopted by the partners are assumed to be maintained by both the individual emotional experience of the partners and the way interactions are organized—that is, by intrapsychic realities and the couple's habitual moves in their interactional dance. These realities and moves are reciprocally determining and constantly recreate one another. Both have to be reprocessed and reorganized if the couple is to attain a positive emotional bond. The creation of such a secure bond is the ultimate goal of EFT.

EFT expands experience and interactions. The first goal of therapy is to access and reprocess the emotional responses underlying each partner's often narrow and rigidly held inter-actional position, thereby facilitating a shift in these positions toward accessibility and responsiveness, the building blocks of secure bonds. The second goal of therapy is to create new interactional events that redefine the relationship as a source of security and comfort for each of the partners. The reprocessing of inner experience is used to expand the interpersonal context (such as when a partner discovers that his wife is desperate rather than malicious). In turn, the structuring of new interactional events expands and redefines each partner's inner experience (as when a spouse expresses his need for his wife, and she then experiences her own fear of responding, rather than staying focused on his unavailability).

When EFT is successfully implemented, each partner becomes a source of security, protection, and contact comfort for the other. Each partner can then assist the other in regulating negative affect and constructing a positive and potent sense of self. The EFT therapist choreographs bonding events in the session, which then powerfully redefine the relationship.

This process is a journey:

- From alienation, to emotional engagement.
- From vigilant defense and self-protection, to openness and risk taking.

- From a passive helplessness in the face of the inex-
  orable dance of the relationship, to a sense of being able
  to actively create that dance.
- From desperate blaming of the other, to a sense of how
  each partner makes it difficult for the other to be
  responsive and caring.
- From a focus on the other's flaws, to the discovery of
  one's own fears and longings.
- But most of all, from isolation to connectedness. This
  is not an easy journey for most couples, even with guid-
  ance of a seasoned therapist.

As the EFT therapist helps each person expand and
reorganize his or her inner experience, the expression of
this experience then involves a new presentation of self, a
new way of relating to the partner, which in turn evokes
new responses from this partner. Stated slightly differently,
new experience creates a new kind of dialogue, and this
new dialogue creates new interactional events. These events
then constitute new steps and initiate new patterns in the
couple's dance.

HOW IS EFT DIFFERENT FROM OTHER APPROACHES?

Role of the Therapist

The EFT therapist is not a coach teaching communication
skills or more effective ways to negotiate with each other. The
EFT therapist is not a wise creator of insight into the past and
how patterns from one's family of origin might influence the
marriage. The therapist is not a strategist employing paradox
and problem prescription. He or she is not primarily a teacher,
who focuses on helping couples modify irrational expectations and beliefs about marriage and relationships.
   The EFT therapist is rather a *process consultant*, helping
partners reprocess their experience, particularly their emotional experience of the relationship, and a *choreographer*,

helping couples to restructure their relationship dance. In therapy sessions, the therapist is a *collaborator* who must sometimes follow and sometimes lead, rather than an expert who tells the partners how their relationship should be. The therapy process presents the couple with opportunities to experiment with new ways to be together, so that they can make conscious choices about the kind of relationship they wish to create.

A Primary Focus on the Present

The EFT therapist focuses on the here-and-now responses of the partners, tracking and expanding both internal experiences and interactional moves and countermoves. Change occurs in the session as the couple experiences themselves differently and interact in a new way. Attention is paid to family-of-origin issues only as they are played out in present sensitivities and the here and now of the interaction, in contrast to object relations or analytic approaches to couple therapy, or systemic Bowenian approaches that focus on techniques such as constructing genograms. There is also less use of future-oriented interventions such as the assigning of future tasks and homework, which are key interventions in the behavioral tradition.

Treatment Goals—Secure Bonding

The goal of EFT is to reprocess experience and reorganize interactions to create a secure bond between the partners, a sense of secure connectedness. The focus here is always on attachment concerns; on safety, trust, and contact; and on the obstacles to the above. There is then no attempt to teach a distressed couple communication skills per se, since from the EFT perspective it is unlikely that couples will use such skills when they are most relevant, that is, when each becomes distressed and vulnerable. Since partners' problems are not generally viewed as resulting from personality flaws, there is little emphasis on insight into unconscious intrapsychic conflicts. Indeed, insight is considered insufficient to create lasting change in emotionally charged interactional patterns. Also, since the relationship is considered primarily as a bond rather than a rational bargain, there is no attempt to help the couple renegotiate new deals, or resolve pragmatic issues by drawing up new agreements or contracts. Once a couple has created a more secure bond, we find that the partners can then use the negotiation skills they have; issues become clearer and less onerous when they are not infused with attachment conflicts and insecurities.

An Emotional Focus

The essence of any short-term therapy is focus. In EFT, emotion is seen as the prime player in the drama of relationship distress and in changing that distress. It is emotion that organizes attachment behaviors, that orients and motivates us to respond to others and communicates our needs and longings to them. In EFT emotion, rather than being minimized or controlled, or simply labeled, is developed and differentiated. We often describe this as *unfolding* a client's emotional reality. Emotional experiences and expression are viewed as targets and agents of change to a much greater extent than in other nonexperiential models of therapy. The expansion and articulation of new or marginalized aspects of emotional experience are primary therapeutic tasks here, and a new corrective emotional experience of engagement with one's partner is the essence of change in EFT. *Unfolding key emotions and using them to prime new responses to one's partner in therapeutic enactments is the heart of change in EFT.*

Taking People as They Are

Distressed partners are not seen as primarily deficient, developmentally delayed, or unskilled. Other authors have also suggested that a general view of relationship problems as necessarily reflecting some form of significant developmental delay is most often inappropriate (Gurman, 1992). Partners' needs, desires, and primary emotional responses are seen here as generally healthy and adaptive. *It is how these needs and desires are enacted in a context of vulnerability and perceived danger that creates problems.* As Freud noted, "We are never so defenseless against suffering as when we love." It is how emotional responses, such as fear, are inhibited, disowned, and distorted that leads to dysfunction. The therapist validates partners' experience and responses, rather than teaching them to be different.

People are seen then as being stuck in particular absorbing emotional states and in self-reinforcing interaction cycles, rather than being generally deficient. Partners are stuck in certain ways of processing, organizing, and regulating emotional experience. They are also stuck in set ways of relating to each other. It is assumed that, given their experience, individuals have coherent and valid reasons for constricting emotional processing and interactions with the spouse. It is the therapist's task to grasp the "hidden rationality" (Wile, 1981) behind seemingly destructive or irrational responses.

WHERE DOES THE EFT THEORY OF CHANGE COME FROM?

EFT is a reflection of the kind of conversation that the experiential therapist Carl Rogers (1951) and structural systems therapists, such as Minuchin or others (Minuchin & Fisch, 1982; Fisch, Weakland & Segal, 1982), might have had if they had discussed a case of relationship distress over tea. Emotion can be viewed as experiential in nature or as a systemic variable (Johnson, 1998) in that emotion, when expressed, pulls for specific responses from others. Emotion is the music of the couple's dance and so organizes key interactions. EFT shares commonalities with traditional humanistic approaches (Johnson & Boisvert, 2002; Cain & Seeman, 2002), which all focus on an empathic understanding of a client's immediate experience, particularly his or her emotions and frame of reference.

EFT is experiential in that it focuses upon:

- The process of how people actively process and construct their experience in interactions with their environment, in the present.

- The power of the therapist's empathy and validation in creating the most positive context for exploration and the creation of new experience. The safety provided by the therapist's acceptance and authenticity allows each client's innate self-healing tendencies to flourish. The therapeutic alliance is egalitarian and collaborative.

- The great capacity that human beings have for growth and the positive adaptiveness of emotional responses and needs. Both Carl Rogers and John Bowlby (1969), the originator of the attachment view of relatedness used in EFT, tended to depathologize clients. Bowlby believed that all ways of responding to the world can be adaptive; it is, as Rogers also suggested, only when those ways become rigid and cannot evolve in response to new contexts that problems arise. In a helping relationship, "one first has to make sure one finds where the other is and starts there" (Kierkegaard, 1948). Rogers believed that therapists had to explicate and validate the client's initial construction of experience and relational stance.

- How inner and outer realities define each other. Emotions are privileged precisely because they orient people to their world and tell people what they need and fear.

- How emotions communicate to others in a way that pulls for emotional responses that are key in relationship definition. Emotions link self and system, dancer and dance. EFT therapists and attachment theorists focus on how identity processes and interactional patterns form crucial feedback loops (Mikulincer, 1995).

- The fostering and heightening of new corrective emotional experiences in the here and now of the therapy session. Experiential therapists see such experience as the main source of significant and lasting change.

EFT is systemic in that it focuses upon:

- The power of context. Each partner's behavior is seen in the context of, and as a response to, the other's behavior. Each partner is seen in some sense creating the responses of the other, often without any awareness of how this occurs. In a typical distressed relationship, then, withdrawal and unresponsiveness pull for criticism and excessive demands, and vice versa.
- The structure and process of interaction, that is, of how interactions are organized and patterns maintained. Degrees of closeness–distance and dominance–submission are monitored and made explicit.
- The rigid negative interactional cycles distressed couples generate are seen as self-maintaining and as a primary factor in the deterioration of the relationship.
- There is a focus on circular rather than linear causality. This lends itself to a focus on pattern and sequence, and on how elements in an interactional pattern reciprocally determine each other, as in, "I withdraw because you nag, and you nag because I withdraw."

EFT synthesizes experiential and systemic approaches, combining the intrapersonal and the interpersonal. The EFT therapist helps partners to reprocess their emotional experience and uses emotional expression to create a shift in their interactional positions. The EFT therapist also directs and choreographs new interactions, which evoke new emotional responses in the partners. As previously stated, new emotional experience impacts how the couple dances together, and a new dance impacts how each partner's emotional experience is organized. The word *emotion* comes from the Latin word meaning "to move." New constructions of emotion help partners move into new stances in their relationship dance, stances that promote secure bonding.

WHAT DOES EFT LOOK LIKE?

EFT is designed to be implemented in 8 to 20 sessions of couple therapy. A positive therapeutic alliance with both partners is considered to be a prerequisite of successful treatment. In the format presented here, it is not designed to be used with violent couples or separating couples. It is most successful with couples who wish to restructure their relationship in terms of a close bond, but have become alienated by negative interaction cycles, often of a blame–withdraw nature. It can be used in a variety of populations apart from maritally distressed couples. For example, it has been routinely used in a hospital clinic in a large urban center, where couples generally have multiple problems, including the symptoms of post-traumatic stress disorder and clinical depression. In a shortened form, it has also been used with nonclinical couples who were experiencing a lack of intimacy and with couples where one partner has suffered a recent stressor, such as a life-threatening illness, which requires a change in the couple's relationship. It has been routinely used with gay couples and those who struggle with chronic and debilitating illness (Kowal, Johnson & Lee, 2003). An observer in an EFT session would see the therapist tracking and reflecting emotional moments and interactional moves. The therapist helps partners crystallize their emotional experience and sets interactional processes in motion with specific tasks (for instance, Can you tell him . . . ?). The therapist moves between helping the client unfold emotional experience and enact new responses.

The couple's change process has been delineated into three stages and nine steps, which are as follows.

Stage 1. The De-escalation of Negative Cycles of Interaction

Step 1. Creating an alliance and delineating conflict issues in the core attachment struggle.

Step 2. Identifying the negative interactional cycle where these issues are expressed.

Step 3. Accessing the unacknowledged emotions underlying interactional positions.

Step 4. Reframing the problem in terms of the negative cycle, underlying emotions, and attachment needs. The cycle is framed as the common enemy and the source of the partners' emotional deprivation and distress.

Stage 2. Changing Interactional Positions

Step 5. Promoting identification with disowned attachment emotions, needs, and aspects of self and integrating these into relationship interactions.

Step 6. Promoting acceptance of the partner's experience and new interactional responses.

Step 7. Facilitating the expression of needs and wants and creating emotional engagement and bonding events that redefine the attachment between partners.

Stage 3. Consolidation and Integration

Step 8. Facilitating the emergence of new solutions to old relationship problems.

Step 9. Consolidating new positions and new cycles of attachment behaviors.

THE PROCESS OF CHANGE

Three major shifts are discernible in the process of change in EFT described above. These are:

- Negative cycle de-escalation at the end of first stage of therapy.
- Withdrawer engagement in Stage Two of Therapy.
- Blamer softening in Stage Two of Therapy.

The first shift, cycle de-escalation, is a first-order change, in that the way interactions are organized remains the same, but the elements of the cycle are modified somewhat. So, for example, withdrawn partners begin to risk more engagement and hostile partners are less reactive and angry. The couple may begin to initiate some close contact such as lovemaking, seem to find their engagement in therapy reassuring, and begin to be hopeful for their relationship.

The other two shifts referred to above represent second-order change, in that they constitute a change in the structure of the relationship.

The second shift occurs when the more withdrawn partner begins to become more active and engaged in the relationship. This shift involves a change in interactional position, in terms of control and accessibility for contact. The withdrawn partner asserts his or her needs and wants, rather than stonewalling or avoiding the spouse, becoming more and more emotionally engaged with the other in the therapy sessions.

A third shift occurs when the previously hostile and more active spouse risks expressing his or her own attachment needs and vulnerabilities, allowing for interactions that challenge the trust level in the relationship. In the interests of clarity, these events are presented as separate and independent. In practice they are, of course, interwoven and reciprocally determining. As a critical spouse becomes less angry, the less engaged partner risks more involvement; as this involvement increases, the critical spouse allows him- or herself to disclose needs and desires more openly. This then makes it easier for the less engaged partner to be responsive. Once these change events have reorganized the couple's interactions, prototypical bonding events, where both partners are accessible and responsive to each other, can take place. Spouses can then be open with each other about their needs and fears and renew their sense of the bond between them.

These three shifts are illustrated here.

A TYPICAL CHANGE PROCESS: SNAPSHOTS

A couple enters therapy with the female partner complaining of lack of intimacy and her partner's absence from the relationship. He complains of her aggression and unreasonableness, from which he withdraws. He believes the solution is to make love more often. She believes the solution is for her spouse to talk to her more. The therapist creates an alliance, assesses their relationship (see chapter 5), and describes their pattern of pursue–blame and withdraw–placate to them, portraying them as creators and victims of the cycle. The highlights of the change process, if caught in snapshots, might then be as follows.

Cycle De-escalation

1. **Gail (pursuing wife):** I am so angry. I have been so let down here. I've never felt so lonely. I want to show him that he can't do this to me.

2. **Ben (withdrawing husband):** No matter what I do, I get the message it's disappointing. I don't speak the language and I don't know how to learn. I know I run away. I hide. I don't know what else to do.

3. **Gail:** I know I push him away with my harping, but I get so panicked (to him) I can't find you . . .

4. **Ben:** I guess I developed the art of hiding. I never really thought that you were looking for me. I think we have got stuck here—I don't know what to do, so I hide and you feel more and more lonely, so you up the ante and get mad. We both get hurt, don't we?

These statements include an awareness of the cycle, an owning of the person's part in the cycle, and a move to articulating underlying feelings, rather than blaming and avoiding. At this point, partners typically make comments like "I'm finding out who you are in these sessions" and "I get how this dance has taken over our relationship and how we both end up hurting."

Withdrawer Engagement

> **Ben:** I'm never going to be the life and soul of the party. I don't want the pressure of that. I need a little recognition when I do take risks with you, for God's sake. If you're going to keep writing report cards, then I'm going to play truant. And I don't want sex all the time. I do want to be held sometimes, and I don't want to feel so careful and timid about asking for it. I need your help here.

In this kind of statement, Ben moves from self-protective distance to active assertive engagement. He talks of his attachment needs and his sense of self in relation to his wife. He is more accessible and engaged.

Blamer Softening

1. **Gail:** I'm not sure this is going to work. I'm afraid. I'll start to count on you and then you'll turn your back. It's been so long since I really felt safe with you.
2. **Gail:** I so desperately want you to tell me that I come first with you. I have to know that I'm important, that you need to be close like I need to be close to you. That I am precious to you, I need to know.

Here this partner reveals her vulnerability and places herself in the other's hands. When he then is able to respond in an engaged and soothing way, a healing, bonding event takes place that begins a new cycle of closeness and affirmation.

The purpose of this chapter has been to give the reader a sense of EFT and to place it in the context of the couple therapy field. Let us now turn to the philosophy behind EFT, starting with the EFT perspective on intimate relationships and continuing with the philosophy of therapeutic change.

2

AN ATTACHMENT VIEW OF LOVE: THE EFT PHILOSOPHY

"Hold me tight—Never let me go."

Every therapist who observes the problems his or her clients bring to therapy has to answer three basic questions. The responses to these questions provide a framework for understanding the multidimensional phenomena he or she is observing, and will determine the therapist's focus and treatment strategies. The three questions are:

1. What is happening here? What is the problem? What is the target of intervention?
2. What should be happening here? What is healthy functioning? What is the goal of treatment?
3. What must the couple do to change the problem and move toward a healthier relationship? How can the therapist foster this change?

A therapist needs a theory of healthy functioning, including a formulation of how problems occur and disrupt such functioning and a theory of therapeutic change. In couple therapy, *the relationship is the client*. A therapist, therefore, needs a theory of adult intimacy, an understanding of the nature of adult love. This is the topic of this chapter.

THE EFT PERSPECTIVE ON ADULT LOVE

If we ask our clients what is the basis of a happy long-term relationship, they inevitably answer with one word, *love.* However, in the field of professional couple and family therapy, love has been conspicuous by its absence. It has been a forgotten variable (Roberts, 1992). Couple and family therapy has generally focused on issues of power, control, autonomy, and the mediation of conflict, to the exclusion of nurturance and love (Mackay, 1996). The recent application of attachment theory to adult relationships is a revolutionary event for couple therapy, because, for the first time, it provides the couple therapist a coherent, relevant, well-researched framework for understanding and intervening in adult love (Johnson, 2003b). This is part of a larger revolution in which science is, at last, beginning to address the "core mysteries of human relationships" (Berscheid, 1999, p. 206).

There is nothing so practical as a good theory. Such a theory directs the therapist to the defining features of the complex multidimensional drama that is a distressed close relationship. Such a theory also gives the therapist a language to capture and legitimize each client's experience. Once the defining features of a relational landscape have been set out, it is easier to map and move through; it is then easier to reach distant destinations. A theory of love not only helps the therapist understand what is wrong in a distressed dyad, but also sets out relevant and meaningful treatment goals and the steps on the road to achieving them. A good theory makes sure that interventions are "on target"; that they go to the heart of the matter.

What are the basic tenets of attachment theory, as first articulated by John Bowlby (1969, 1988), then developed and applied to adults by social psychologists such as Shaver

(Shaver & Mikulincer, 2002) and by a growing number of couple and family therapists (Johnson & Whiffen, 2003)?

The Tenets of Attachment Theory

The 10 central tenets of attachment theory are:

1. Attachment is an innate motivating force. Seeking and maintaining contact with significant others is an innate, primary motivating principle in human beings across the life span. Dependency, which has been pathologized in our culture, is an innate part of being human rather than a childhood trait that we outgrow. Attachment and the emotions associated with it are the core defining feature of close relationships; it is the "heart of the matter" for the couple therapist. This theoretical perspective can claim considerable cross-cultural validity (van Ijzendoorn & Sagi, 1999). It also draws links to the evolution of humans as social animals and offers a universal perspective. It reminds us that when the wind blows, it stings the eyes of all. The fear of isolation and loss is found in every human heart.

2. Secure dependence complements autonomy. According to attachment theory, there is no such thing as complete independence from others or overdependency (Bretherton & Munholland, 1999). There is only effective or ineffective dependency. Secure dependence fosters autonomy and self-confidence. Secure dependence and autonomy are then two sides of the same coin, rather than dichotomies. Research tells us that secure attachment is associated with a more coherent, articulated, and positive sense of self (Mikulincer, 1995). The more securely connected we are, the more separate and different we can be. Health in this model means maintaining a felt sense of interdependency, rather than being self-sufficient and separate from others.

3. Attachment offers an essential safe haven. Contact with attachment figures is an innate survival mechanism. The presence of an attachment figure, which usually means parents, children, spouses, and lovers, provides comfort and security, while the perceived inaccessibility of such figures creates distress. Proximity to a loved one tranquilizes the nervous system (Schore, 1994). *It is the natural antidote to the inevitable anxieties and vulnerabilities of life.* For people of all ages, positive attachments create a *safe haven* that offers a buffer against the effects of stress and uncertainty (Mikulincer, Florian & Weller, 1993) and an optimal context for the continuing development of the personality.

4. Attachment offers a secure base. Secure attachment also provides a *secure base* from which individuals can explore their universe and most adaptively respond to their environment. The presence of such a base encourages exploration and a cognitive openness to new information (Mikulincer, 1997). It promotes the confidence necessary to risk, learn, and continually update models of self, others, and the world so that adjustment to new contexts is facilitated. Secure attachment strengthens the ability to stand back and reflect on oneself, one's behavior, and one's mental states (Fonagy & Target, 1997). When relationships offer a sense of felt security, individuals are better able to reach out to and provide support for others and deal with conflict and stress positively. These relationships tend then to be happier, more stable, and more satisfying. The need for a secure emotional connection with a partner, a connection that offers a safe haven and a secure base, is the central theme of couple distress and the process of effective relationship repair.

5. Emotional accessibility and responsiveness build bonds. In general, emotion activates and organizes attachment behaviors. More specifically, the building blocks of secure bonds are emotional accessibility and responsiveness. An attachment figure can be physically present but emotionally absent. Separation distress results from the appraisal that an attachment figure is inaccessible. It is emotional engagement that is crucial and the trust that this engagement will be there when needed. In attachment terms, any response (even anger) is better than none. If there is no engagement, no emotional responsiveness, the message from the attachment figure reads as "Your signals do not matter, and there is no connection between us." Emotion is central to attachment, and this theory provides a guide for understanding and normalizing many of the extreme emotions that accompany distressed relationships. Attachment relationships are where our strongest emotions arise and where they seem to have most impact. Emotions tell us and communicate to others what our motivations and needs are; they are the music of the attachment dance (Johnson, 1996). As Bowlby has suggested, "the psychology and psychopathology of emotion is . . . in large part the psychology and psychopathology of affectional bonds" (1979, p. 130).

6. Fear and uncertainty activate attachment needs. When the individual is threatened, either by traumatic events, the negative aspects of everyday life such as stress or illness, or by any assault on the security of the attachment bond itself, powerful affect arises and attachment needs for comfort and connection become particularly salient and compelling. Attachment behaviors, such as proximity seeking, are then activated. A sense of connection with a loved one is a primary inbuilt emotional regulation device. Attachment to key others is our *"primary protection against feelings of helplessness and meaninglessness"* (McFarlane & Van der Kolk, 1996). This theory helps the couple therapist understand how a particular event, such as a flirtation at a party or a short period of distance at a time of need, can threaten a relationship and begin a downward spiral of distress.

7. The process of separation distress is predictable. If attachment behaviors fail to evoke comforting responsiveness and contact from attachment figures, a prototypical process of angry protest, clinging, depression, and despair occurs, culminating eventually in detachment. Depression is a natural response to loss of connection. Bowlby viewed anger in close relationships as often being an attempt to make contact with an inaccessible attachment figure and distinguished between the anger of hope and the anger of despair, which becomes desperate and coercive. *In secure relationships, protest at inaccessibility is recognized and accepted.* An emotionally focused therapist sees the basic dramas of distress,

such as demand–withdraw, as variations on the theme of
separation distress.

**8. A finite number of insecure forms of engagement can be
identified.** The number of ways that human beings have to
deal with the unresponsiveness of attachment figures is limited. There are only so many ways of coping with a negative
response to the question "Can I depend on you when I need
you?" Attachment responses seem to be organized along two
dimensions, anxiety and avoidance (Fraley & Waller, 1998).

When the connection with an irreplaceable other is threatened but not yet severed, the attachment system may become
hyperactivated or go into overdrive. Attachment behaviors
become heightened and intense as anxious clinging, pursuit,
and even aggressive attempts to control and obtain a response
from the loved one escalate. From this perspective, most criticism, blaming, and emotionally loaded demands in distressed relationships are attempts to deal with and resolve
attachment hurts and fears.

The second strategy for dealing with the lack of safe emotional engagement, especially when hope for responsiveness
is tenuous, is to attempt to deactivate the attachment system
and suppress attachment needs. The most commonly
observed ways of doing this are to focus obsessively on tasks,
and limit or avoid distressing attempts at emotional engagement with attachment figures. These two basic strategies—
anxious preoccupied clinging and detached avoidance—can
develop into habitual styles of engagement with intimate
others. Angry criticism, viewed through the attachment lens,
is most often an attempt to modify the other partner's inaccessibility, and as a protest response to isolation and perceived abandonment by the partner. Avoidant withdrawal
may be seen as an attempt to contain the interaction and
regulate fears of rejection and confirmation of fears about the
unlovable nature of the self. A third insecure strategy has
been identified that is essentially a combination of seeking
closeness and then fearful avoidance of closeness when it is
offered. This strategy is usually referred to as disorganized in
the child literature and fearful avoidant in the adult literature

(Bartholomew & Horowitz, 1991). This strategy is associated with chaotic and traumatic attachments where others are, at one time, the source of and solution to fear (Johnson, 2002; Alexander, 1993).

The anxious and avoidant strategies were first identified in experimental separations and reunions with mothers and infants (Ainsworth, Blehar, Waters & Wall, 1978). Some infants were able to modulate their distress on separation, to acknowledge their distress and engage in clear support seeking when the mother returned. They were able to give clear signals and so make reassuring contact with the mother, and then, confident of her responsiveness if she was needed, to return to exploration and play. They were viewed as *securely attached*. Others became extremely distressed on separation. They did not seem to be confident that the mother would return and then clung to, or expressed anger to, the mother on reunion. They were difficult to soothe and were viewed as preoccupied with making contact with the mother and *anxiously attached*. Another group showed signs of significant physiological distress but showed very little emotion at separation or reunion. They focused on tasks and activities and were seen as *avoidantly attached*. These styles are "self maintaining patterns of social interaction and emotion regulation strategies" (Shaver & Clarke, 1994, p. 119). They echo the display rules for emotion that Ekman and Friesen identified (1975), namely exaggerating—substituting one feeling for another, as when we focus on anger rather than fear, and minimizing.

Recent research into adult attachment has added to our understanding of adult attachment style. For example, anxiously attached adults seem to experience separation from their attachment figure as a catastrophe that parallels death, while more secure adults are more open to new information and able to revise beliefs in relationships, as well as being able to seek reassurance more effectively. Anxious partners are more prone to strong anger, whereas avoidants seem to experience intense hostility and to also attribute this hostility to their partners. Moreover, avoidant partners tend to feel hostile when the other partner expresses distress or seeks support. Research suggests that avoidant partners can be socially skilled in general but avoid seeking or giving support when attachment needs arise within them or their partner. Avoidant partners also tend to be more prone to promiscuous sexuality (Brennen & Shaver, 1995; Shaver & Mikulincer, 2002). In general, anxiety and avoidance foster a rigid hypervigilant attitude to novelty and uncertainty and an equation of letting down one's guard with helplessness. All couple therapists will recognize these factors as preludes to and part of narrow rigid patterns of interaction and a constriction of the flexible openness necessary for closeness and connection.

These insecure habitual forms of engagement can be modified by new relationships, but they can also mold current relationships and so can easily become self-perpetuating. They involve specific behavioral responses to regulate emotions and protect the self from rejection and abandonment, and cognitive schemas or working models of self and other. In the attachment literature the term *attachment styles*, which implies an individual characteristic, is often used interchangeably with the term *attachment strategies*, which implies behavior that is more context specific. The use of the third term, *habitual forms of engagement* (Sroufe, 1996), further stresses the interpersonal nature of this concept. These forms of engagement can and do change when relationships change and are best thought of as continuous, not absolute (one can be more secure or less secure). The literature on these forms of engagement in the attachment dance helps the couple therapist see past all the content issues and dramatic subplots to the key moves and stances in that dance. The description of these strategies or patterns also fits with descriptive research on marital distress, for example, the delineation of the blame–pursue followed by defend–distance pattern as a prelude to relationship breakdown.

It is hardly surprising given the above that research confirms that attachment style affects marital satisfaction. Individuals with insecurely attached spouses report lower satisfaction; couples where both are securely attached report better adjustment than couples in which either or both partners are insecurely attached (Feeney, 1994; Lussier, Sabourin & Turgeon, 1997). When we consider these habitual responses and self-perpetuating patterns of interaction, it is easy to see that attachment is a systemic theory (Johnson & Best, 2002), and is concerned with "a reality-regulating and reality-creating not just a reality-reflecting system" (Bretherton & Munholland, 1999, p. 98).

9. Attachment involves working models of self and other. We define ourselves in the context of our most intimate relationships. As stated above, attachment strategies reflect ways of processing and dealing with emotion. Some spouses catastrophize and complain when they feel rejected; some become silent for days. Bowlby outlined the cognitive content of the representations of self and other that are inherent in these response patterns. Secure attachment is characterized by a working model of self that is worthy of love and care and is confident and competent, and indeed research has found secure attachment to be associated with greater self-efficacy (Mikulincer, 1995). Securely attached people, who believe others will be responsive when needed, also tend to have working models of others as dependable and worthy of trust. These models of self and other, distilled out of a thousand interactions, become expectations and biases that are carried forward into new relationships. They are not one-dimensional cognitive schemas; rather they are *procedural scripts* for how to create relatedness and ways of processing attachment information. These models involve goals, beliefs, and attachment strategies, and they are heavily infused with emotion. *Working models are formed, elaborated, maintained, and, most important for the couple and family therapist, changed through emotional communication.* The couple therapist will recognize in his or her clients' emotional self-disclosures the models of self and other that naturally well up in highly charged interactions with loved ones. Once distressed partners step beyond their angry protests, for example, they often begin to disclose fears about their own lovableness and worth.

10. Isolation and loss are inherently traumatizing. Lastly, it is important to recognize that attachment is essentially a theory of trauma. Bowlby began his career as a health professional by studying maternal deprivation and separation and its effects on children. Attachment theory describes and explains the trauma of deprivation, loss, rejection, and abandonment by those we need the most and the enormous impact it has on us. Bowlby viewed these traumatic stressors, and the isolation that ensued, as having tremendous impact on personality formation and on a person's ability to deal with other stresses in life. He believed that when someone is confident that a loved one will be there when needed, "a person will be much less prone to either intense or chronic fear than will an individual who has no such confidence" (1973, p. 406). The couple and family therapist knows the stress of deprivation and separation well. It is an essential part of the ongoing drama of "ordinary" relationship distress. Indeed, clients often speak of such distress in terms of trauma, that is, in life-and-death terms. As a theory of trauma, attachment theory specifically helps us to understand the weight behind emotional hurts such as rejection or perceived abandonment by a loved one. Distressed partners who are dealing with the traumatic helplessness induced by isolation and loss tend to adopt stances of fight, flight, or freeze that characterize responses to traumatic stress. The trauma perspective, with its focus on the power of helplessness and fear, helps the couple therapist tune in to the reality of distressed partners and deal with that reality constructively.

Adult Attachment—A Note

Due to our cultural focus on the individual and valuing of self-sufficiency, it is difficult for some clinicians and some couples to think of adult relationships in attachment terms. John Bowlby always believed that attachment was a lifelong affair, and it is perhaps worth pausing and explicitly noting the basic similarities in the features of infant/child–caregiver and adult love relationships (adapted from Shaver, Hazan & Bradshaw, 1988).

In both kinds of relationships, there is a deep desire for attention, emotional responsiveness, and reciprocal interest. A child or an adult lover feels more confident and secure, and therefore more able to cope with stressful events, when the other is perceived as on hand and dependable. In both relationships, people are happier and more outgoing and show a greater threshold for distress and tolerance of ambiguous or negative relationship events if the other is seen as basically accessible and responsive. When an attachment figure is distant or rejecting, both infants and adult lovers become anxious, preoccupied, and unable to concentrate or explore their environment. Both kinds of relationships are typified by contact seeking and high levels of physical contact, such as caressing, hugging, holding, and kissing. When afraid, sick, or distressed, adults and children want particularly to be held and comforted by their loved one. At all ages, there is distress at separation from and loss of an attachment figure, and fear of this loss. Reunion is a source of joy and comfort expressed by reaching and greeting; this is especially true when there was any doubt concerning the reunion. In both relationships, experiences and gifts are shared, confiding is valued, and people actively reflect on how a loved one would react to events or interesting sights. These are the only relationships typified by prolonged eye contact—gazing and a fascination with the other's physical features and a desire to explore them. Nonverbal communication is also very important, and both lovers and parent–child dyads coo and sing to each other.

There can be more than one attachment figure, but for both child and adult there is usually one key primary person who represents a safe haven and secure base. Adversity and stress increase a person's need for the other and intensify attachment behaviors, no matter what the age. Empathic attunement is part of falling in love and playing with a child, and when the attachment relationship is not going well there is a hypersensitivity to nonreciprocity and disapproval. Both lovers and parent–child dyads get enormous pleasure from the attention, approval, and responsive caring of the other.

Conversely, across the life span, relationship disruption tends to cause great distress and increase susceptibility to physical and psychological problems and illnesses. From the cradle to the grave, humans desire a certain someone who will look out for them, notice and value them, soothe their wounds, reassure them in life's difficult places, and hold them in the dark.

Given all of this, it is also important to note that adult attachments tend to be different from parent–child attachments in three important ways:

1. Adult love relationships are more representational. Adults find it easier to carry their loved ones around in their minds and use this representation for comfort and reassurance. The smaller the child, the more there is a need for tangible physical contact.

2. Adult relationships are more sexual. Sexuality can be seen as an attachment behavior as well as a seeking after orgasm or reproduction. Attachment theorists make the point that oxytocin, titled the cuddle hormone, is released during nursing and at sexual climax. In this context it is interesting to note that prostitutes, for whom sex is a rational bargain, commonly refuse to engage in kissing, nuzzling, or face-to-face contact with their clients.

3. Adult relationships are more reciprocal in nature. A parent is expected to take the lead and frame the attachment relationship with a child. Adult partners expect this to be a reciprocal process.

There is also the possibility that adult bonds take longer to develop from the stimulation mode of friendship into the emotional bond of attachment. Some theorists suggest that adult relationships of two years' duration are more likely to display attachment features (Hazan & Zeifman, 1999). These theorists also stress that in both child and adult primary relationships, it makes *excellent adaptive sense to react with anxiety and protest to even the temporary "loss"*

*of an attachment figure who is the primary source of emo-
tional and/or physical security.* This anxiety and protest
shows up in the couple therapist's office as a "communication
difficulty" or a lack of closeness.

Given the above, it is also useful to note that the most often
accepted model of marital distress and divorce, a model
where negative emotion, conflict, and negative interactions
lead to a decrease in positive feelings like love, trust, and
affection, is probably incorrect (Roberts & Greenberg, 2002;
Huston et al., 2001). An alternative model, and one that fits
with the attachment perspective, is that it is the absence of
disclosing and responsive interactions that begins the process
of relationship distress. Individual attachment needs are then
left unsatisfied, and it is this deprivation and distance that
eventually lead to conflict and distress. Once responsiveness to
attachment cues is established in a relationship and bonding
becomes more secure, couples can resolve many long-standing
arguments and can also argue without such disagreements
threatening the relationship.

Attachment as an Integrative Perspective

Couple therapy is generally becoming a more integrative
endeavor, and attachment theory is an integrative perspective. It is a systemic theory that focuses on behavior in context
and patterns of communication (Kobak & Duemmler, 1994;
Erdman & Caffery, 2002). This theory takes an evolutionary
perspective and sets out a wired-in control system designed
to maintain proximity and caregiving between primary caregivers and children and partners who need to cooperate to
raise their children. It can also be seen as an individual
dynamic theory that focuses on affect regulation and ways of
perceiving others (Holmes, 1996). There are some attachment
theorists who focus on attachment as only an inner state of
mind, but other theorists and couple and family therapists
see attachment and attachment styles from a transactional
perspective—that is, as being continually constructed and
reconstructed in interactions with loved ones. Individuals

may have qualitatively different relationships with different caregivers, and attachment styles can and do change as people learn and grow in relationships (Davilla, Karney & Bradbury, 1999). At best, attachment, like the practice of couple and family therapy, integrates self and system. Modern versions of attachment theory also integrate care-seeking, caregiving, and sexual behavior (Feeney, 1999).

Attachment theory, in its focus on emotion and validation of dependency needs, is consonant with and easily integrated with feminist viewpoints, such as those expressed by Baker Miller and Pierce Stiver (1997) or Fishbane (2001). Attachment theorists concur with the feminist focus on the power of close relationships and the dangers of pathologizing our need for connection with others (Vatcher & Bogo, 2001). The feminist and the attachment theory models of healthy relationships are congruent. Both perspectives see such relationships as characterized by "egalitarian mutuality, reciprocity, intimacy and interdependency" (Haddock, Schindler, Zimmerman & MacPhee, 2000). But most important of all, attachment is a clinical theory that takes the mystery out of adult love and shows us the plot underlying the drama of distress so that we can redirect this drama effectively.

The theorizing and research on attachment form an integrative whole in that it addresses how relational partners deal with their emotions, process and organize information about the self and others, and communicate with loved ones. For example, this perspective helps the couple therapist understand the emotional reactivity of the anxiously attached and the tendency of avoidant partners to withdraw from emotional engagement at the precise moment when they or their partners experience vulnerability or need (Simpson, Rholes & Nelligan, 1992). Attachment security promotes openness to new evidence and alternative perspectives and so aids collaborative problem solving. This knowledge encourages the couple therapist to create emotional safety and attachment security before setting up pragmatic problem-solving or skill building interactions. Once partners can deal with a certain level of uncertainty, they are also more able to step outside interaction feedback loops such as demand–withdraw and take a metaperspective on conversations. Secure attachment fosters openness, coherence, and competence in communication. As Goleman notes in his book on emotional intelligence, "attunement to others demands a modicum of calm in oneself" (1995, p. 112). Research has linked attachment security to distinct behaviors of crucial interest to the couple therapist. Secure attachment is associated with balanced assertiveness and lack of verbal aggression. Secure partners offer more support and use rejection less. These points are further summarized elsewhere (Johnson, 2002).

Finally, it seems important to note there is a general convergence of theory, research, and practice in the modern discipline of couple therapy, and attachment theory is part of this coming together. The data on the nature of distress in couple partnerships that stress the corrosive power of cycles such as demand–withdraw and the necessity for soothing and sustained emotional engagement (Gottman, Coan, Carrere & Swanson, 1998), the nature of adult love as outlined by attachment theory and research, and the research on outcomes and change processes for models such as emotionally focused therapy *all point in the same direction*. This direction integrates a focus on emotion and on specific interactional patterns and suggests that the business of couple therapy is essentially the business of addressing the security of attachment bonds.

Changes in Attachment

Changes in attachment can be considered on the level of changes in behavioral responses, for example, becoming more open and empathic, changes in ways of regulating emotion, or changes in relationship-specific and general models of self and other and ways of organizing information in attachment relationships. Changes can occur, then, on different levels, but generally the couple therapist wants to foster new attachment responses that restructure a couple's relationship into a more secure bond.

In his writings, Bowlby focused on how a therapist might help to create insight for an individual client, and so help to change that client's general negative models of attachment. However, modern attachment-oriented therapists focus more on compelling new emotional experiences in specific ongoing attachment relationships as the main route to change in attachment responses and models. These new emotional experiences can disconfirm past fears and biases (Collins & Read, 1994), allowing models to be elaborated and expanded and new behaviors to be constructed and integrated (Johnson & Whiffen, 1999).

From a systemic perspective, it seems useful to think of changes in attachment in terms of constriction and flexibility. Health in systemic terms is about flexibility and the ability to adapt inner models of the world and behavioral responses to new contexts. Bowlby stressed that to be useful, working models of attachment had to be open to revision and kept up to date (1969), and that restricted or defensive processing of ongoing experience could interfere with this process. The attachment-oriented therapist will focus on expanding clients' attachment behaviors, and how habitual and new attachment experiences are understood and dealt with. Change happens, then, in the heart, the head, and also in specific kinds of interactions. For anxiously attached spouses to become more secure, they may have to look at their propensity to be vigilant and easily disappointed, and they will also have to have new experiences of being able to ask for and achieve secure connection with their loved ones. Many models of couple and family therapy have tended to focus on either behavior, interactional pattern, or inner realities. An attachment perspective on change argues for integrating all these foci. Both attachment and systems theory use the concept of circular causality to explain the creation and maintenance of interactional patterns. However, attachment theory also suggests that specific kinds of anxiety and ways of regulating this anxiety organize key responses in close relationships (Johnson & Best, 2003). Attachment realities are created by how individuals dance together and how they grasp and internally attune to that dance.

The Significance of Attachment Theory for Couple Therapy

Attachment theory offers answers to some of the most fundamental questions about human relationships. How do we become caught in futile strategies that rob us of the love we desire from our partners and family members? Why does distancing so often fail to cool down conflictual interactions with attachment figures? Why do certain events define the nature of relationships more than others? And, most fundamental for the couple therapist, how can we best focus our repair attempts and foster the precious bonds with those we love?

Attachment theory, especially recent formulations and findings on adult attachment, offers the couple therapist a way to see and so to shape relationship interactions. More specifically, attachment theory offers the couple therapist:

- A clear conceptualization of the health in close relationships and pivotal moments that define health or dysfunction. This then naturally leads to a set of process goals and a final destination point for the therapist's journey with a couple. A major goal of effective couple therapy has to be to address attachment concerns, reduce attachment insecurities, and foster the creation of a secure bond. EFT therapists choreograph prototypical bonding events that build trust and secure attachment. There is, then, in these events, an explicit shaping of mutual accessibility and responsiveness, the building blocks of a secure bond. It is my belief that it is the impact of these change events that protects couples receiving EFT from the relapse commonly associated with other models.

- A clear depathologizing perspective on the essential nature of distress that offers the therapist a language for clients' hurts and dilemmas and so makes a safe haven of the therapy session and accelerates learning. This approach also offers a powerful way of reframing each partner's responses in a distressed relationship that fosters compassion and contact rather then mistrust and alienation.

- A way to grasp, articulate, and so hone in on the leading elements in relationship dramas: attachment emotions, fears and longings, and the ways patterns of interaction maintain separation distress. The therapist is concerned with helping partners to articulate attachment insecurities and deal more constructively with deprivation and the loss of trust and connection. All couple therapists know the struggle to stay focused in the chaotic drama and content issues of a relationship in distress.

- New ways to understand and so effectively address impasses and wounds in relationships. Chapter 12 details an attachment-oriented EFT approach to forgiveness and reconciliation.

Many years ago, Lyn Hoffman (1981) suggested that couple and family therapy had many ideas about how to create change but no clear ideas about what to change. As she put it, "Family therapy is better with how to change it than what to change. Descriptions of the creative that family therapists are out to get have been notoriously unsatisfactory. Clinicians know that something is rustling about in the bushes but nobody has done a good job of finding it or explaining what it is." This changed with John Bowlby and the adult attachment theorists. Once we can make sense of the drama of a distressed relationship, we need a theory of change—an approach to intervention. The next chapter presents the integration of the humanistic experiential and the systemic approach to therapy, as used in EFT.

3

THE EFT THEORY
OF CHANGE:
WITHIN AND BETWEEN

EFT is a synthesis of experiential and systemic approaches to therapy. It views marital distress as being maintained by the manner in which people organize and process their emotional experience, and the patterns of interaction they engage in, which take on a life of their own and become self-reinforcing. A distressed couple is in an absorbing state of compelling, automatic emotional responses and a corresponding set of rigidly organized interactions, both of which narrow and constrict interaction and experience. The emotional music and the pattern of both partners' dance steps pull for and reinforce each other in a circular loop of hurt and despair. This narrow absorbing state—where everything leads in and reinforces this state, and nothing leads out—renders emotional accessibility and responsiveness almost impossible. Research has shown that distressed couples are distinguishable by their rigid structured interaction patterns and their intense negative affect. What do the two approaches to change—the experiential and systemic therapies—tell us about how to help couples redefine their relationships? The humanistic experiential perspective focuses upon how to help partners to reprocess and expand their experience and the systemic perspective focuses upon how to help partners modify their interaction patterns.

THE EXPERIENTIAL VIEWPOINT—CHANGING
INNER EXPERIENCE

EFT is essentially a humanistic approach to therapy (Johnson & Boisvert, 2002). The humanistic approaches have always recognized the importance of emotion and have focused on it more systematically as part of the change process than have other models and approaches. What are the main tenets of humanistic experiential approaches to therapy that are relevant to the practice of EFT?

1. A focus on process. Human beings are constantly processing and constructing their experience, symbolizing that experience from moment to moment, and *creating meaning frameworks* (Cain, 2002). The client, not the therapist, is the expert concerning his or her own experience. The therapist's role is to help each client expand his or her awareness of that experience in the present moment in the session, integrate aspects that were excluded from awareness, and create new meaning frameworks. The focus of therapy is then on *present process*. It is *how* events are processed, not simply the content or facts of an event or experience, that matters in this perspective. The therapist is a process consultant. Therapy is then a collaborative process of discovery for therapist and client. As Rogers (1961) stated, the process of therapy is one in which the therapist can "enjoy discovering the order in experience" (p. 24). This ordering process is unique to each person. The experiential perspective is one that respects individual differences and views each person and relationship as a unique culture that the therapist must get to know. The experiential therapist's stance of "informed no knowing" (Shapiro, 1996) fits well with the focus on diversity in the field of couple and family therapy.

2. A focus on the necessity for a safe, collaborative therapeutic alliance. Humanistic therapists view people as primarily social beings who need to belong and feel valued by others and are best understood in the context of their relationship to others (Cain, 2002). It is not surprising, then, that the acceptance and empathy of the therapist are considered to be a key factor that fosters a reprocessing of experience, the construction of new meanings, and a new sense of agency. The acceptance of the therapist, or what Rogers termed the therapist's "unconditional positive regard" (1951) for each client, allows clients to encounter their experiences in new ways. Rogers suggested that empathic reflection of a client's experience, for example, is not in fact a reflection but a "revelation" that more fully orders and structures this client's experience in a way that allows the "frightening crannies of inner experience" to be encountered and dealt with (Rogers, 1961, p. 34). As in other postmodern perspectives (Anderson, 1997), the therapist attempts to be egalitarian, authentic, and transparent and so to create a safe haven in the therapy room. In this safe haven, people can begin to see the choices they make in their relationships, such as to shut down and shut the other out, and take responsibility for the impact of those choices on themselves and their partner. In couple therapy, the creation of safety involves a conscious effort to validate each partner's experience without invalidating or marginalizing the core elements of the experience of the other partner. In couple therapy, the ultimate goal is also the creation of a safe, accepting connection with the partner.

3. A focus on health. Human beings are naturally oriented toward growth and development, and in general have healthy needs and desires. It is the constriction, disowning, and denial of these needs and desires that create problems. This view of problems arising out of a narrowing or rigidity, a "stuckness" in processing experience, parallels the more interpersonal systemic perspective that focuses on the problematic nature of narrow patterns of interaction. Health in this model, as in systemic models, is openness to experience and responsive flexibility that allows for new learning, new choices, and adaptation to new environments. The experiential approach is then essentially nonpathologizing. The focus here is on growth through new experience and new ways of processing that experience, rather than on the correction of inherent deficits or deficiencies. This approach assumes that the ways people cope in dire circumstances when choices are few often become limiting and inadequate for creating positive relationships and lifestyles. All ways of responding can be adaptive (Bowlby, 1969), providing these ways can evolve in response to new contexts.

4. A focus on emotion. Emotion is given a prime place in this approach, as it is in attachment theory, and is seen as essentially adaptive. Bowlby and emotion theorists (Frijda, 1986) point out that emotions tell us and others what we want and need and prime key actions, especially relationship responses. More specifically, recent experiential theorists suggest that emotional frames or *blueprints* are constructed in relation to situations that frustrate or satisfy needs and goals. These frames then guide people in the differentiation and classification of experience, and in organizing expectations and reactions (Greenberg, Rice & Elliot, 1993). These frames help us predict, interpret, respond to, and control our experience. Emotions are not stored, but are reconstructed by the appraisal of a situation that activates a frame, an organized set of responses. In therapy, such blueprints are activated and made available for exploration and development; they may then also be modified by new experience. Emotion is accessed, developed, and restructured, and is also used to transform ways of constructing experience from moment to moment and responding to others. It is a target and agent of change.

5. A focus on a corrective emotional experience. Change occurs, in the present, as a result of the expanded processing of experience and the generation of powerful new corrective emotional experiences. Change is not then primarily the result of insight, the ventilation of emotion, or improved skills. It arises from the formulation and expression of new emotional experience that has the power to transform how the individual structures key experiences, views him- or herself, and communicates with others. In general, there is more and more acknowledgment and research evidence that emotional arousal and depth of experiencing in therapy predict positive outcome, not only in experiential therapies but even in cognitive behavioral interventions (Greenberg, Korman & Paivio, 2002).

A couple therapist who is using an experiential approach would then:

- Focus upon and reflect each partner's emotional experience.
- Validate and accept that experience, rather than trying to marginalize or replace it.
- Attune to and empathically explore such experience, focusing upon what is most alive and poignant, the not-yet-quite-formulated felt sense that emerges in specific interactions.
- Expand the client's experiencing by questions, usually process questions such as *what* or *how*, and by conjectures.
- Direct the client to engage in tasks that foster a new kind of processing of experience, such as attending to new elements in a problematic reaction (the stimulus or trigger, rather than the reaction itself), and broadening and deepening this awareness until new facets emerge that reorganize the experience as a whole. Such a task might be, in experiential individual therapy, to ask a client to hold an imaginary conversation with a key attachment figure who has impacted this client's definition of self, and to examine his or her emotional reaction. Working with emotion will be dealt with in more detail in the next chapter when therapeutic tasks are discussed.

These experiential interventions were originally designed for use in individual therapy. In couple therapy, the partner is observing while the therapist is helping his or her spouse reprocess experience. But the partner is also present, so that in-session interactions can influence that experiencing. The therapist here is not conducting individual therapy in the presence of the other. *The goal for the exploration of intrapsychic experience is to foster a new kind of contact with the partner in therapy sessions and at home.* This goal influences the kinds of experience that the therapist will choose to focus on and how the therapist will intervene. In couple therapy, there has to be a balance among exploring each partner's intrapsychic experience, validating each partner's very different experience, and encouraging interaction between the partners. The therapist also has to be aware that partners are witnessing and reacting to the therapist's interventions with the other and to be acutely sensitive to how the other is hearing the therapist's comments. The therapist must be sure, for example, that in validating one spouse he or she does not discount the other's experience.

If we answer the questions posed at the beginning of the chapter in the light of humanistic experiential theory, the following answers emerge. Problems arise or are maintained when partners organize or process their experience in a constricted manner, limiting awareness and rendering behavioral responses inflexible. The goal of therapy is to help clients to expand their manner of processing, to symbolize their experience in a way that enables them to connect with their needs and goals, and to respond to their environment, including their partner, in new ways. Awareness of emotion is central to healthy functioning in this perspective, since emotional responses orient the individual to his or her own needs and longings and prime the struggle to get those needs met. The process of change here involves a more intense engagement with one's own experience and the creation of new experience and new meanings that prime adaptive action.

SYSTEMS THEORY: CHANGING
INTERACTIONAL PATTERNS

What are the main tenets of systems theory (Bertalanffy, 1956) that are relevant to the practice of EFT?

First, since many different kinds of systems orientations exist, it is best to define how this term is used. *Systems theory* here refers to the systemic structural approach as exemplified by the work of Minuchin and Fishman (1981). Systems theory places the focus on present interactions and the power of those interactions to direct and constrict individual behavior. The hallmark of all family systems therapies is that they attempt to interrupt repetitive cycles of interaction that include problematic or symptomatic behavior.

1. Systems theory encourages us to look at a particular context as a whole and how elements of that context interact, rather than at one or two elements in isolation. The focus is upon patterns and sequences of behavior. Parts can only be understood in the context of the whole, so one partner's behavior can only be understood in the context of the other partner's behavior. Patterns and cycles of interaction are the focus here.

2. The elements of a system stand in consistent relationship to each other; they interact in predictable, organized ways. This organization produces stability and coherence (Dell, 1982). In order to create change, a systems therapist will focus on changing the ways in which the elements in a system relate to each other; the way the system is organized, rather than the elements themselves. A change in the nature of elements (for example, a partner becoming less hostile) is called level-one change and is considered insufficient. A change in the organization of a system is titled level-two change (Watzlawick, Weakland & Fisch, 1974). A focus on the process of interaction and how it is organized into stable self-maintaining patterns naturally arises from this perspective. Once a pattern exists, the coherence of the pattern acts to limit the effect of exceptional or unpatterned behaviors. For example, when a usually withdrawn spouse opens up and reaches for his or her spouse, this spouse often does not trust the unusual response and

continues to attack; the withdrawer then retreats into withdrawal.

3. Causality is circular, so no one behavior simply causes another; rather, each is linked in a circular chain to other behaviors, as when one partner nags in response to the other's withdrawal, and the other withdraws in response to the nagging. The focus is not on inner motives and intentions, but on the *pull of each partner's behavior on the other.* This perspective encourages the therapist to discover how each partner inadvertently helps to create the other's negative responses in the circular feedback system of mutual influence.

4. The emphasis is on the communicative aspects of behavior, on the command or relationship-defining element inherent in *how* things are said, which then defines the role of the speaker and listener, rather than on content. This allows the therapist to focus on each partner's interactional position in terms of closeness and distance, autonomy and control. This is of crucial importance in understanding cycles and each person's behavior in the cycle. How participants are defined in communication with significant others also influences how they see themselves, so changing relationship structure also affects intrapsychic responses to the self.

5. The therapist's task is to change the negative rigid interactional cycle the couple consistently engage in. This can be done in various ways: by reframing interactional positions to create new perceptions and responses, or by interrupting interactional patterns with tasks, such as sharing fears, that create a new kind of dialogue. To be effective, the therapist has to join with the couple system and create an alliance.

6. The goal of structural systemic interventions is to restructure interactions in such a way as to foster flexibility (which allows partners to adapt effectively to

changing contexts and needs), and the growth of individuals in the relationship—in other words, to create a system that supports belonging and autonomy and fosters contact, while allowing for individual differences and desires. Where there is a secure bond, individual differences are not threatening, but are in fact enlivening. As Minuchin said, "to be more fully connected is to be more fully oneself" (1993, p. 286). This being said, systems theorists have often focused exclusively on boundaries and control issues rather than nurturance and connection.

How does systems theory answer the questions posed at the beginning of the chapter as to the nature of the problem, the goal of therapy, and the nature of change? The problem in systemic terms is the structure of the relationship, the positions the partners adopt, and the process of interaction; that is, the tight repetitive sequences of self-reinforcing responses typically found in distressed relationships. The goal is to foster more flexible positions and new kinds of interactions, which allow each partner to have a sense of control and belonging in the relationship.

INTEGRATING SYSTEMIC AND EXPERIENTIAL PERSPECTIVES

These two ways of creating change work well together. They make good partners. They are easily integrated and also complement each other, each bringing a different perspective, one intrapsychic and one interpersonal. They also have certain similarities.

Both view the person as a fluid system constantly in the process of creation, rather than as possessing a fixed character based on psychogenetic determinants. Both focus on the present, rather than on historical determinants as important causes of specific behaviors. There is a focus on process—how experience and the interactional dance are structured.

In both approaches, people tend to be seen as "stuck" rather than deficient or sick. In the experiential approach, people are caught in constricted ways of processing information and in absorbing states of negative emotion that limit their responses. In systemic approaches, people are constrained by the interactional patterns or rules of the relationship.

In both approaches, it is crucial that the therapist join or ally with the couple and help them create new more flexible positions, patterns, and ways of processing their inner worlds.

The EFT perspective is that it is necessary for the couple therapist to use a model of change that incorporates the intrapsychic and the interpersonal, and that these foci complement and expand each other. Systems theory has in fact been criticized for its impersonal techniques, abstract epistemologies, and lack of attention to how family members experience their relationships (Nichols, 1987). In systemic approaches, dependency or high cohesion has also often been incorrectly equated with "enmeshment" or an unhealthy lack of separateness (Green & Werner, 1996). The experiential focus of EFT adds the intrapsychic half of the feedback loops delineated by systemic theorists and a focus on nurturance and safe connection. From the EFT standpoint, secure attachment enables maximum differentiation (it is easier to be completely yourself if you are securely connected to those you depend on), and maximum intimacy and connection. Secure connectedness also enhances flexibility and the ability to reflect on rather than react to situations. What many systemic Bowenian therapists would then see as enmeshment, the EFT systemic therapist would see as anxious or fearful avoidant attachment.

Rigid interactional patterns are not then just about systemic coherence and feedback loops. They are also about how specific interpersonal stances mesh with attachment emotions and how these emotions "move" people and organize their steps in the relationship dance. Bertalanffy, the father of systems theory, suggested that a small change in a leading or organizing element in a system could cause significant changes in the total system. If attachment emotions are viewed as such a leading element in a system, as a primary signaling system between intimates, it is easy to integrate emotion and emotional change processes into the systemic perspective (Johnson, 1998).

As other theorists have suggested (Nichols, 1987), it is better in therapy to use both a telescopic lens (exploring individual experience) and a wide-angle lens (exploring the interpersonal dance). In fact, using only one can mislead and distort realities. The experiential model gives the therapist a guide to accessing and reprocessing emotional experience, and the systemic model gives the therapist a complementary guide to restructuring interactions.

SUMMARY: THE PRIMARY ASSUMPTIONS OF EFT

Using attachment theory as the basis for understanding adult love and an experiential and systemic approach to therapeutic change, what are the main assumptions of EFT?

1. The most appropriate paradigm for adult intimacy is that of an emotional bond. The key issue in marital conflict is the security of this bond. Such bonds are created by accessibility and responsiveness, by emotional engagement. These bonds address our innate need for security, protection, and contact.

2. Emotion is key in organizing attachment behaviors and in organizing the way the self and the other are experienced in an intimate relationship. Both attachment and experiential theory stress the importance of emotional experience and expression. Emotion guides and gives meaning to perception, motivates to action, and communicates to others. It is both a crucial target and agent of change in couple therapy. The creation of new emotional experience is considered the most important factor in both intrapsychic and interpersonal change.

3. Problems in relationships are maintained by the way interactions are organized and the dominant emotional experience of each partner in the relationship. These elements operate in a reciprocally determining manner, and can be used in therapy to mutually influence and redefine each other.

4. The attachment needs and desires of partners are essentially healthy and adaptive. It is the way such needs and desires are enacted in a context of perceived insecurity that creates problems. Both attachment theory and the experiential view of human functioning emphasize the potentially adaptive nature of most needs and desires, and see problems arising from the disowning and constriction of such needs. The recognition and validation of such needs is a key part of EFT.

5. Change in EFT is associated with the accessing and reprocessing of the emotional experience underlying each partner's position in the relationship. The creation of new elements of emotional experience and new ways of expressing that experience tend to modify the positions partners take with each other, and allow for key new interactions to occur that then redefine the bond between partners. Change does not occur primarily through insight, through some kind of catharsis, or through negotiation. It occurs through new emotional experience and new interactional events. As Einstein suggested, "All knowledge is experience: everything else is just information."

This chapter has outlined the theoretical perspectives that the EFT therapist uses to guide his or her interventions and summarized the assumptions of EFT. The next chapter outlines the basic therapist skills necessary for the successful implementation of EFT.

4

THE BASICS OF EFT: TASKS AND INTERVENTIONS

EXPANDING EXPERIENCE AND SHAPING DANCES

Therapist: So when he reaches for you, right now, as he leans forward and says he needs you, what happens to you? (She clasps her hands tight and looks at the floor) This is hard to take in—you are holding on to you—your hands?

Wife: Yes, I want to hold on tight. I don't believe him—I'll respond and then (she lets go of her hands and lets them fall).

Therapist: Then—if you let yourself hope and trust— if you risk—suddenly he might not be there—and the fall would be awful—unbearable—? (She nods emphatically)

Wife: (to therapist) If you weren't here I'd run out of the room—right now.

Therapist: Aha—I make it a little safer—yes? (She nods) Can you tell him, I am so afraid to hope—to put myself in your hands? Can you?

Husband: (to therapist) She won't risk it.

> **Therapist:** It is hard for her. Can you help her? Can you lean forward and look at her—so she can see you reaching for her? Can you help her with her fear—I remember you did that in the last session . . .

In the short piece of dialogue above, the three tasks of EFT are implied or apparent. These are:

1. Fostering a safe therapeutic alliance to enhance engagement in the change process.
2. Accessing, unfolding, and expanding emotional responses in an attachment context.
3. Choreographing response sequences to restructure key interactions.

The EFT therapist has to be able to create a safe context—a secure base, in attachment theory terms—for both partners to access and work with emotion, and to restructure interactions. This involves an ability to flexibly move from processing inner experience with an individual partner to choreographing interactions between partners. The therapist moves from following and tracking experience and interactions to also expanding and directing and so moving such experience and interactions forward. The therapist needs to be able to hold multiple realities—experiential and systemic perspectives—simultaneously; to see how a particular spouse's silent withdrawal is an almost inevitable response given his partner's behavior, and at the same time to see how this spouse's way of organizing his experience, his attachment strategies and ways of coping, play a part in this withdrawal and tend to dictate his partner's behavior. The overall frame of attachment theory assists the therapist's ability to focus in a way that includes inner and interactional realities. One way of conceptualizing this process is that in this context, this attachment dance, each partner's steps dictate the emotional music, and the emotional music and the way it is played dictate the way each partner dances and the steps each partner takes.

It is easier to learn EFT if the therapist's personal style includes, as well as the flexibility mentioned above, a certain comfort with emotional experience and with being active and directing interactions. At key moments, the process of EFT involves fostering intense experience and pointed, sometimes dramatic, encounters. It is an up-close style of therapy, rather than one that advocates a detached therapeutic stance. The therapist needs to have some level of comfort with relatively close contact. The EFT therapist is active, engaged, and flexible, discovering with his or her clients the possibilities in their relationship. The person of the therapist is an important factor here, but there are also set techniques and interventions. The EFT therapist uses his or her personal style and resources to create a context for techniques and interventions, and to connect with each client's experience. The three basic tasks involved in the successful implementation of EFT are the creation of a collaborative alliance, the accessing and refining of emotional experience, and the restructuring of interactions. They are discussed below.

THE KEY ROLE OF EMPATHY

Before discussing the key tasks of EFT, however, it seems essential to discuss the nature and significance of empathy. Empathy is a necessary prerequisite for and integral part of all EFT interventions and of humanistic approaches to therapy in general (Bohart & Greenberg, 1997; Rogers, 1975).

The word *empathy* comes from the German word *einfuhlung*, which means "to feel into." The EFT model parallels Rogers's stance when he said that "the ideal therapist is first of all empathic" (1975, p. 5). We can articulate the myriad ways that therapist empathic responses impact clients in therapy. An attuned, accurate empathic response can:

1. Reassure a client that his or her experience makes sense to another human being. This tends to lessen

"one's fear of the unknown in one's experience" (Warner, 1997, p. 134). Less articulated elements of experience are then easier to grasp and own. Increased openness to experience promotes the ongoing revision of this experience.

2. Encourage clients to listen in a more attuned way to themselves and to loved ones. An empathic response from the therapist *models an accepting stance* toward each client's experience that enhances the recognition of and engagement in new elements of this experience and new ways of seeing. As the therapist attunes to the client and does not judge, this client tends to feel safe; this lessens the need to defend against difficult experiences as they come into focus. Empathy is necessary as a precursor to the validation that is one of the hallmarks of EFT. It is hard to validate what you cannot make sense of or connect with.

3. Focus attention on the processing and unfolding of specific experiences, and slow this processing down so that clients can "hold" experiences in awareness and process them further. The client can then see things in a new light and engage in ongoing experience on a deeper level.

4. Organize and order experience that is chaotic or ambiguous, or put elements of such experience into an integrated and meaningful whole.

5. Comfort and reassure clients so that they are not overwhelmed by difficult emotions. Empathic responses can modulate the intensity of a session and so maximize client engagement. Empathy can be seen as the primary way in which a therapist creates a "working distance" from emotion. Empathic reflections hold, support, and contain when experience becomes overwhelming. As Siegel (1999) noted, what is sharable is bearable.

6. Allow the meaning of key experiences to be felt, checked, explored, differentiated, and revised.

In general, then, sensitively communicated empathy enhances a client's sense of safety, promotes a focus on the construction of experience and its meaning, and so enables new responses. The therapist is a processing partner who, through various forms of empathic responsiveness, *orders* and *deepens* each client's experience. This enables each partner to connect with another, the therapist or the other partner, while staying engaged with his or her own emerging realities.

This emphasis on empathy reflects the concern in experiential therapies with the concrete experience or immediate "felt sense" of the client and the process of its construction. Experience and the making sense of experience is always a work in progress. Experience is the "knowing without words: a knowing that precedes words and from which words emerge" (Vanaerschot, 1997, p. 142). In healthy functioning, experience is always evolving, and meanings and action responses evolve with it.

Empathic attunement and responsiveness can be a demanding task. The EFT therapist has then to be willing to engage with and attune to each client's experience and to *resonate* with this experience. This is a skill that can be developed, but it also implies an openness on the part of the therapist and a propensity to be genuinely inquisitive and curious. The therapist and each client *discover* the client's experience. To achieve high levels of empathic understanding, the therapist not only has to immerse him- or herself in a client's world but also has to have access to his or her own experience as a reference point, so as to be able to tune in to the shape, color, and form of an emerging or only dimly sensed experience a client is accessing. The therapist has then to actively "use" his or her self to connect with the client's experience, while keeping the "as if" quality so as to not get lost or overwhelmed by this experience. He or she can then often find the words that the client cannot find and help the client to unfold the implicit or hidden aspects of key experiences. To stay focused and empathically engaged, the therapist also has to be able to cope with any elements in the client's world that elicit his or her own raw places or insecurities, and to be able to suspend his or her own preconceptions and frames of reference if need be. The therapist has to be able to communicate empathy to each client, and to do this without invalidating the other spouse. Empathy is at once then a state of intense focused attention, a multileveled task that involves constant effort, a complex skill, and a genuine connection—a way of relating to the client.

The focus of empathic questions in EFT is often emotions— more specifically, the needs and fears that arise in the partners' unfolding attachment drama. The therapist's empathy, like a soft light, then selects some moments and elements of experience for further exploration and quietly directs and focuses the therapy session. Empathic attunement allows the therapist to track and to taste the client's moment-to-moment experience. The therapist will inevitably make mistakes in formulating the client's experience, but as Bohart and Greenberg pointed out (1997), the usefulness of an empathic response is not in its objective accuracy but in its ability to engage with and carry forward the client's experiencing and his or her exploration.

TASK 1: THE CREATION AND MAINTENANCE OF A THERAPEUTIC ALLIANCE

In EFT, this alliance is characterized by the therapist's being able to be with each partner as that partner encounters his or her emotional responses and enacts his or her position in the relationship. The therapist is a *collaborative partner* in the piecing together and processing of experience, and a guide in the creation of a new relationship dance. As stated previously, the therapist acts as a *process consultant*, not an expert on the contents of each partner's psyche, or on the right way to construct an intimate relationship. A positive alliance has three elements (Bordin, 1994). It is one in which the client has a *bond* with the therapist and sees the therapist as appropriately warm and supportive, views the *tasks* presented by the therapist as relevant and helpful, and shares the same therapeutic *goals* as the therapist. A bond with the client ensures that this person then has confidence that the therapist will be accepting and ready to help him or her with the painful experiences and destructive cycles that are part of marital distress. The task element was found to be the most important element of the alliance in terms of predicting outcome in EFT (Johnson & Talitman, 1996). This makes sense in that it is the experience of EFT therapists that engagement in the tasks of therapy is the crucial factor in outcome. We assume that the perceived relevance of focusing on emotions and on attachment needs and fears is the reason why there are so strikingly few drop-outs in EFT treatment studies. Clients know they are dealing with the heart of the matter and feel heard and supported. The formulation of common goals is also an essential part of the therapeutic alliance and an essential part of first sessions. The goal of a more secure emotional connection, rather than simply less conflict or better problem solving, seems to be one that resonates with most clients, although it has to be translated into their language and terms of reference.

The relevance of the quality of the alliance is supported in a study of EFT process (Johnson & Talitman, 1996) where it accounted for 20 percent of the variance in therapy outcome. This is higher than the 10 percent of outcome variance usually associated with the alliance in psychotherapy research (Beutler, 2002). Generally research suggests that a positive ongoing alliance with the therapist is necessary for positive outcome, but it is not the whole story; it is not sufficient in and of itself. It makes sense that a positive, reassuring alliance is particularly important, however, when change involves significant emotional engagement in the process of therapy and dealing with difficult, risky interactions with loved ones.

The building of the alliance is a crucial and inherent part of the interventions used in the beginning sessions of EFT, both in interventions that focus on individual experience and in those that focus on interactions. Both the reflection and validation of each partner's experience of, and position in, the relationship, and the nonjudgmental description of how interactions are organized are powerful interventions in and of themselves; they also build a strong alliance. Both partners then experience the therapist as someone who can and does empathize with them, and also understands the powerful web of interactions in which they are caught. These interventions are described in more detail in chapters 5 and 6.

In more general terms, the most powerful element in the building of an alliance is the stance the therapist takes toward the couple, their distress, and change. In EFT, this stance is characterized by the following:

1. Empathic attunement. As mentioned above, there is a constant attempt by the therapist to empathically attune to each partner, and to connect on a personal level. Empathy has been described as an *act of imagination*, an ability to inhabit each client's world for a moment (Guerney, 1994). In experiential approaches, the taking of this stance, together with its communication to the client, has traditionally been seen as curative in and of itself (Rogers, 1951). As stated previously, empathy reduces a client's anxiety and allows for a more complete engagement in ongoing experience. The therapist is not concerned with evaluating the client's comments in terms of truth, realism, or dysfunction, but rather in making contact with the client's world. The focus is, what is it like to be this client in this context and what is the essence of this person's experience? Therapists' ability to listen, to connect what they hear with their own experience, and then to stay with this subjective perspective enables them to answer this question. It has been noted in developmental and clinical research that attunement often involves a focus on a speaker's nonverbal messages and an imitation or reflection of these physiological cues and the emotions implicit in them (Stern, 1985; Watson, 2002).

2. Acceptance. A nonjudgmental stance is essential in the creation of a powerful alliance. This stance is somewhat a function of who the therapist is and how aware this person is of his or her own human frailties and vagaries, but it is also a function of the theories and beliefs he or she holds. It is difficult to hold and communicate a nonjudgmental stance if the therapist adheres to a model of therapy that views people as deficient or defective. It is easier to maintain such a stance if the therapist has a relatively positive view of human nature and a belief in people's ability to change and grow. The experiential approach to therapy has emphasized the need for the therapist to *honor and prize clients as they are*, and to be able to tolerate ambiguity and aspects of clients that even they themselves do not prize or accept. This stance of respect and acceptance allows partners to face, with the therapist, what they could not face alone, or reveal to the other partner. There are times when the therapist is hard pressed to honor a client's specific behaviors but can honor the emotional reality that primes these behaviors. For example, it is possible to honor the fear of loss and associated desire to control a partner, while reflecting the abusive comments that arise from this fear and their negative impact on both partners and the relationship. Attunement to and acceptance of what is true for a client come before any attempt at change or finding remedies. This acceptance is active rather than passive; it involves an *actively validating stance* toward each partner. This involves not just nonpathologizing but explicitly framing negative behaviors as creative adaptations to impossible circumstances and the willingness to learn as bravery and strength (Johnson, 2002).

3. Genuineness. The genuineness of the therapist, how real and present he or she is able to be, is a crucial aspect of the alliance. This does not mean that the therapist is impulsive or always self-disclosing, but that the therapist is accessible and responsive to the client in a way that the client can trust. The therapist can then admit mistakes, and *allow clients to teach him or her about their experience*. In short, the therapeutic relationship is a real human encounter, which the therapist takes on with integrity, although the alliance with marital partners may not have the intensity of the alliance in individual therapy. This intensity is mediated in couple therapy by the presence of probably the most important attachment figure in each individual's life, the other partner. Part of the therapist's genuineness is also a certain transparency or willingness to be seen. For example, in EFT it is usual for the therapist to be willing to explain what he or she is doing in terms of intervention and how this will help the therapy process. Therapist self-disclosure is discussed later in the chapter.

4. Continuous active monitoring. If this kind of alliance is to be maintained throughout therapy, the therapist must take an active, deliberate role in monitoring, probing, and, if necessary, restoring this alliance. The therapist monitors his or her engagement with each spouse, actively seeking and processing each partner's responses to him or her. If the therapist has any hint that there may be a rupture in the alliance, the mending of this alliance becomes an immediate priority. The therapist might ask questions as to a client's reactions to his or her comments or interventions, encouraging the client to express his or her views and desires. An empathic question from the therapist can prevent a rupture in the alliance and/or strengthen it; for example, at the end of a session, a therapist might state that the couple had worked pretty intensely and invite their reactions, particularly concerns or worries about the process or content of the session. The therapist then explicitly encourages the partners to give feedback to him or her.

5. Joining the system. The couple therapist engages not only each partner but also the relationship system. The therapist sees and accepts the relationship as it is structured at the beginning of therapy. In systemic terms, the therapist joins the system. This involves the therapist not only piecing together and being able to describe the positions, patterns, and cycles of the relationship, but also being able to accurately reflect to the couple their own idiosyncratic version of the patterns distressed couples evolve together. The most common of these patterns is demand/criticize/pursue followed by defend/distance/stonewall. The therapist reflects the sequence and pattern of interactions, in an empathic and respectful manner, helping the couple to take a metaperspective on their interactions. They can then begin to own a part in the creation of the pattern, while also being acknowledged as its victims.

The therapist has to be able to validate each partner's experience of, and position in, the relationship in the presence of the other, without in any way invalidating the other's experience. Each partner also sees the therapist and the other spouse relating to each other; this may be a crucial part of the alliance and of the general change process. The spouse, for example, may reveal him- or herself in a new way in the interaction with the therapist. For the therapist, this demands a high level of awareness as to how his or her interventions with one spouse may affect the other, and a willingness to focus on this. For example, the therapist may ask for a partner's reaction to the dialogue he or she has just had with the other spouse and find out that this partner sees the other as receiving preferential treatment from the therapist, or that witnessing the dialogue evoked resentment as to why a spouse could reveal to the therapist what he or she could not reveal to the partner.

The stance described above elicits a collaborative partnership between the couple and the therapist, which is explicitly delineated in the early sessions by an exploration of the goals of therapy and the kinds of tasks that the therapist will be asking the couple to engage in. Part of the assessment process in EFT is clarifying each partner's goals and ascertaining whether these are compatible, as well as clarifying what partners can expect from therapy.

TASK 2: THE ACCESSING AND REFORMULATING OF EMOTION

Emotional experience is focused upon, expanded, reformulated, and restructured throughout the process of EFT. *The expression of new and/or expanded emotional experience then allows for a reorganization of the interactional positions partners take with one another.* The accessing of desperate loneliness in a critical, attacking partner, for example, (a) creates a new meaning context for this partner's hostility, (b) allows this hostility to be reprocessed as desperation, fostering a new presentation of self to the other, and (c) challenges the other's perceptions of this hostile partner's behavior and thus fosters new responses toward this partner. The accessing and deepening of emotion are particularly crucial at particular times in therapy, specifically in Steps 3 and 5, and in key change events as described later.

Emotion in EFT

Before describing the basic skills involved in this task, it is important to clarify how emotion is conceptualized in EFT. It is not seen as a primitive irrational response but as a high-level information processing system. In fact, as a therapist, I have never seen an emotion that did not make sense, if placed in context. It is also important to note, since *emotion* is a global label applied to many different experiences from embarrassment to despair, that the term refers here to the *small number of basic universal emotions* identified by key theorists in this area (Plutchik, 2000; Tomkins, 1991; Izard, 1977). More specifically, in this volume, it refers to anger, fear, surprise, joy, shame/disgust, hurt/anguish, and sadness/despair.

These emotions each involve a unique and universally recognized facial expression, an inborn neurological foundation, a social function that helps us survive and have an effect on others, a quick and compelling onset, and early development soon after birth (Izard, 1992).

Emotion is seen here in information processing terms, as an integration of physiological responses, meaning schemes, and action tendencies, as well as the self-reflexive awareness of this experience. If emotion is considered as a *process*, it is useful to think of it as a sequence, as Magda Arnold first suggested many years ago (1960). If your eye catches a glimpse of a long black shape on the forest path, the first response is an *appraisal,* usually brief, rapid, compelling, and global. Is this good or bad, threatening or safe? The essence of this response is speed rather than accuracy, and it takes place in the limbic area of the brain, specifically the amygdala. *Physiological arousal* follows. If the appraisal is "snake"—"danger," the heart pumps and the body gets ready to run. Most often there then follows a *reappraisal* that is more complete, involves more cognitive processing, and takes place in the neocortex part of the brain. Here meaning is assigned, as in "it is just a piece of wood" or "it is a large viper." A *compelling action tendency* then kicks in; the person either smiles and relaxes in relief and surprise, or runs away from the dangerous snake. If we translate this into a couple therapy event, it may appear as follows: She asks him if he loves her, he grimaces and raises an eyebrow, she appraises this ambiguous response as negative and dangerous, her mouth sets and her body stiffens as for a fight. She then says, "And what is that silly grimace supposed to mean?" He then looks away, and we hear her reappraisal as she says, "As usual nothing comes back— why do I ask—so stupid." She then leans forward and attacks: "You are an emotional cripple. I don't know why I am even here today." Emotion has "moved" her into an attack position, and this response then cues a massive defensive shutdown from her partner. This process orientation to emotion opens doors for the therapist to focus on, to clarify and expand, or to recast any part of the emotional response and so expand the whole.

Emotion is then a rich source of meaning: It gives us powerful, compelling feedback as to how our environment is affecting us. This feedback regulates our responses and organizes our behavior. Emotional expression, by communicating with others, also regulates social interaction, and the social functions of emotion are being more and more clearly articulated. The primary social function of emotion is perhaps to mobilize us to deal rapidly with important interpersonal encounters (Ekman, 1992). In general, emotions, like an internal compass, orient us to our world and provide us with crucial information about the personal significance of events; they tell us what we want and need. Indeed, it is almost impossible to make action decisions without reference to emotion (Damascio, 1994). They are a primary and compelling motivating force. Anger energizes us for a fight, intimidates attackers, and defends against injury. Sadness protests loss and evokes nurturing and help from others. Shame bids us hide from others and retreat so as to keep our place in a social group. Fear energizes us for fight or avoidance and evokes protection.

Emotion is seen here as basically adaptive, providing a response system that is able to rapidly reorganize a person's behavior in the interest of security, survival, or the fulfillment of needs. In intimate relationships, emotion tends to:

- **Focus attention and orient partners to their own needs and particular environment/social cues.** So when I am sad, I am acutely aware of how much I need contact, and I am particularly sensitive to any sign of distancing by my partner.
- **Color perceptions and meaning construction.** So my anger primes me to see the other's behavior as an affront to me and reminds me of all the other incidents I experienced in the same way.
- **Prime and organize responses, particularly attachment behaviors.** When I am anxious, I am particularly likely to seek out my partner for reassurance and comfort.
- **Activate core cognitions concerning, self, other, and the nature of relationships.** When I am engaged in an emotionally hot interaction, key defining concepts about myself naturally arise, such as, "Perhaps I deserve this response. I am a failure."
- **Communicate with others.** Emotion is intrinsically social. It is the primary signaling system in relationship-defining interactions. Displays of emotion pull for particular responses from others, thus playing a crucial role in organizing interactions. These displays evoke

complementary emotional responses in others. In an attachment context, for example, expressions of fear or distress evoke sympathetic distress and a desire to comfort. These complementary responses are core elements in courtship, bonding, and reconciliation (Keltner & Haidt, 2001). More generally, when vulnerability is expressed, it tends to disarm and pull for compassion, while anger tends to pull for compliance and/or distance. Intense emotion also tends to override other concerns and elicit compelling responses, such as fight–flight or approach–avoid. These responses are difficult to inhibit or control and tend, in distressed relationships, to constrain the responses of the other partner. *Emotion is then the music in the dance of adult intimacy.* When we change the music—we change the dance.

Emotion is so compelling and powerful, particularly in intimate relationships, that if it is not enlisted into the service of therapy, it is at the very least a powerful force left unused, and at worst an active undermining agent. A focus on emotion is also efficient, in that strong affective responses are able to reorganize responses quickly and create broad changes of perspective or meaning frameworks. As Sartre suggested, emotion involves a transformation of the world; to a sad man, it is always raining. It can also be used to transform the world into a more positive place, full of new possibilities.

Emotion is supremely relevant here. In distressed attachment relationships, where responses have high emotional impact, a corrective experience has to evoke emotion. It is the difference that makes a difference. It has been suggested that "while thinking usually changes thoughts, only feeling can change emotion" (Guidano, 1991, p. 61). It is interesting to note here that when partners are trying to cope with and reorganize threatening emotions, they often do so by evoking a competing alternative emotion. Fear, for example, is often dealt with by moving into an angry stance.

Emotion can be differentiated into primary, secondary, and instrumental responses (Greenberg & Johnson, 1988). Primary emotions are here-and-now direct responses to situations; secondary emotions are reactions to, and attempts to cope with, these direct responses, often obscuring awareness of the primary response. For example, angry defensiveness is often expressed in marital conflict, rather than hurt, fear, or some other primary affect. Instrumental emotions are used to manipulate the responses of others.

Emotion can also become maladaptive or enhance problematic behaviors in the following ways:

- Emotional responses, if they remain unprocessed, may arise out of context and constrict how present situations are processed. For example, the present relational experience of abuse survivors is often colored by the panic associated with the original abuse. Painful emotion is often suppressed rather than processed and integrated. However, the evidence is that this suppression is hard work and does not offer an escape from emotional pain (Gross & Levenson, 1993).

- Overwhelming emotion that cannot be regulated can flood the senses and narrow focus. Intense fear, in particular, exercises such tight control over information processing that it often eliminates all parts of the perceptual field that do not seem to offer a direct escape route (Izard & Youngstrom, 1996). When we are overwhelmingly afraid, we look only for danger cues and ways out.

- Limitations of emotional awareness or expression can limit responsiveness and trap a person into *spirals of negative emotions and interactions.* Distressed couples generally interact on the level of secondary reactive emotions that then pull for negative responses from their partner and so maintain negative emotions.

It is the primary emotional responses that are unattended to, undifferentiated, or disowned that the EFT therapist

focuses upon, although therapy often begins with the thera-
pist reflecting and validating the secondary responses that
the couple habitually presents as part of the cycle of distress.
In the process of EFT, emotions are processed and regulated
differently, resulting in more adaptive responses. Constricted,
overwhelming, or unprocessed emotional responses can be
acknowledged and clarified in the safety of the therapy session. As change occurs, the client's relationship becomes a
place where difficult emotions can be regulated in a different manner, expressed in an adaptive manner, and eventually
reorganized. For example, when a partner can acknowledge
to self and other the panic that arises during close physical
contact, this often evokes compassion and comforting behavior from the other spouse, allowing new healing emotional
experiences to occur in the present relationship that reduce
and change the nature of the panic response.

It is, then, the experience and expression of the primary
emotions underlying interactional positions, the sense of loss
underlying critical anger, or the helplessness and sense of
failure underlying withdrawal that have the potential to create new levels of emotional engagement and to modify problematic interactional cycles in couple therapy. The differentiation of the kinds of emotion outlined above is not difficult
to make in clinical contexts, and emerges naturally out of the
process of therapy.

It is also important to clarify issues concerning the level of
emotion and how it is used in EFT. These issues can be
outlined as:

• **Involvement.** Generally, emotional experience is not
  discussed from a distance with limited involvement.
  Labeling emotions and discussing them from a distance
  is not effective. Emotion is then evoked and experienced as vividly as possible. It is this engagement with
  emotional responses that allows for the discovery of
  new aspects of each partner's emotional life and the
  reorganization of emotional responses. The therapist
  tends to use simple, concrete words and images that

connect the person to that experience, rather than abstract terms or interpretations. If, however, emotion begins to be overwhelming, the reflection and ordering of emotional experience by the therapist tends to calm the client. Placing emotions in the context of the negative cycle and attachment insecurity also offers a way to make sense of them and so renders them more manageable. Gendlin (1996) has pointed out that experiential therapists help the client create a *safe working distance* from emotion, where they are intensely engaged but not overwhelmed. Such a concept fits with the recent writing on emotional intelligence (Salovey, Hsee & Mayer, 1993). This intelligence involves being able to recognize feelings as they arise, regulate them so they do not overwhelm, reflect on and control emotional impulses when necessary, and use the wisdom in emotion to guide meaning making and action. Since empathic attunement is the essence of secure attachment interactions, the therapist also actively helps a partner attune to, recognize, and respond to the other's primary emotions.

• **Exploration.** The goal here is *not* to place labels on experience or teach clients "better" ways to express themselves. Rather, a process of emotional exploration and discovery is engaged upon that expands each partner's experience of self in relation to the other. This involves a continuous focus on the as-yet-unclear edges and marginalized aspects of experience and the differentiation and symbolizing of that experience. For example, this may involve *unpacking* a label like anger into different elements, such as exasperation, bitterness, helplessness, and fear. It may also involve focusing on the different elements of emotion, such as the sensation of falling in the pit of the stomach that is experienced fleetingly just before a person becomes numb and distances from the spouse. When such elements are explored, new facets emerge that expand the experience as a whole and can be used to reorganize it. For example, numbness, when more fully processed, may become hopelessness and defiance. The experience and expression of these emotions then allows the partner's experience of self to evolve beyond numbness. To articulate that one is numb is often the first step away from numbness and toward connection with the partner. It also places this person's distance in a new meaning context for the partner and so creates a new kind of dialogue.

• **New emotion.** The indiscriminate ventilation of negative emotion to create catharsis is not part of the EFT process and can be detrimental in couple therapy. The repetitive expression of secondary reactive emotions is a recurring part of distressed couples' everyday problematic interactions. It is the discovery and development of new or unrecognized emotional experience that is useful in couple therapy. In EFT, emotion is expanded and revised or restructured from the bottom up, not top down. The EFT therapist does not attempt to reason a client out of a compelling emotional state, but encourages a new level of engagement and elaborates on new experiential elements to revise existing emotional states.

WHICH EMOTION TO FOCUS ON?

In terms of which emotion to focus on, the EFT therapist has three general guides:

1. The therapist focuses upon the *most poignant and vivid aspect of experience* that arises in the therapy process—for example, the tear, the dramatic nonverbal gesture, the potent image or label.

2. The therapist focuses upon the emotion that is *salient in terms of attachment* needs and fears. Anger is the usual response to an unresponsive attachment figure. Sadness and grief, as well as the anguish of loss and helplessness follow. Shame is also often key when

clients cannot ask for needs to be met or show their longings for closeness. However, fear and vulnerability are at the heart of attachment theory and, most often, the core negative affect in the definition of distressed relationships.

3. The therapist focuses on the emotion that seems to *play a role in organizing negative interactions* and restricting accessibility and responsiveness. The therapist focuses then upon the brief look of fear that occurs just before a withdrawn partner's statements of resignation, triggered by his spouse's complaints.

The question of which emotion to follow and unfold is more complicated in situations such as trauma cases where many powerful and conflicting emotions arise at the same time (for an example, see Chapter 6 in Johnson, 2002). In a typical couple, the EFT therapist generally begins by acknowledging the anger inherent in criticism and the anxiety and helplessness inherent in withdrawal and then follows the trail of fear, anxiety, and attachment insecurity.

The stage of therapy generally shapes the emotion and the level of emotion that the therapist will focus on, follow, and work with. The process in beginning sessions will move from *making implicit secondary emotions explicit*—for example, having a partner directly acknowledge his or her anger rather than listing the spouse's faults and recounting incidents of injury—to *placing both partners' secondary emotions in context*, the context of the negative cycle, and validating them. The therapist will then begin to *focus on primary attachment emotions* that seep through the couple's interactions. In the middle phase of therapy, the therapist will focus more on and *deepen each client's engagement with primary underlying emotion*, such as the helplessness that fuels the angry response. These underlying emotions are often implicit but not yet clearly formulated and/or articulated. They have an emerging or leading-edge (Wile, 1994) quality to them. People also may have feelings about their feelings, such as being afraid of their anger or ashamed of their fear. The therapist then has to validate and support the client to accept his or her own emotions.

Therapists also have to be able to deal with their own anxieties around strong emotions. Most therapists can name particular catastrophic fears about the evoking of such emotion, and clients, especially traumatized clients, tend to have the same fears. We may fear that if emotions are unleashed, they will go on forever. We may fear that we will be taken over by such emotions and our ability to organize our experience, our very sense of self, will disappear. We fear that we will lose control and be slaves to the impulses inherent in these emotions, and so we may makes things worse or actively harm ourselves or others. We fear we will not be able to tolerate these emotions and will go "crazy." We fear that if we express certain emotions, others will see us as strange and/or unacceptable. These kinds of fears can then block the therapist's ability to attend to, accept, unfold, and use emotional experience to create change.

The client's readiness and ability to respond to intervention also dictate the intensity of the therapist's focus. *The EFT therapist stays close to the client's experience, to where the client is in the here and now.* The readiness of the client to stay with and inhabit an emotion is a factor here. A particular partner may be willing at a particular point in time to include confusion or discomfort in his or her construction of experience, but may not yet be ready to formulate certain elements of his or her experience as fear. Clients also frame their emotions in idiosyncratic ways, and the therapist accepts this frame. For example, a partner may balk at the word *anger* and insist on *frustration* instead and then be quite willing to explore this frustration; or an older man may be able to talk about *upset* but seems to feel too exposed if this experience is termed *sadness.*

Another way of thinking about this is to consider the different entry points where the EFT therapist accesses and begins to work with emotion. Emotional experience can be unfolded by focusing on and expanding an in-session *comment* by a partner or an *abstract label/image*—for example, a partner says "This is too difficult," or "I feel upset by this" or "This is like boom, boom for me"; the therapist might explore a reaction to a specific interaction or a *dialogue sequence* between clients—for example, the therapist might ask, "How do you feel as you say to him . . ." or "What happens to you as your spouse says . . . ?" The therapist can also reflect the emotions spoken or implicit in *an example of the couple's core negative cycle*. The therapist tracks and explores the emotions contained in a *narrative* given by a couple. In-session and out-of-session *events* that have attachment significance can also be unfolded.

An example of accessing and expanding an emotional response follows:

A couple comes into an early session of EFT, and both partners are distant and constrained. The husband, usually the blamer and the pursuer, then tells this story. The couple had gone to a party the night before. He had been thinking on the way to the party that his wife had refused his sexual advances for the last few weeks, and so he deliberately went and found himself a few large drinks when he arrived at the party to "calm" himself. He then went to find his wife, whom he saw engaged in apparently intense conversation with a very attractive man who looked like a "stupid model from the front of some magazine." He then "marched" across the room and inquired if she was going to "flirt and whore around" all night with this "idiot." She coldly replied that her conversation was "delightful" and he could leave anytime so that she could continue it. He stormed out and drove home, enraged. After this, they had not spoken until they came for the EFT session. The therapist frames this event as an example of a key part of the couple's negative pattern, a pattern in which the husband becomes agitated and angry or demanding and his wife, hurt and hopeless, withdraws. The EFT therapist will then typically slow down and recap these steps in the event with the husband, focusing on the parts of the emotional response listed above: the initial cue, the bodily sensation, the reappraisal or meaning construction, and the action, as well as its consequences. In this case, the therapist reflects the client's anger and focuses on the cue for this emotional response.

What did he see when he looked across the room at his wife engaged in conversation? What stood out for him in the picture? What exactly was so upsetting in the picture? The client at first simply repeats his derogatory comments about his wife, but the therapist slowly and softly repeats the questions above. The client then begins to focus on his memory and says, "It was the way she was looking up at him." The therapist then follows this cue, and the client suddenly begins to tear and states in a choked voice, "She doesn't look at me that way anymore." This then opens the process up to an exploration of the client's attachment needs and fears and his expression of these to his wife, who then requires considerable support to begin to be able to recognize the vulnerability underneath his hostile behavior. In this event, the husband bypassed the experience of anguish and fear of possible loss and the sudden racing of his heart and focused instead on the secondary coping response of rage. The therapist could also have expanded this client's response by focusing on other elements such as how his body felt as he looked across the room, or as he speaks about this incident. The therapist could access his meaning frame and appraisal process by asking what he said to himself as he crossed the room or focus on his motivation—for example, what additional things he wanted to say to her, such as "You can't do this to me." Expanding any one of these elements can expand and reorganize the whole picture and then the drama between the couple.

The therapist's goal, especially in Task 2 of EFT, is then to explicate, expand, and reformulate key attachment emotions, use newly formulated emotions to expand meaning frames, use emotion to "move" clients into new responses, and use expanded emotion to expand the ways couples are able to engage each other.

To take a different perspective, if we look at the elements of emotion and how the therapist could use those in therapy, what would that look like? These elements are: the cue or trigger for the emotion, the initial appraisal or perception, body arousal, reappraisal (meaning making, usually regarding cycles, identity, attachment), and action tendency.

Example

> **Wife:** You are so difficult—I can't tolerate your attitude.
>
> **Husband:** (Throws up his hands and turns to look out the window)
>
> **Therapist:** What happens to you as your wife says, ". . . ?"
>
> **Husband:** Nothing—I am used to this. She says this stuff all the time.
>
> **Therapist:** You feel nothing as she says, ". . . ?" (*Repeat cue*)
>
> **Husband:** This happens lots—I just try to roll with it—forget it— (*Shifts to coping*)
>
> **Therapist:** You try to forget these times when she tells you that you are too difficult for her to tolerate? (He nods) But in that split second before you try to push it aside and "forget" her words—what happens to you? When she tells you, you are too difficult?
>
> **Husband:** Don't know. I just move away.
>
> **Therapist:** There is something here that is hard?—upsetting?—you can't take it in—that is too hard? (He nods) What do you hear her say? (*Initial appraisal is focus*)
>
> **Husband:** (*appraisal—threat*) She's saying that I'm hopeless—this relationship is doomed—down the tubes.
>
> **Therapist:** (*focus is body arousal*) You threw up your hands—like this—that is the hopelessness—the defeat? (*Moving to meaning reappraisal*)
>
> **Husband:** I guess so—yes—
>
> **Therapist:** It's like you throw up your hands and you give up—it's hopeless—
>
> **Husband:** Yeah— (Looks down at shoes—quiet voice) There is nothing I can do.
>
> **Therapist:** (*focus on meaning*) You hear her say—you are too difficult—you feel hopeless—try to push it

aside—but your body expresses the hopelessness and you say to yourself—what?—I have blown it—already lost her?

Husband: Yep. I have totally blown it. I'll never make it with her. She has her standards and I can't . . . I'll never . . . (tears)

Therapist: (*action tendency*) So you give up and withdraw to protect yourself—to try to shut down the pain and helplessness. And then you (to the wife) get even angrier (she nods) and that is the cycle that has taken over the relationship and leaves you both alone (*attachment significance*). And that brings tears for you?

Husband: No—my eyes are just watering—

Therapist: You say to yourself—"I have blown it—lost her—I'll never make it with her"? Some part of you wants to throw up your hands—like—"I will never please her—have her love"—Is that it? (*Repeat meaning frame*)

Husband: Right—My brother said—there is a time to get married and he told me I was too young—but you do what you do—all my family got married young. (*Exit into side topic*)

Therapist: I'd like to go back. (*Refocus*) So when you hear your wife's anger you move away—try to forget it—and she sees—what did she say?—she sees "coldness" (she nods). But in fact, you throw up your hands—you are trying to deal with a huge sense of defeat—a sense of failure—a fear that you can never please her—so you shut down and shut her out. Am I getting it? (*Summary of all elements of emotional experience in context of cycle*)

Husband: Yes—that's it—I think that's it—that's it. (He weeps)

Once the emotional experience has been unfolded and synthesized into a meaningful whole—and the client is fully emotionally engaged—then an enactment is usually initiated.

Therapist: (suggest enactment) Can you look at her and tell her please— "I hear that I'm hopeless— I have already lost you, so I shut down to stop the pain"— can you tell her?

The therapist will then help the wife formulate and develop her response to this message.

Let us now look at the specific skills the EFT therapist uses in the process of therapy.

SKILLS AND INTERVENTIONS: ACCESSING AND REFORMULATING EMOTION

1. Reflection

The therapist attends to, focuses on, and reflects present poignant emotion. The therapist conveys understanding of the client's experience and directs the client's attention to that experience. Reflection here is not simply echoing and paraphrasing the client's words. It requires intense concentration from the therapist and an empathic absorption in the client's experience. The therapist tracks the client's experience, processing that experience with the client and being aware of how this particular client constructs his or her experience moment to moment. The therapist will pick up on and articulate shifts in the flow of experiencing—for example, if a client suddenly shifts in level of emotional engagement or becomes stuck and cannot find words.

If such reflection is skillfully done, the client feels seen and acknowledged. The therapy session then becomes a safe place and the therapist is seen as an ally. Such reflection also *directs the client's attention* to the unfolding of inner experience, *sharpens the client's grasp of this experience*, and *slows down* the interpersonal process in the session. Reflection underscores the significance of particular comments and creates a focus for the process of therapy. *Reflection can be seen as a way of turning and turning an experience to the light so that new facets appear.* It can be seen as helping clients to grasp and taste what may be vague and abstract. It can soothe and it can heighten, depending on how it is used. It also is the basic tool the EFT therapist uses *to focus and direct the session.* A good reflection is the first step in making a client's experience vivid, tangible, concrete, specific, and active (versus something that happens to you).

Example

> **Therapist:** So, help me understand, Ellen, what you are saying to Peter is, I don't see that you want me and miss me. What I see and hear is that I am never enough. I disappoint you. I am analyzed and found wanting. I feel put down and defeated. Is that it?
>
> **Wife:** Yes, that's it. Exactly. I am condemned.

2. Validation

The EFT therapist conveys to both partners that they are entitled to their experience and emotional responses. If necessary, the therapist explicitly differentiates one partner's experience from the other's intention and/or character: One partner can legitimately feel hated, without the other being hateful. The therapist takes the stance that there is nothing wrong, irrational, deficient, shameful, or strange about their responses. Empathic reflection, if it is done with respect and caring, conveys this message, but it is also necessary to *explicitly* validate each partner's experience of the relationship. The therapist's affirmation, and the security created by this acceptance, act as an antidote to the general level of anxiety and the climate of disqualification and self-protectiveness that characterizes distressed couples. This acceptance also acts as an antidote to the constricted experiencing and presentation of self, which result from self-criticism or from the anticipated judgment of others. Empathic reflection and validation encourage partners to become more engaged with their experience, so that this experience can be expanded upon and crystallized.

Example

> **Therapist:** I think I understand. It's like when he would say how depressed he was, you would feel

overwhelmed and a little scared. You felt like this
heavy weight was descending on you, crushing the
breath out of you. So after a while, it was natural to
push back at the weight, so you could breathe, and to
get angry at your husband for not finding a way out.
So you would withdraw or tell him to snap out of it.
Is that it?

3. Evocative Responding: Reflections and Questions

These responses focus upon the tentative, unclear, or emerging aspects of a partner's experience and encourage exploration and engagement. The word *evocative* comes from
the Latin *evocare*—"to call." The therapist bypasses the
more superficial content issues in a conversation and calls
to the emotions of the client. The therapist attempts to
vividly capture the quality and the implicit elements of this
experience, tentatively expanding such experience, often by
the use of evocative imagery. This then helps the client to
construct this experience in a more vivid and differentiated
way.

These reflections are offered *tentatively*, for the client to
taste, try on, correct, reshape, or take on, not as an expert
synopsis of his or her responses. The reflections may focus
upon how cues are perceived and processed, the most
poignant elements of an emotional or body response, the
desires and longings that arise from a particular response, the
conflicting elements within that response, or the action
tendency or intention that is inherent in the emotional experience. The therapist guides clients to the *leading edge of
their experience* and invites them to take another step in
formulating and symbolizing the experience. Consider the
following examples:

Examples

1. **Therapist:** So what is it about Mary's tone of voice
   right now that seems to trigger the sense of the floor
   dropping away?

2. **Therapist:** When you say that, Sam, there is a catch in your voice, like it hurts you to even put it into words, that you may not be what Mary needs.

3. **Therapist:** I'm unclear here. I think I hear you saying that when you see that expression on her face, you have this incredible desire to run and hide. Is that it? Help me understand.

4. **Therapist:** You want to run and hide, but some other part of you insists that you try to stand your ground, is that it?

5. **Therapist:** So when you hear that, part of you, the defiant part, wants to yell, I'm never going to let you hurt me like that again. Is that it?

Questions such as: What happens to you when . . . How do you feel as you listen to . . . or as you say . . . What is it like for you . . . directly ask the client to expand his or her awareness of present experience. The focus here may be on inner experience or on the process of interaction:

6. **Therapist:** What happens to you when you begin to feel this sense of hopelessness you just mentioned?

7. **Therapist:** What just happened there? Mary, you flinched when Jim hit his leg with his hand, and then you remained silent; what happened for you right then?

As part of capturing a client's experience, the therapist may direct attention to a specific element. This may be done by simply repeating a poignant phrase that the client glossed over or did not emphasize, or by asking the client to repeat it. For example:

8. **Therapist:** Can you say that again, Mary, that piece where you said, I'm not going to let you destroy me?

These interventions are invitations to partners to explore and reprocess their experience. As they become more and more engaged with, and immersed in, their experience, new elements begin to arise that reshape that experience. Evocative responding is a main tool the therapist uses to help a client move from a denial of any emotion, or acting out an emotion by blaming or belittling another (as in "You're just a jerk"), to a direct owning of secondary affect (as in "I am very angry at you"), to the formulation of underlying primary emotion (as in "I get so helpless. I smack you down just to get a response").

There is also a specific kind of evocative responding where the therapist evokes parts of a person or the voice of a partner's attachment figure to expand and reprocess experience. The therapist might then *evoke a contrasting part of a client* to highlight a dilemma or deepen experiencing. The therapist might also *evoke the voice* or speak as an attachment figure to validate a client's fear or to provide an antidote to overwhelming fear.

Examples

1. **Therapist:** So, Amy, one part of you says, "Don't do it. Don't take the risk. You have been hurt before." But another part of you feels so sad—so alone. This other part tells you to reach for him—to reach for what you long for. Is that it?

2. **Therapist:** So right now, the fear says, "Just shut down—just stay away and numb out." Is that it? The fear says, "This is hopeless."

These interventions increase engagement in the process of the present moment. They may vary in focus from helping clients contact their general experience of self and other in the relationship, to helping clients reprocess a particularly loaded response that underlies their interactional position, to developing and restructuring specific compelling emotional responses in a way that helps to create accessibility and responsiveness in self and other.

4. Heightening

As the therapist tracks the internal and interpersonal processes, within each partner and between the couple, he or she may choose to highlight and intensify particular responses and interactions. These responses and interactions are often those that seem to play a crucial role in maintaining the couple's destructive interactions, although if positive or new interactions occur, these too are heightened. The therapist can use this heightened emotion to help partners engage with their emotional experience in a new way, and create a different kind of dialogue with the other. Heightening brings a particular response from the background into the limelight, so that it can be used to reorganize experience and interaction. There are several ways of achieving this:

- Repeating a phrase to heighten its impact.
- Intensifying the experience by how something is said. The EFT therapist typically leans forward and lowers and slows his or her voice when heightening a soft or vulnerable response or raises the voice when heightening an assertive response.
- Using clear, poignant images and metaphors that crystallize experience.
- Directing partners to enact their responses; to turn intrapsychic experience into interpersonal messages.
- Maintaining a specific and sometimes *relentless* focus. The therapist blocks exits or changes in the flow of experience that are likely to lessen the emotional intensity of the moment.

Example

An excerpt of therapy illustrating the above interventions follows.

> **Therapist:** So can you say that again, Jim, I just can't open up and let myself commit to her.
>
> **Jim:** Yes, I just can't. I can't make myself. I hold back. Keep her out.
>
> **Therapist:** How do you feel as you say this, Jim?

Jim: I feel sad, but it feels right, it's right. It feels better.

Therapist: It feels safer to keep her on the other side of the door, to keep her at a distance.

Jim: Yes, it's just the way it is. In my country . . .

Therapist: You want to keep her out. It feels better behind the door.

Jim: Yes.

Therapist: So can you tell her: I'm going to keep you out, at a certain distance. It really doesn't matter what you do. I'm not ready to put myself in anyone's hands. I'm not going to let you really connect with me.

The client begins to give his version of the therapist's statement and bursts into tears. In this moment, Jim's experience is intensified and his interactional position is enacted explicitly.

5. Empathic Conjecture/Interpretation

Here the EFT therapist infers the client's current state and experience from nonverbal, interactional, and contextual cues to help the client give color, shape, and form to his or her experience and take this experience one step further. The aim here is not to comment on psychogenetic causes or patterns, or to help the client interpret his or her experience in a "better" way, but to extend and clarify that experience, so that new meaning can naturally emerge. Such conjectures are not cognitive labels that categorize and therefore provide closure to experience, and are not meant to give clients new information about themselves. The goal is to facilitate more intense experiencing from which new meanings spontaneously arise, not to create insight per se. The inferences used here arise from the therapist's empathic immersion in the client's experience, and knowledge of the interactional positions and patterns of the couple. Such inferences are also guided by attachment theory, the perspective on adult love that forms the basis of EFT.

There is a concern, from an experiential perspective, that these interpretations not be in any way imposed upon the client by the therapist and so impede the client's discovery of his or her own awareness. This danger is reduced in couple therapy since the system and problematic responses are visible to the therapist, and therefore immediate corrective feedback is available to challenge incorrect inferences. The inferences are also given in a tentative manner, and partners are actively and explicitly encouraged to guide and correct the therapist throughout therapy.

Inferences in EFT might typically concern *defensive strategies, attachment longings, and core catastrophic attachment fears and fantasies.* These conjectures may take the form of statements concerning the need for self-protection apparently experienced by the partners, and formulations of attachment responses such as helpless mourning, the longing for comfort, or the classic human fears of engulfment/ subjugation, rejection, and abandonment. The definitions of self implicit in partners' dialogue, such as the perceived unworthy or unlovable nature of the self, are also made explicit in this manner. The therapist thus elaborates on the partners' experience, or makes explicit the elements in that experience that they seem unable to formulate or cannot yet own.

Examples

1. **Therapist:** So, the sense I get, Sam, is that you're caught between telling Marie to go to hell, no one is going to crowd you with expectations and demands, no one is going to take you over, and desperately fearing her anger and rejection, her dismissal of you. Is that right?

   Sam: Yeah, that sums it up; that's it exactly.

2. **Therapist:** Where are you right now, Carrie?

   Carrie: Don't know.

   Therapist: What is happening?

   Carrie: Don't know . . . just feel quiet.

Therapist: It's like you're a long long way away.

Carrie: Yes, far away.

Therapist: Where no one can hurt you, yes? (Carrie nods vigorously) It's the only way to feel safe right now, is that it?

Carrie: Right, I space right out.

Therapist: What's it feel like, being spaced out?

Carrie: Empty, but it's better than, than . . . (long pause)

Therapist: Than being humiliated and shamed, is that it?

Carrie: Yes, I asked him, and he laughed at me, just now, he laughed.

Therapist: Like you didn't matter, your longing didn't matter, like you were nothing, yes?

Carrie: I won't plead and beg, he'll wait a long time for that. I won't fight for him to listen.

Therapist: You'll go where he can't find you, and so defeat him, right? (Carrie nods) It's empty and lonely, but you're intact, then?

A particular kind of conjecture is used in change events in the second stage of EFT, when the therapist is restructuring interactions and fostering withdrawer reengagement and blamer softening. This conjecture is called *seeding attachment.* It is also a form of heightening and a form of validation. The therapist expands on the client's fears by stating what the attachment moves are that are blocked by this fear. This intervention has been observed as regularly occurring in successful softening events. This inference validates the impasse created by the client's fear and also gives a vision of what might occur if the fear were not so powerful. The intervention always begins with "So you could never . . ." The attachment longing and behavior blocked by the fear are made explicit. This intervention gives an image of possible attachment bids for connection that the therapist will try to foster later in the therapy process.

Examples
1. **Therapist:** (in a low, evocative voice, to a client who is identifying a fear of exposing herself to her partner and asking for him to respond to her) So you could never, never turn to him and say, "Come and be with me. Come and be with me because I need you and, right now, I need to come first. (The client shakes her head) You could never do that, never do that. That would be too scary. You don't deserve that even. Is that right?

   Prue: I can't do that—I can't.
2. **Therapist:** (to a client who is attempting to reengage with his partner) So you could never let her know how the "constant testing" as you put it defeats you and pushes you to withdraw. You could never ask her directly to risk and give you a chance to learn to be close?

This intervention challenges the client, gives him or her an image of a possible and more engaged stance with the partner, but still remains empathic and validating.

The EFT therapist also occasionally uses a particular and more elaborate form of conjecture called a *disquisition*, when partners are particularly resistant to exploring their experience and the above techniques prove ineffective. A disquisition is a story constructed and presented by the therapist about couples in general, or about types of marital problems. Presented as perhaps having some similarity to, or relevance for, the couple in therapy this story is designed to be an elaborate metaphorical description of the key responses of the couple in therapy, with conjectured underlying emotions woven into the story. The narrative is set up to reflect the therapist's understanding of the present couple's intrapersonal and interpersonal realities, in a discursive, nonthreatening manner. It is usually an expanded version of the story the couple have presented in therapy, but one that is more elaborated in terms of emotional experience and the links between that experience and how the couple respond to each other. The usual effect of this intervention is that one or both partners will identify with some aspect of the story and begin to relate it to their own experience. This is an indirect and very non-threatening way of probing for certain experiences with a relatively closed partner or couple.

Examples

The therapist can use disquisitions to elaborate on a partner's experience in the destructive cycle:

> **Therapist:** There's something here that reminds me of some of the other couples I have worked with, and this may be completely different for you, of course, it may not even be similar, but in some couples the more active partners get to the point where they want the other person to hurt, too. To see that they can have an impact, an effect on this seemingly impervious contained person, and they end up just hammering away, just to show the other partner that they won't just be ignored and discounted. The other partner experiences this as an attack, relentless and over-whelming, and just digs deeper and deeper into a trench, burrows down, builds up defenses. It's like a kind of "you can't get me," but it gets a bit tiring, always listening for distant guns and getting ready to duck, always having to be ready to run or to hide. This all ends up being pretty awful for both of them. I'm not sure if you can relate to this at all?

The therapist can also use disquisitions to conjecture about experience that the client does not own. For example, a disquisition might be made in response to intrusive jealous behavior on the part of a very uncommunicative husband who listened in on the wife's phone calls to friends and is unable to discuss this behavior in the session.

> **Therapist:** (to the wife) Well, I hear that you really find it hard to understand this behavior of Ted's, and

he seems to have a hard time talking about it. I'm not sure what it's all about. I see that it makes you angry. The only chord it strikes for me is that it reminds me of a client I had, who couldn't stand to go to parties with his wife. He slowly realized that when he heard her talk to her friends with a lilt in her voice, he felt so much anguish and longing, because it reminded him that she used to talk to him that way once, and he used to feel special and loved. It reminded him that it wasn't that way anymore, that he had lost that somehow; she didn't talk to him like that anymore. He felt excluded and sad, so he'd get very angry and ask her lots of questions about her conversations, and she would end up feeling intruded upon. But that was this other client. It may not be relevant or similar to you at all.

This intervention is aimed primarily at accessing the husband's experience, but is directed to the wife in the form of a story about someone else.

6. Self-Disclosure

This is not a large part of the EFT therapist's repertoire, particularly when EFT is compared to other humanistic experiential approaches (Kempler, 1981). It is generally limited and used for a specific purpose, such as to build an alliance and intensify validation of clients' responses, or as a form of joining with clients to help them identify elements of their own experience.

Examples

1. **Husband:** I feel so foolish, I guess I feel that I shouldn't let my anxieties get out of hand to the point where I can't even hear my wife.

   Therapist: Hm, well I know I find it hard to really take in anything when I'm scared. Being scared tends to take up so much space.

2. **Husband:** I think I can deal with anything. I don't feel much right now at all.

   Therapist: You see yourself as pretty resilient. (He nods) Well, I'd like to just share that for me when I see the struggle you two are engaged in, with your wife reaching out and you staying behind your wall, I get sad. Right now it seems sad to me.

These interventions normalize, validate clients' responses, or attempt to evoke a more emotional response from a partner who seems cut off from his or her feelings.

Summary

The therapist's interventions presented above are based upon first accepting both partners as they are, and by this acceptance creating a context for the exploration and elaboration of experience. Particular responses and positions are generally developed and elaborated, rather than confronted or replaced by more "skillful" approaches. The EFT therapist will validate and help the partners explore potentially negative responses such as anger or silent withdrawal, rather than suggest or teach different responses.

Helping clients access, reprocess, and, if necessary, reorganize their experience of self and other in an intimate relationship is a process of discovery and creation. The client discovers new elements of his or her experience that have been previously denied, brushed aside, or simply not formulated.

TASK 3: RESTRUCTURING INTERACTIONS

The two tasks, accessing/reformulating emotions and restructuring interactions, are separated here for the sake of clarity; in practice they are always intertwined. The EFT therapist is always using new emotional experience to create new kinds of dialogue and then using that dialogue to create new interactional events, which then impact the inner emotional life of the partners. How we regulate, engage with, and express emotion and how we engage with others are two sides of the same coin. Thus, the expression of vulnerability creates a new dialogue about one partner's longing for comfort from the other spouse, which tends to elicit new responses from that spouse. In turn, the new dialogue, in which a vulnerable spouse risks being needy and then receives caring, expands this partner's sense of longing and creates the first glimmers of trust. Self and system, dancer and dance, reflect and create each other.

In Task 3, the therapist does the following:

- Tracks and reflects the patterns and cycles of interaction.
- Reframes problems in terms of context, that is, in terms of cycles and attachment processes.
- Restructures interactions by choreographing new events that modify each partner's interactional position.

1. Tracking and Reflecting

The therapist tracks and reflects the process of interactions, in a similar manner to the way in which the therapist tracks and reflects the process of inner experience as each partner constructs that experience. The therapist, by describing the process and structure of interactions, focuses in on and clarifies the nature of the relationship between partners. Early in the therapy process, the therapist pieces together, from the couple's descriptions and from direct observation, the typical problematic interactions the couple engage in. This sequence of interactions is reflected back to the couple and identified in terms of a recurring pattern, the most common being some form of blame–defend or pursue–withdraw. As stated previously, the partners are framed as both the unwitting creators and victims of these negative interactional cycles.

The identification and continuing elaboration of the negative cycle of interaction throughout therapy externalizes the problem in a manner not unlike the narrative approaches to therapy (White & Epston, 1990). This provides an antidote to versions of the relationship problem that involve defects within either of the partners, and tends to defuse blaming and destructive arguments aimed at assigning responsibility for relationship distress. This formulation allows the partners to take some responsibility for the way the relationship has evolved, while framing the destructive cycle, rather than the other partner or personal failings, as the enemy. This destructive pattern of interactions is framed as having a life of its own and as defeating the couple's attempts at contact and caring. The partners can then begin to move toward each other, facing together the enemy that is robbing them of their relationship. The experience of a common external enemy creates a pull toward cohesion in the couple.

The description of interactional patterns, like the descriptions of inner experience, continues throughout therapy and becomes more elaborated and differentiated as time goes on. The EFT therapist focuses upon *prototypical moments* in the interaction when such negative patterns are operating and either accesses underlying emotions to expand the interaction or reflects and/or replays the interaction to crystallize the dance between the couple. The therapist may ask questions such as:

- What just happened there? You said . . . , and then you said . . .
- How do you react, want to respond, when he talks about this in this way?

The interaction is then replayed, described, and summarized in order to clarify and heighten interactional sequences and the positions the partners take with each other in terms of closeness/contact and power and control.

Examples

The following is a reflection of a destructive cycle in Session 1:

> **Therapist:** So, let's see if I understand. What usually happens here is that you want more closeness with

Walt, and you try to talk to him about your feelings and the relationship, and Walt, you prefer to be doing activities or to be with lots of friends, so you find it hard to make the time for this. You are not sure you even know what Jane means by talking. And this has gotten to the point where, Jane, you see Walt as a roommate rather than a partner, and so you get pretty angry and critical of him, and Walt, you try to avoid her anger, so you go out even more and are spending less and less time with Jane. Is that it?

The following is a reflection of the same cycle later in therapy:

Therapist: This is one of those times, Jane, is it, where you start to feel all alone, like Walt is indifferent to you? You feel invisible, and that stirs up indignation in you (invisible *and* indignation *are Jane's words from a previous session*), and you protest. You get mad and you "get in his face" as you put it.

Jane: Yes, and then he does his "I'm out of here" thing.

Therapist: Aha.

Walt: There's no point in staying.

Therapist: The way you experience it, there's nothing you can do then. It seems hopeless.

Walt: Right, right, so I run. I go and find my friends.

Therapist: You run to a safer place, where nobody gets mad at you, tells you they are disappointed in you. That's very difficult for you to hear?

In the following, the therapist replays a specific instance or enactment of the cycle and further differentiates a partner's position.

Therapist: Mary, what happened just then, you bit your lip, went silent, and turned to look out of the window. And Peter, you said, "You never listen, maybe I should find someone who will" and Mary, you replied, "That's right, maybe that's right." It sounds like what you are saying to Peter is, "I won't listen. I won't be critiqued anymore. I'll become quiet and distant and shut you out." (*Position is made explicit and active*) Peter, you sounded pretty angry and accusing. You were letting Mary know that you could leave, which is a pretty big threat, heh? Is that what it is like for you Mary, it's like you're saying, "I'll shut you out"?

Mary: Yes, that's the place I get to. I won't be constantly criticized, analyzed, destroyed, I won't, so I go watch TV and all the other things he says I do. I shut him out.

Therapist: It's like you're protecting yourself; if you don't, you'll be destroyed.

Mary: If I listened to him I'd feel like nothing, like no one. I'm never enough. Why does he want to be close to me if I'm so awful.

Therapist: If you let him close, the message you expect to hear is that you are awful, nothing, almost unlovable. (Mary agrees) So you shut him out. (Mary nods)

Reframing

As a result of the tracking, identification, and elaboration of the cycles of interaction referred to above, the EFT therapist is able to reframe each partner's behavior in terms of such cycles and in terms of the other partner's behavior. This is not reframing in the strategic sense of the term; the frame is not arbitrary, but arises from the increasingly elaborated emotional reality of the partners. As in the work of structural systemic family therapists such as Minuchin and Fishman (1981), each partner's behavior is constantly placed in the context of the other's response.

A voiced desperate desire for contact with the other would be framed here, not in terms of the deficits in the desperate spouse's character structure (she is too needy), or in terms of family of origin (she is seeing her partner as if he were her ungiving father), but in terms of the present relationship. Such desperation would most likely be framed as a reflection of the present distant position her partner takes in the relationship and her subsequent deprivation. The distancing behavior of the other spouse might then be framed as self-protection in the face of the other's angry pursuit, rather than a reflection of indifference. Such reframes help partners to see how they unwittingly help to create the other's distress and resulting negative responses.

In EFT, each partner's behavior is placed, not only in the context of the other's behavior and the pattern of interactions, but also more specifically in the context of intimate attachment, since this is the lens through which the EFT therapist views romantic love. *Interactional responses are framed in terms of underlying vulnerabilities and the attachment process.* Anger may therefore be framed as desperate protest at the partner's perceived unavailability and a response to separation distress. Stonewalling on the part of a distant spouse, which is one of the behaviors associated with marital breakdown (Gottman, 1991), might be framed as this partner's attempt to regulate attachment fears and to protect the relationship from escalating negative interactions. The therapist might frame angry and withdrawing responses as a response to how vitally important the other spouse is as an attachment figure. This is in contrast to the way distressed partners usually understand these responses, which is as a lack of love and caring. These reframes are not simply exterior labels placed on interactional responses by the therapist. If they are to be effective, they must arise from the client's exploration of his or her own experience, how that client symbolizes his or her experience, and the process of interaction.

The three most basic and often used reframes in EFT are that anger is framed as attachment protest, withdrawal is framed as fear, and the cycle is framed as the enemy and the problem, rather than the other spouse and his or her "flaws." Withdrawal and defense are also framed in terms of how crucial this attachment is to a person—as a way of

coping with attachment insecurity—rather than as indifference
or coldness.

Example

> **Therapist:** So, of course, it's difficult to open up and
> show her who you are, when you feel sure she won't
> like who you are and will tell you that, or when you
> are sure she will be angry.
>
> **Gary:** I just go numb. This voice says, she'll leave me,
> like all the others. I freeze, and she gets madder and
> madder.
>
> **Therapist:** You freeze, 'cause it's like you've lost her
> already, almost. It's dangerous.
>
> **Gary:** If I go real quiet maybe it will stop and she'll
> calm down and cool off, if I'm still.
>
> **Therapist:** If you stay completely still the danger
> might pass? (He nods) It's so scary, the idea that she
> will leave, you freeze and hide.
>
> **Gary:** Yeah, and I know it makes her madder than hell.
>
> **Sue:** I can't find you.

The frames proposed above, which place a response in the
context of the other partner's behavior, the interactional cycle,
and the nature of attachment, provide a metaperspective on
the way the relationship is constructed, moment by moment.
The couple engages in a process that demonstrates to them,
in an immediate way, how the moves each one makes then
push the dance in a particular direction, as well as how each
is trying, in the best way he or she knows, to foster a safer
attachment bond.

RESTRUCTURING AND SHAPING INTERACTIONS

The therapist directly choreographs new interactions
between the partners to create new relationship events that
will redefine the relationship. This is the most directive part

of EFT, and often the most dramatic. The therapist directs one partner to respond to the other in a particular way, encourages the expression of new emotional experience to the other, or supports each to state needs and wants directly. At these moments, the relationship moves into new and unfamiliar territory, and each partner requires the direction and the support of the therapist.

The therapist may use such directions to:

1. Crystallize and enact present positions so that they may be expanded.
2. Turn new emotional experience into a specific new response to the partner that challenges old patterns of relating.
3. Heighten new or rarely occurring responses, which have the potential to modify a partner's position.
4. Choreograph change events.

1. Enacting Present Positions So That They May Be Directly Experienced and Expanded

Key interactions that serve to maintain the structure of the relationship are focused upon, highlighted, and enacted more and more explicitly. This is an immediate and powerful way to capture the impasses in a relationship interaction and make them accessible for modification.

Example

In a 10-year relationship in which the male partner holds back from commitment, insisting on keeping his own apartment, periodically breaking away only to reconnect after a few weeks in a highly romantic manner, he says:

> **José:** I cannot quite make the leap, you know. I like my tranquility. Perhaps we should stop the sessions for a few months, that is the best decision, the only one I can make. You are so beautiful, please don't take this personally.

Marie: Well, I know this leap, this getting closer, is hard for you.

Therapist: José, the decision is? Help me understand?

José: Perhaps if we have a few months apart, then I will feel the loss.

Therapist: The decision is to hold back, yes (He nods), to stay separate? (He nods) So can you tell her please: I'm not going to let you in, I'll let you come so far, but no farther.

José: Well, I . . . I'm not sure, I don't think I can say it.

Therapist: Can you tell her: I'm not going to let you in. I never have. I've never let any woman into where she can really hurt me and I don't want to.

José: (sighs) Do I have to say this? This is sad.

Therapist: Does it fit for you. Perhaps I said it wrong?

José: No, I think that it's right. (Long silence) But it's hard to say. (Therapist nods, agrees)

Therapist: I think it's important. You guys have been here, at this point, many times before. (They nod)

José: (looks at his partner) I, I will not let you in. I've never let anyone in (He weeps), never . . . no.

Therapist: Is there anything she could do to change this, José? She has been trying so hard for so long.

José: No, no . . . (to his partner), there's nothing you can do. I have to decide to risk.

The therapist may also ask the couple to replay specific, crucial interactions that seem to capture the essence of the negative cycle or a stuck point in that cycle. The therapist extracts and lifts up a small, significant part of the interaction; one that seems to present a microcosm of the relationship, out of the ongoing dialogue. For example:

1. **Therapist:** What was that there? Alison, you said, "I hurt," and Tim, you said, "I disagree with that." This

seems to happen all the time, doesn't it? You say "I hurt," and then Tim, you say, "No you don't. I didn't do anything bad." Can we go back there? Can you tell him about your hurt, Alison?

2. **Therapist:** What just happened here was the same as what happened in that incident you described at home, wasn't it? Chris, you took a tiny, tiny risk. You moved your knee close to hers last night, at home. And you were hoping she would leave her knee close to yours. But she moved it away—yes? And right here, Mary, Chris took a tiny risk and you said, "Well, I see it. But if he thinks I am going to respond—to begin to let him come close—he's wrong." It's like he has to prove himself first. (Mary nods) And then Chris, you give up and move into depression, and Mary, this confirms your hopelessness and need to protect yourself. So these risks, small risks, the beginning of a new path, go nowhere. Is this right?

2. Turning New Emotional Experience Into a New Response to the Partner

This occurs when the therapist has helped an individual partner explore an emotional experience and a new synthesis of this experience has emerged. This new experience is then expressed to the spouse in a direct way. This is the first step to creating a new kind of positive dialogue and modifying partners' positions. Change in EFT comes not from a reprocessing of inner emotional experience per se, but from new dialogues that arise as a result of this experience. The therapist crystallizes this experience in interpersonal terms, that is, as it relates to the other spouse, using the client's own words as much as possible, and then asks the client to express this version to the other partner. The client usually complies, often modifying the message slightly to make it completely his or her own. If the client cannot express his or her feelings to the other, then this is focused upon and explored.

Examples

1. **Therapist:** So can you look at her? Can you tell her, "I'm so afraid, I'm so afraid to risk reaching for you. I know you'll turn away."

2. **Therapist:** There seems to be this great longing. (Client nods) It's never really said. Can you let him know a little about that? About how much you long to just be held and comforted?

3. **Therapist:** So have I got it right? Even in your anger you are still saying: I want to give myself, to love you. (Client nods) I protect myself with my coldness. I want to be safe and close, too, but not on your terms. (She nods again) Can you tell him this, please?

3. Heightening New Responses

Here the therapist draws attention to and heightens any response that is outside of the usual negative pattern and has the potential to create a new kind of engagement. In the normal course of events, such responses might sometimes occur, but they tend to become submerged in the usual pattern of dialogue between partners.

Example

Therapist: What just happened there? That was different. What was that like for you, Mike, to say what you just said?

Husband: Well, I guess it is a bit different . . . maybe I was a bit different, it was like, like a risk, like coming out.

Therapist: Can you tell Joan that again, I think it was something like: "Don't tell me who I am, it pushes me away"? (*The therapist summarizes and clarifies what was said and asks the person to enact this new response again*)

4. Choreographing Change Events

As new emotional experience and new aspects of self emerge in therapy and attachment issues come to the fore, the therapist is able to facilitate interactions that more and more redefine the relationship in terms of autonomy–control and closeness–distance, and create the basis for more emotional engagement and a more secure bond. The term *choreograph* is used deliberately in that, like a choreographer, the therapist has an overview of the dance and gives step-by-step direction and structure, but the dance is also the dancers' own creation and a vehicle for the expression of self.

There is a sense in which all of the interventions described above lead up to the events of engagement and bonding. Once these events take place—or alternatively, there is a clear definition of the relationship in terms of separateness— a new dance begins. All the new experience and new interactional moves that have evolved in the therapy session are synthesized here to redefine each partner's position and the bond between them.

In a typical blame–withdraw cycle, the two necessary shifts in position are the following: The withdrawn partner becomes more accessible, more emotionally engaged with self and spouse; the blaming partner moves from anger and coercion, asking for attachment needs to be met from a position of vulnerability. This invites contact and allows for bonding events where both partners can be accessible and responsive to each other. *In change events, a spouse explicitly takes a new position with the partner, and this new position then elicits a reorganization of the interaction.*

The therapist keeps the interaction focused, curtailing detours and exits, directs and crystallizes emotional expression, and gently guides the couple in the direction of emotional engagement. Let us look at one brief example of an EFT therapist choreographing the continued engagement of a usually withdrawn husband, and the subsequent beginning of a softening in his critical spouse, culminating in a bonding event.

Example

> **Mary:** So why didn't you tell me you were so depressed? I asked you and you said you were fine, and then went off and tried to hurt yourself. You took all those pills.

Ted: Because I expected you to tell me to go and tell my therapist. I didn't believe you would understand.

Therapist: It would have been such a risk and you were already so raw (he nods), but in fact it was her you wanted, not your therapist.

Ted: Sure it was. If I could have reached out to her and gotten comfort that would have made all the difference, but I couldn't risk it.

Therapist: You couldn't bear the thought that she might reject you, so you gave up?

Ted: Yeah, and now I want her to (therapist motions to him to direct his speech to his spouse), I want you to climb down from your tank, your steamroller, stop solving problems and interrogating me, so we can be together, that's what I need. (Mary looks away)

Therapist: What's happening, Mary?

Mary: I feel confused, I'm good at solving problems, it's my style. I don't know what to say.

Therapist: What happens for you when Ted says he needs you?

Mary: It feels good, but, I don't know what to do. It's like I've lost my bearings. Do you think you need me more than your friends at work? (*Exit to old response of questioning spouse*)

Therapist: Mary, can you tell him: I feel confused.

Mary: Yeah . . . it's hot in here . . . if I can't problem solve, what does he want? (Therapist looks at Ted)

Ted: I want you . . . more than a problem solver . . .

Mary: (weeps) Well, that's it . . . if I'm not the great director, the bulldozer, the manager . . . it feels vulnerable. I'm not sure of myself here. (Starts furiously rubbing her hands)

Therapist: This is strange territory, huh? (Mary nods) You're uncertain, feeling vulnerable, and knowing that Ted sees that. It's a little different, a little scary perhaps?

> **Mary:** Sure, sure it is. I'm not as tough as everyone thinks I am.
>
> **Therapist:** Can you tell him: It's scary to step out of that tank and be vulnerable.
>
> **Mary:** (to Ted) It is. I'm unsure of myself here. Do you want that? I've never done that.
>
> **Ted:** (weeps) I want us to be together (cups his hands and clasps them together in front of his chest), not you managing me. Can we? (*He is now emotionally engaged and asserting his needs with his wife*)
>
> **Mary:** I'll try.

Here the therapist not only helps one partner formulate new responses to the other, but also fosters the creation of a new dialogue based upon these new responses. In the above example, the process went smoothly; at other times the therapist may have to help the partners attend to, process, and acknowledge these new responses from the other spouse. After such an intervention, the therapist also makes explicit the new positions the partners are taking with each other and the implications of these new positions and dialogues for the relationship.

TECHNIQUES SPECIFIC TO DIFFICULT THERAPEUTIC IMPASSES

There are also specific techniques the EFT therapist uses in difficult impasses. These are:

- Presenting diagnostic pictures and narratives of the couple's interactions and positions in a manner that makes the impasse explicit and confronts the couple with the consequences of this impasse for their relationship.
- Conducting individual sessions to explore specific blocks in the therapy process. These blocks may take the form of attachment injuries. These injuries are addressed in a later chapter.

Diagnostic Pictures or Narratives

Here the therapist paints pictures of the couple's positions and cycles and elaborates on the nature of the present process. In effect, it is as if the therapist says, "We are stuck here, aren't we? How can we move and what happens if we can't?"

The picture the therapist paints is concrete and specific. It is based on the process of previous sessions and the couple's own perceptions of this process. This graphic presentation of the present status of the relationship heightens the partners' sense of the impasse. It also presents them with a limited number of choices about the future nature of the relationship. Often this process results in a new risk being taken, or a new response given, that will break the impasse.

The most common form of impasse encountered in EFT seems to be when a previously less engaged partner is now available, but the other partner cannot bring him- or herself to risk trusting and allow emotional engagement. The therapist might first recount the story of therapy up until the present time, then paint a picture of the present interactional patterns and describe how they place the relationship in neutral.

Example

> **Therapist:** So this seems right to you? We have come to the point where, Terry, you are really wanting to connect with Sarah. I see you inviting her to come and be with you, not hiding or trying to force her to come, but holding out your hands, yeah? (He nods) And Sarah, you see it too?
>
> **Sarah:** I guess so, yes, yes, he is. I know, he's different.
>
> **Therapist:** But you're still, as you describe it, behind your wall. You're not sure you want to learn to trust him, is that it?
>
> **Sarah:** I just wanted the fights to stop, and they have really. I'm not sure about closeness, that's a whole other thing. Perhaps I want a more distant relationship than he does.

The therapist helps Sarah articulate her reservation about creating a closer relationship; for her this is, as she describes it, "bungee jumping." The couple can then talk about the consequences of staying where they are, in the impasse. *The therapist's task is to present the choices that are available to them.* It is important that the therapist not judge the appropriateness of their choices, or impose values and choices on the couple. The couple have to decide what they can and will live with. This may be very different from the therapist's view of a good relationship, or one which the therapist might want for him- or herself.

The essential nature of an impasse can sometimes be captured in a dramatic narrative or disquisition. For example, a male partner suffering from post-traumatic stress disorder was in crisis and becoming dangerously coercive and demanding with his wife. He was told a story that attempted to capture the emotional reality of, and the couple's positions in, the relationship. The story began, "Once upon a time there was a little boy, and he lived in a very scary cold place; the boy met a girl and asked her to hold him. She agreed, because she loved the little boy, but her arms began to ache and she asked to put him down for a moment. The little boy became terrified and believed she would leave, so he insisted that she hold him. In the end her arms hurt so badly that she put him down. He was enraged and kicked her. Then, very reluctantly, very sadly, she left." This kind of narrative allows the partners to see the larger picture and can expand an obsessive focus on one aspect of the relationship. It is, of course, only useful if the couple are "caught" by it and use it to reprocess their own situation.

INDIVIDUAL SESSIONS

Individual sessions, if used, are always balanced between partners. If one partner is given one, the other partner is also given one. In these sessions, experiential techniques are used to address specific emotional responses that seem to block emotional engagement in the marital sessions, or to focus intensely on problematic responses that undermine progress in the marital sessions. The therapist might focus, for example, on a partner's threats to leave the relationship (discussed elsewhere, Johnson & Greenberg, 1995), or explore responses (such as shame) that can inhibit risk taking in the couple sessions, making it very difficult for one partner to ask the other to respond to attachment needs.

In addition to experiential techniques for reprocessing problematic reactions, an attachment frame and dialogues with attachment figures are actively used. With very self-deprecating partners, who judge themselves unworthy of love, the therapist, for example, might use previous positive attachments to challenge this negative view of self. The therapist does this in the form of an imaginary encounter with this attachment figure. The client is asked to articulate, for instance, how his mother might see his present situation in his marriage and what she might say to him. He is thus asked to formulate, with the therapist's help, a more compassionate and accepting view of himself. Again, such techniques are only useful if the client becomes emotionally engaged in the process.

Individual sessions can also be useful when a crisis occurs that threatens to swamp the therapy process—for example, when the death of a parent results in a sudden withdrawal from the couple relationship that threatens to undermine all the progress already made in couple therapy sessions.

SUMMARY

The therapist in EFT acts as a guide, a process consultant, to the reprocessing and reorganization of emotional experience in relation to the partner, and to the reorganization of interactions in such a way as to promote emotional engagement and secure bonding. This is a powerful change process, involving an exploration not only of each partner's habitual ways of connecting to and engaging with intimate others, but also with his or her own emotions, attachment needs, and core representations of self. The purpose is to generate a corrective emotional and interactional experience of self in relation to other, and also to empower people to create the kinds of relationships they want in their lives.

In a typical session of EFT, the therapist might be focused upon the following activities:

- **Monitoring the alliance.** "I sense this process is difficult for you. Is there some way I can be more supportive?"

- **Reflecting secondary emotion.** "And you get very angry when this happens, because it feels like such a no-win situation. I understand (to the other partner) that to you the anger seems to come out of the blue."

- **Reflecting underlying emotions.** "So, what it's like is, there is a kind of panic when he turns his back, is that right? And you feel it right now—as he turns away from you."

- **Validating present responses.** "I think I'm starting to understand. For you, 'shutting down,' as you call it, is your natural way to cope. In fact, it has protected you all through your life, so when alarm bells go off, it just comes up as the only thing to do."

- **Validating newly experienced underlying emotion.** "It is very hard for you when you hear your wife say that you've disappointed her. You might seem impervious, but in fact it's like a knife in your heart. It hurts so much that you go numb."

- **Evocative responding.**
  a. "What happens when you hear your wife talking like this, John? When she talks about feeling cornered and confined. How do you feel as you listen to her say this?"
  b. "What happened right there, Alan? Mary said that she has never felt taken care of in this relationship; then you closed your lips and folded your arms across your chest?"

   c. "What does that part of you—the part that told you
      never to open up—to never get hurt again—what
      does that part tell you right now?"

- **Heightening.** "Can you say that again, Evan: 'Where are
  you? I can't find you.' Can you look at her and say that
  again?"

- **Engaging in empathic conjecture.** "I'm not sure I quite
  understand. Is it like, if she doesn't desire me every day,
  I've lost her. That's the signal I rely on to reassure myself
  that she's still here, that she wants me. Is that it?"

- **Tracking and reflecting interactions.** "What just happened there, you said . . . and then you said . . . ?"

- **Reframing each partner's behavior in the context of the
  cycle.** "So this is dangerous ground for both of you right
  now. You feel that you have to protest; protest how distant Jim is, but actually that scares you, Jim. It adds to
  your sense that you'd better find a place to hide, yes?"

- **Reframing each person's behavior in the context of
  attachment needs.** "When you do this, what you call
  ambush, it's like you have to get him to respond, to
  know that you do have an impact and that there is still
  a relationship, a connection, is that it?"

- **Restructuring interactions.** "So can you tell her that,
  Tom, can you tell her, I don't know how to come and
  be close, I don't know how."

THE HOW OF INTERVENTIONS

The congruence of the therapist—the match of the therapist's
nonverbal messages and verbal messages—is of supreme
importance in EFT. The nonverbal aspect of communication
is designated as the "command" aspect of communication
for a good reason. It colors communication content and
commands the listener's response. The EFT therapist must

then be aware of his or her nonverbal messages. In training, we speak of how a therapist can *hold a client with her or his voice and keep this client in the present moment.* Not only does a certain kind of stance and voice and eye contact promote safety and contact with the therapist and promote a strong alliance, but the EFT therapist also thus *invites* clients to engage with their experience on a deeper level. This combination of safety and engagement creates a working distance from powerful emotional experience, so that it can be developed and refined. In particular, when the therapist wishes clients to contact and engage with difficult emotions, the following *RISSSC* acronym is useful. In EFT training, we offer the scaffold below to increase awareness of nonverbals, especially when emotional risk (hence the acronym) is present:

- **Repeat.** It is important to repeat key words and phrases a number of times.
- **Image.** Images capture and hold emotion in a way that abstract words cannot.
- **Simple.** It is essential to keep words and phrases simple and concise.
- **Slow.** Emotional experience unfolds in a session; a slow pace enables this process.
- **Soft.** A soft voice soothes and encourages deeper experiencing and risk taking.
- **Client's words.** The EFT therapist notes and adopts the client's words and phrases in a collaborative and validating way.

This manner and tone are crucial when *unfolding* and working with absorbing emotions. It is not essential at other times when the therapist is engaged with other tasks, such as delineating the cycle or discussing an argument.

In the process of helping the client to unfold and engage with experience, an EFT therapist will take an abstract or undifferentiated label used by a client and slow down the process of therapy to focus on a word or a label such as *dark* or *complicated* or *impossible* or *frozen* using the RISSSC manner described above.

Example

Dennis: (high voice, fast pace, distracted demeanor) This is impossible to talk about. There are other matters—all these issues with the cottage and the finances—I have nothing to say really. Everything between us is too complicated. I feel nothing—empty.

Therapist: (slow pace, low soft voice) So when your wife tells you—as she just did—that she is giving up—she is despairing of being able to be close to you—you feel you have nothing to say—you feel nothing—just empty—? (He nods) And that nothing place—what is that like?

Dennis: (slower, low voice) Don't know. Well—it's just dark.

Therapist: Just dark. When you wife tells you she is despairing—giving up on the relationship, you go into nothing—into darkness—into emptiness?

Dennis: Yes—What is the point anyway. I just freeze up. What is the point? I don't know how to do this relationship stuff right.

Therapist: (*using RISSSC*) So you freeze, go into darkness, emptiness, and I guess then, if this was happening at home, you would just withdraw?—yes. (He nods) And she would think you were indifferent—uncaring. When, in fact, you are overwhelmed—it is all so "complicated" as you put it, and you are in darkness—you don't know what to do. (He nods and tears) That dark place must feel awful—we get lost in the dark—and maybe it's kind of scary?

Dennis: You bet it is— (He shrugs)

Therapist: But there is nothing you can do—or at least it looks that way—you are lost in the darkness without a sign—a direction—and it feels scary and empty. Can you tell her, when you tell me . . . I . . . ?

The EFT therapist here stays focused on the present moment and unfolding this moment. But it is not just the focus and the interventions that encourage the client to walk deeper into his or her experience and expand and differentiate it—it is also the manner the therapist uses.

Couple therapy is a multileveled drama that evolves across a number of sessions, and interventions will vary according to the goals and tasks of different stages and steps in the change process. However, at this point it seems useful to also focus on the recurring process that occurs in each session of EFT.

In-Session Processes and Interventions

EFT is a *process-oriented* approach. In every session, the therapist focuses on and develops the evolving process of how both partners construct their relational experience, particularly their attachment emotions, and how both then engage their spouse. The therapist will then continually track and reflect inner responses and interactional moves and patterns. The therapist allows clients to gradually taste and savor their relational experience and then places this in the context of patterns of interaction, and vice versa. The therapist trusts clients' innate ability to grow, the power of corrective emotional experience, and the power of attachment longings and strivings. In general, the EFT therapist turns and turns experience and interaction to hold them up to the light. The therapist constantly frames emotion as the music of the couple's dance and the dance as creating the music. The therapist also turns both to the light so as to make the following shifts:

- From vague to vivid.
- Obscure to tangible.
- General to specific.
- Then to now—immediate.
- Global to personal.
- Passive to active.
- Abstract to concrete.

In every session, then, an observer would see the EFT therapist circling through the following process:

- Track, reflect, validate, and unfold emotional processes— place in context of attachment and cycles of interaction— create enactments—unfold the drama of the enactments.
- Track, reflect moments of interaction—place in context of attachment and complete cycles of interaction—listen to the emotional music of these moments of interaction— unfold key attachment affects.

The EFT therapist is always focused, then, on the moment-to-moment creation of *emotional moments* and interactional *moves* and patterns and so on the creation of attachment realities.

It is now time to turn from techniques to the process of therapy, in which these interventions are woven together to accomplish particular tasks at particular times.

5

ASSESSMENT: DEFINING THE DANCE AND LISTENING TO MUSIC

EFT: STEPS 1 AND 2

This chapter describes the first two steps in the EFT treatment process: the delineation of conflict issues and the identification of the negative interaction cycle that maintains the couple's distress and precludes secure bonding.

Assessment is not separated from treatment in experiential models of therapy such as EFT. The EFT therapist is, in a sense, always learning about his or her clients and assessing their needs. However, the first two conjoint sessions of EFT, and the two individual sessions that usually follow, are conceptualized as assessment.

The therapist's general goals in the first sessions are:

- To connect with both partners. To create an alliance where both partners feel safe and accepted by the therapist, and begin to have confidence that the therapist understands their goals and needs and will be able to help them.

- To assess the nature of the problem and the relationship, including its suitability for couple therapy in general, and for EFT in particular.

- To assess each partner's goals and agendas for therapy and to ascertain whether these goals are feasible and compatible, not only in terms of the partners' individual agendas, but also with the therapist's skills and the nature of the therapy.
- To create a therapeutic agreement between the couple and the therapist, a consensus as to therapeutic goals and how therapy will be conducted.

Such agreement is not possible if, for example, couples have widely divergent and/or conflicting therapy agendas. In a couple where the husband has already left the relationship, but the wife has coerced him into seeking couple therapy in a desperate attempt to change his mind, the partners are usually advised to seek some kind of individual help. However, a few sessions of couple therapy can clarify the nature of the relationship, perhaps helping the still-engaged partner to begin the grieving process.

Partners also occasionally come for therapy with agendas that the therapist cannot engage in—for example, the partner who is enraged that his wife will not conform to his demands and whose one agenda for therapy is to get the therapist to agree that his wife's noncompliance is a sign of mental illness and to persuade her to comply with his requests. There are times when the most therapeutic intervention is not to engage in couple therapy.

More specifically, there are contraindications for the use of EFT. These will be discussed in more detail in chapter 10 EFT is not used, for example, where there is ongoing abuse and violence in a relationship, or where there is evidence that the exposure of vulnerability will place a partner at risk, as in the case of a highly verbally abusive husband who in the session unrelentingly demeans his partner, mocking her when she speaks of her suicidal depression. The issue of how to assess violence in the context of deciding the appropriateness of couple therapy is very well addressed by Bograd and Mederos (1999).

PROCESS GOALS

If there are problems such as those mentioned above, they will emerge in the process of the assessment as the therapist follows the process goals outlined below:

- To begin to enter into the experience of each partner and sense how each constructs his or her experience of this relationship.
- To begin to make hypotheses as to the vulnerabilities and attachment issues underlying each partner's position in the relationship.
- To track and describe the typical recurring sequences of interactions that perpetuate this couple's distress, and crystallize each partner's position in that interaction.
- To begin to understand how the present relationship evolved and what prompted the couple to seek therapy. To hear the couple's story of their relationship.
- To begin to hypothesize as to the blocks to secure attachment and emotional engagement within and between partners and to explore these. Are they both wanting the same kind of relationship? Are they both committed to the relationship?
- To sense how this couple responds to interventions and how easy or difficult the process of therapy is going to be. Do they each take some responsibility for the problems in the relationship? How open and willing are they to take risks in the session? The level of rigidity in the enactment of positions and the reactivity of responses are noted.
- To note the strengths of the partners and the positive elements in the relationship.

By the end of the assessment, as the therapist turns toward Step 3 of EFT, he or she has a topographic map of the prototypical interactions that define the attachment bond between this couple, a clear sense of their positions and patterns. The therapist also begins to have a sense of how these are experienced on an emotional level by each partner. He or she begins to sense the *tone* of the relationship; the music of the dance.

THE THERAPY PROCESS

What do the first few sessions of EFT look like? What is the usual process as a therapist guides the couple through the first two steps of therapy?

Let us try to get an overview of a typical session by considering the questions that go through the therapist's mind as the first sessions evolve. They might be as follows:

- Who are these people? What does the general fabric of their life look like? The therapist gathers basic information.
- How did they decide to come for therapy at this particular time?
- How does each of them see the problem in the relationship? Can they sustain a dialogue about their views, or are they radically different and/or rigidly held?
- Does each of them see strengths in the relationship? What keeps them together? How do they describe each other? As they tell their stories, what kinds of problematic interactions are described, and how did they attempt to deal with them?
- How do they view the history of the relationship and understand how they originally connected?
- How does each of them present him- or herself and his or her own history to the therapist? Does each person's story suggest any particular attachment issues and/or problems?
- How does the couple generally interact in the session? If asked to interact around a particular topic, how does

the dialogue evolve? What messages are conveyed by each partner's nonverbal responses?

The couple generally experiences these sessions as relatively intense and emotionally engaging. They are encouraged to tell their story of marital distress, describe their fights and problems, as well as their positive moments, and dialogue about difficult topics. The therapist, while allowing the couple the space to describe the last fight, to state their point of view, or tell how their differing approaches to conflict are typical of their family histories, also asks directive questions and focuses the session on attachment issues, emotional experience, and interactional sequences.

In a couple session so much occurs, on so many different levels, that the key issue, even for an experienced therapist, is where to look or what to pay attention to in the crowded landscape of facts, feelings, incidents, and interactions. In first sessions, partners usually share key pivotal relationship incidents that define how the relationship is for each of them, and contain implications about how the self is defined in relation to the other. They also enact powerful interactional sequences, sometimes heightened by the therapist, which capture the essential quality of the relationship. These moments are like *personal and interactional landmarks* in the landscape of the marriage and help to clarify the therapist's emerging picture of the couple's predicament. These landmarks are always characterized by a shift toward more deeply experienced affect. Particular note is taken of how, in the process of describing or enacting such incidents, one partner defines the other, labeling his or her experience and character, and also how partners define themselves in relation to their partner. To give the reader a sense of these kind of incidents, some examples are given below.

Personal Landmarks or Incidents

Such incidents have attachment significance that is often not understood by the other partner, and are continually referred to in the interactions, often as ammunition in an argument. They cannot be forgotten or left behind, and they cannot be resolved in the present emotional climate of the relationship.

- A wife recounts that her parents wanted a boy and told her she was ugly and retarded. The real punch, however, comes when she tearfully recounts that when her husband told his family about her, he described her as a good woman, from a good family, even if she was not very pretty. As she recounts this, she weeps, while her partner smiles and minimizes the incident, thus fueling her anger and her alienation from him. She goes on to note that she has never been clear as to her value to her partner.

- A wife tells how her husband refused to come to a potentially traumatic medical appointment at the hospital with her, because his friend had called and asked to see him.

- An apparently very reserved man, who presents as very rational and detached, insists that for him there is no problem in the marriage. His wife is alienated by his accommodating reserve. He then begins to describe how he once, 10 years ago, had had a very brief affair during which his lover once told him that he was physically beautiful and desirable, and he begins to weep uncontrollably.

All these incidents are like a door opening onto the partners' experience of their marriage. They also provide clues as to the nature of their pain and their sense of self in relation to the other partner. Such incidents can be seen in attachment terms as abandonments and betrayals, and/or as ways into the attachment wounds and longings of these partners. The EFT therapist will stay with and validate these experiences, helping the client elaborate on them and their significance for the relationship. The therapist will also use them in future sessions as a reference point for partners' emotional experience in the relationship.

Interactional Landmarks

In the first sessions, interactions occur that vividly demonstrate the positions of the partners and their negative cycle. These are noted and may be reflected back to the couple. They can also be expanded and elaborated as part of the assessment process. This expansion must be particularly respectful and carefully done, since it is early in the therapy process and only a preliminary alliance exists between the partners and the therapist. For example, interactions may occur that one partner dominates or effectively controls. The therapist notes how the other partner responds, as well as how and when the more controlling partner acts in this way:

- A husband tearfully states that he cannot go on with the very extensive infertility treatments that his wife is insisting on. She then cuts him off and explains in a calm, controlled manner that she cannot help it if he is infertile. He must, therefore, continue with the agreed-upon procedures. The husband then looks resigned and visibly withdraws from the conversation.

- A wife describes how humiliated she feels when her spouse criticizes her in front of her family. He states that if she would improve her behavior, for example, do her chores more conscientiously, he would not have to criticize her. She cries at this point, while he continues to point out to her that even here in the session her communication skills are deficient. The wife then begins to plead with her partner to be less of a perfectionist.

- One partner accuses and threatens, while the other remains calm and detached. The first partner increases the tenor of the accusation and the other definitively labels this partner as sick or deficient in some way. The first partner then weeps and withdraws. After a short pause and perhaps a change of topic, this pattern occurs again.

These kinds of incidents may just be noted by the therapist, or may be focused on, depending on the process of the session. For example, the wife who did the chores imperfectly might be asked to continue to try to get her husband to hear her distress, with the therapist providing support to both of the partners. As the couple tries to complete this task, they demonstrate the rigidity or relative flexibility of the present interaction pattern and how the responses of each partner contribute to the pattern.

Interactions also usually occur that demonstrate the quality of contact and support in the relationship and the blocks to such contact and support. One spouse will become vulnerable, for example, and the therapist will note the other's response or lack of response:

- A woman cries over the death of a newborn child and states that she feels alone in her grief. She then asks her husband if he ever feels this way. The spouse looks at the ceiling and states that crying will not bring the child back and there is no point to it. His wife then attacks him for all the ways she sees that he disappoints his children by his long absences from home.

- The wife states that her partner is emotionally crippled and cannot feel. Later in the session, he weeps. The therapist asks the wife, who is looking out the window, what is happening with her as her husband weeps. She states that she does not believe in, or trust, his response and sees him as manipulating the therapist.

- A highly intellectualizing and withdrawn spouse breaks down at the end of a first session and, with tears in his eyes, states that he does not know how to show his wife that he loves her very much, and that she is the source of his happiness in life. His wife, who has previously complained bitterly about not being loved or feeling important to her spouse, looks confused but then indignantly attacks him and states that she is not any house flower and feels demeaned by his tone and comment.

The couple usually shows the therapist, who fosters and heightens their interactions, not only the control and affiliation aspects of the positions they take in relation to each ther, but also how in a negative cycle, the position taken by spouse recursively evokes the position taken by the other. The speed, automaticity, and rigidity of the cycle are noted. Couples will vary in *how aware* they are of the cycle, *how compelling* the cycle is, whether they have *any ways of exiting* and reinitiating a different form of contact, and *how much of the relationship it has encompassed*. Often couples wait until the cycle can be more accurately described as a spin before they seek out a therapist. The word *spin* captures the speed and self-perpetuating, absorbing nature of the negative cycle. This cycle often absorbs and defines every element in the couple's relationship.

INDIVIDUAL SESSIONS

As part of the assessment process, the EFT therapist often conducts an individual session with each of the partners, usually after the first or second conjoint sessions. The purpose of these individual sessions is:

1. To foster the therapeutic alliance with each partner.
2. To observe and interact with each partner in a different context, one in which the spouse is absent.
3. To obtain information and check hypotheses that are difficult to explore in front of the spouse. For example, the therapist can seek information on commitment level, extramarital relationships, or previous personal attachment traumas that impact the present relationship. The therapist also can explore how each partner perceives his or her spouse; such uncensored key perceptions of the other may be useful in later therapy sessions. The therapist can also check for contraindicators for couple therapy, such as violence in the relationship.

4. Such sessions allow the therapist to refine his or her impression of the underlying feelings and attachment insecurities that influence each partner's interactional position and to begin to articulate these insecurities with individual partners.

The issue of the therapist being stuck with secrets that undermine his or her therapeutic effectiveness does not seem to arise here. In the collaborative partnership of the alliance, if information arises that is likely to undermine therapeutic attempts to improve the relationship, such as an ongoing emotional involvement with another person, this is explored in terms of the client's goals for the therapy sessions and effects on the marital relationship. The therapist then requests that this information be shared with the other partner in order to meet the goals of therapy. He or she helps the individual explore any fears or reservations about such disclosures. The therapist also helps this partner share the information with the spouse in the next session.

In the first sessions, assessment and treatment are intermingled. If first sessions are considered as treatment, what are the therapeutic processes and interventions that usually occur? The following section will discuss this in the format that will be used in the following chapters to discuss all nine steps of EFT. This structure consists of: the *markers* (points of intervention) and *tasks* in the therapy process, therapeutic *interventions*, couple *change processes* and how these processes are understood in EFT, as well as the *end state* of such processes.

THERAPEUTIC PROCESSES

Therapeutic Markers

A first session in couple therapy can be compared to suddenly finding oneself in the middle of a play, without knowing the plot or the characters. One of the first steps in a therapy model is to formulate what the therapist notes and responds to in the session. A marker is a point in therapy where a particular type of expression or interactional event signals to the therapist an emotional processing or interactional problem, or an opportunity to intervene in the above. The occurrence of particular markers suggests particular tasks and interventions to the EFT therapist, which lead to particular client responses or activities and contribute to change in the session. Markers in EFT are prototypical reactions—both emotional responses to the partner and interactional events that define the relational experience and the structure of the couple's marriage. They are signals to the therapist to pay attention and to intervene.

The kinds of markers that usually occur in the first sessions, both intrapsychic and interpersonal, are:

Intrapsychic Markers

1. As one partner tells his or her story of the relationship and the problems in the relationship, *strong emotional responses* interrupt the narrative. At this point, partners usually exhibit nonverbal signs of strong affect—crying, flushing red, turning away, biting the lips, clenching the fists—and the flow of the narrative or dialogue is interrupted. The task here is to focus on and acknowledge the affect, thereby creating a secure base in the therapy session for such experiencing.

2. As one partner tells his or her story, *the lack of emotion* is very marked. Dramatic and often traumatic events are reported from a detached stance, as if they had happened to someone else. The incongruity between what is being said and the manner in which it is reported—in a sense, emotion that is conspicuous by its absence—grabs the therapist's attention. The task here is to explore the lack of engagement in personal experience and what this signifies concerning the couple's engagement in, and definition of, the relationship.

3. During moments of intense affect, partners articulate *beliefs* concerning themselves, the other partner, or their relationship that appear rigidly organized and/or destructive in the present context. These beliefs are often stated as definitions of identity. The self, the other, the relationship or relationships in general are defined and declared to be constituted in a particular way. The partners often convey the meanings that they have given to key relational events in terms that preclude the possibility of change, or the development of any new perspective or information. The task here is to reflect and elucidate such beliefs and begin to frame them as part of the destructive cycle that controls the couple's relationship.

4. Particular *attachment issues are identified, but are not owned*, or are responded to in ways that block resolution of such issues; for example, a wife blames her partner for being a "workaholic" but does not seem willing to focus on her own sense of abandonment and loss. The task here is to begin to focus on such issues and frame them as central to the ongoing problem in the couple's relationship.

Interpersonal Markers

1. In the first sessions, the therapist particularly notes *position markers*, that is, comments or responses that appear to define power or control and closeness–distance in the relationship. These markers occur in dialogue between the therapist and each partner, in the dialogue between the partners, as well as in the stories of the relationship that each partner tells. The task here is for the therapist to get a clear picture of the position each partner takes in relation to the other and each partner's perception of and emotional responses to such positions.

2. The therapist also notes *negative cycle markers*. By far the most common cycle in distressed couples is some form of pursue/criticize–withdraw/avoid. However, withdraw–withdraw cycles, where both partners are

relatively disengaged, and volatile attack–attack cycles are also seen. In withdraw–withdraw cycles, the story the couple tells often makes it clear that this cycle has developed from the pursue–withdraw pattern; by the time they come for therapy, however, the pursuer has also begun to disengage and withdraw. The couple tells the therapist about, and enacts, the manner in which the positions they take with each other interconnect to create negative self-reinforcing patterns in the relationship. *The therapist tracks and clarifies such cycles.* The task is to become clear about what the cycle is and to frame it in such a way that the couple finds it relevant and true to their experience. They can then begin to integrate it into their way of thinking about the relationship. Individual responses are placed in the expanded context of the cycle.

3. The therapist particularly notes the way the partners interact when there is an opportunity for positive contact and emotional engagement, particularly how that contact is blocked. This illustrates how the attachment insecurities of each partner are played out in the interaction. The task is to note if and how the couple makes positive contact, and to note and explore exits from such contact, such as when one partner reaches for the other and the other rapidly shifts to an inaccessible position. If such contact is created in the first sessions, the task is to focus on it and acknowledge it as part of the strength of the relationship.

INTERVENTIONS

The interventions the EFT therapist is most likely to use at this point in therapy are:

1. Reflection

In early sessions, this often consists of empathic reflections of each partner's experience of the relationship and of the sequences of interaction, positive and negative, that characterize the relationship.

Example

> **Therapist:** So, help me get this straight, Dan. You're saying that you once found Yvonne's more distant, quiet style alluring and mysterious, but now it frustrates and enrages you and usually ends up with you questioning her, or what she experiences as "badgering." Is that it?

2. Validation

This is particularly crucial in the first sessions. The therapist conveys the message that the partners' emotions and responses are legitimate and understandable, and their responses are the best solutions they could find in the light of each partner's experience of the relationship. This proactive acceptance of each person is essential to a strong alliance and to the process of EFT.

Example

> **Therapist:** I think I understand, Marie. You are talking about feeling so desperate, so desperate to know how Rob feels about you, that threatening to hurt yourself with those pills was your way of trying to get relief from this dreadful doubt. The doubt that he doesn't care, or wishes he could be rid of you. I understand that for you, Rob, it doesn't feel like this. You feel tricked and enraged, like Marie is pulling your strings.

3. Evocative Reflections and Questions

These interventions are always offered in a tentative and respectful fashion; this is especially true in the first few sessions, when the therapist is learning about the relationship and the alliance is not yet formed. The therapist focuses upon unclear or emerging aspects of experience to clarify how each partner perceives and experiences the problem in the relationship and to identify the interactional positions and cycles. However, this is done with deliberate care and respect. Any issues concerning the partners' engagement in the process of therapy, their reservations, anxieties, and doubts, are also the focus of such reflections. The task here is not so much the active reprocessing of experience, but the accessing of each person's experience of the relationship.

Example

1. **Therapist:** So what is it like for you to hear Mary talk about you in this caring way?
2. **Therapist:** So what has it been like for both of you to talk to me? You have shared some very difficult and painful things.

Heightening and empathic conjecture are used much less in beginning sessions, although the therapist may summarize partners' responses in an evocative or dramatic manner to crystallize the cycle and/or each partner's experience of the relationship. The partners are also *explicitly* encouraged to correct the therapist and help the therapist understand, if they feel that he or she is in any way painting a picture that they cannot relate to, appears inaccurate, or makes them uncomfortable.

4. Tracking and Reflecting Interactions

At this stage, the therapist focuses especially on typical behavior sequences that seem to define the relationship and reflect attachment issues. This is an essential part of identifying the patterns of interaction. The sequences of interaction are then plotted from the narrative presentation of the relationship, from the description of specific incidents, and from observation of interactions in the session.

Example

> **Therapist:** So how it goes, then, is that a lot of your relationship is taken up with Fred feeling left out and getting "feisty" and "prickly," and you refusing to be "picked on," as you put it, and moving even farther away. Is that it? Just like what happened here a moment ago, he reached over and poked you and you brushed him off and moved your chair away.

5. Reframing

This intervention may be used in the first sessions, but on a relatively superficial level. Even in the first session, the therapist may begin to frame one spouse as deprived, for example, and the other as needing to protect the self through distance. However, this depends on whether the partners express their experience in a way that is amenable to such formulations. Such reframes can be incorporated as part of the description of the cycle. In a general sense, the moment that the couple makes contact with the therapist, the kinds of questions he or she asks, and the focus taken, begin the process of reframing the couple's problems and issues. Certain reframes are consistent throughout therapy. The couple's problem is framed as the self-reinforcing negative cycle and its impact on attachment security, and problematic responses are often framed in terms of fears around the partner and the attachment significance of the partner, rather than as character flaws or indifference to or hostility toward the partner. However, the central task at the very beginning of therapy is to engage the couple in therapy and to begin to grasp the intrapsychic and interactional struggles that structure the relationship.

Example

> **Therapist:** The moving away is your way of standing up for yourself, protecting yourself, from his "poking," yes? And for you, poking is your way of saying "I'm here, here I am, let me in, see me." Is that it?

COUPLE PROCESS AND END STATE

The desired outcome of the first sessions in EFT is that both partners feel understood and acknowledged by the therapist. They begin to feel safe in the session and to have confidence in the therapist as a person who will respect them, and as a professional who can understand the struggles in their relationship. The therapist instills hope in the partners by structuring the session so that each is heard, by validating each partner's experience and strengths, and by conveying directly that, for every couple, close relationships are a struggle, but a struggle that the therapist expects to be able to help them with. The summary at the end of the first sessions always includes a description of the struggles they have already engaged in and won, even if the only apparent one of this kind is that they have decided to come for help. By the end of the first session, the therapist is also creating an alliance where he or she is an accepted partner in the creation of a more loving relationship.

If the result of the first sessions is that the therapist does not recommend EFT, then the couple is given feedback and a diagnostic picture, which usually includes a description of their interaction cycle and a summary of how each seems to experience this relationship, as well as the reasons why EFT is not being offered. Other forms of help are then discussed and referral sources offered, whether they be individual therapy, groups for addictions or learning to overcome anger problems, or other forms of couple-oriented interventions such as divorce mediation.

During the course of the first sessions, the couple usually travels from uncertainty about the process of therapy to more comfort and confidence in it; from anxiety about the therapist to a sense of being accepted by the therapist and being able to rely on him or her for help; from a sense of confusion and desperation about the relationship to the beginning of a sense of hope and agency; from a sense of stuckness in dead-end interactions, such as fights about who is to blame for the present state of the relationship, to a sense of new possibilities and discovery; from a constricted picture of the relationship and its impact on the self to an expanded view of the cycle and how it keeps both partners trapped and helpless.

At the end of the first sessions, and indeed at the end of every session, the therapist summarizes the high points, themes, and developments of the session in such a way as to validate both partners and give them hope. It is also important to allow a little time to invite clients to ask questions about the process of therapy and about EFT in particular. In a collaborative therapy, such inquiries are encouraged and fully responded to. Sometimes such questions are general, and sometimes they are very specific—for example, a client may ask why the therapist focuses so much on emotion or why he or she was asked to talk directly to the spouse about difficult issues, as in enactments. The EFT therapist responds to such questions in as open and transparent a manner as possible.

A transcript from a first session of EFT may be found elsewhere (Johnson & Greenberg, 1992). A training tape of EFT also shows the process described in this transcript (Johnson, 1993).

6

CHANGING THE MUSIC: TOWARD DE-ESCALATION
EFT: STEPS 3 AND 4

"I feel so small, so naked when I ask. So I make myself
bigger, pushier."
"It sure works, you terrify the hell out of me—I go hide."
"I get so frustrated. I'm more alone than when I was single.
So I bang on the door—louder and louder. So he will hear
me. I am so lonely—so exhausted."
"I guess I just put up a wall. I can't take all the
negativity—all the criticism. It kills me."

This chapter describes Steps 3 and 4 in the therapy process: accessing the unacknowledged feelings underlying interactional positions, and reframing the problem in terms of the negative cycle and these underlying feelings and attachment needs. At this point in therapy, the first task of the therapist is to access the music of the couple's dance, that is, the primary emotions that are usually excluded from individual awareness and not explicitly included in the partners' interactions. The second task is to use these emotional responses, and the attachment needs reflected by such responses, to expand the context of the couple's problems. The problem is framed in terms of the way the couple interacts, and the emotional responses that organize such interactions.

This chapter presents the markers and tasks, therapeutic interventions, couple change processes, and end state of this part of therapy. As previously stated, the steps of therapy do not occur in a set linear fashion; rather, each step tends to be integrated into the next step or steps, so that the EFT therapist will continue to access emotion during the process of Steps 4 through 9, building on the framework constructed in Step 3. Later sessions and steps of EFT therefore contain elements of previous steps, which are then integrated into the tasks of the present session. When underlying emotions are first accessed in Step 3, they are related to the position each partner takes in the relationship. Later, this step is integrated into Step 5, where such emotions are experienced more fully and related to the way each partner perceives self and other in the relationship. In Step 7, these emotional experiences form the basis of the expression of needs and wants.

Each partner also progresses through these steps at a different rate. Sometimes one partner will take the lead and begin in Step 3 to move a little ahead of the other. But generally in Stage 1 (Steps 1 through 4), the therapist alternates between working with both partners in an equal fashion, helping withdrawn partners to begin to find their voice and blaming partners to voice more than hostility.

Accessing emotion in Step 3 of EFT does *not* involve:

- Reiterating the past emotional experience of the relationship, to blame the other or justify the self.
- Ventilating negative emotions in the hope that uninhibited expression will diminish such responses.
- Labeling one partner's emotional responses to teach the other partner to behave differently.
- Discussing emotions from a cognitive distance or, to use an analytic term, from the point of view of the observing ego.

Accessing emotion here *does* involve the following:

- An active engagement in, and focus on, emotional experience occurring in the here and now.
- An expansion of that experience so that the experience can be refined and revised.
- A reprocessing of experience that involves a process of discovery and creation, so that new aspects of experience are encountered.
- A naming of that experience in terms that are relevant to and elucidate the way this partner responds to his or her spouse.

MARKERS

In Step 3, the therapist intervenes at moments when:

1. One of the partners expresses the reactive secondary emotions that make up a large part of a distressed couple's interactions. This is often anger or frustration that is expressed in the process of blaming the other or justifying the self. The task here is first to acknowledge and validate these secondary responses, but then to engage with the client in the process of exploring specific experiences and eliciting emotions that are minimized, discounted, or avoided. This can occur as the partner tells the therapist the story of the relationship and the distress in the relationship, or as he or she recounts a particular incident that is particularly relevant to how he or she perceives the relationship. It can also occur as a couple interacts in front of the therapist in the session.

2. One of the partners exhibits nonverbal behavior in response to his or her partner that is noteworthy due to its incongruity, intensity, or effect on the interaction. As a wife complains and weeps, for example, a husband taps his foot and frowns with apparent

impatience. His wife then looks at him and lapses into silence. In another couple, a wife states that she is going to leave the relationship and the husband begins to laugh and talk about possible summer holidays. The task here is for the therapist to slow down the process of interaction and focus attention on the emotion implicit in the nonverbal behavior.

3. A partner begins to explore his or her emotional responses in the session, and to encounter a new, alive sense of how he or she experiences this relationship, or to symbolize this experience in a new way, but exits from this process rapidly, often becoming caught up in the negative interaction cycle with the partner. The other partner may also discount this experience and elicit the usual fight–flight response, which then takes precedence over the beginning exploration. The therapist's task is to redirect the process in the session back to the exploration and help the partner engage in it more fully.

4. The couple exhibits the interactional cycle that has been identified in Step 2. The partners themselves may now identify the interaction as part of the cycle, or the therapist may comment on it. The task now is to focus on one person's position in the interaction and how this person experiences the other partner and his or her own compelling emotions in this interaction.

On one level, each couple has their own idiosyncratic ways of interacting and experiencing the relationship. Indeed, the process of therapy has to be a process of discovery for them, the discovery of the unique, particular aspects of their inner and outer worlds and how they create their own distress and happiness. For the EFT therapist, however, certain relationship positions can be predictably associated with particular underlying emotions, even though how these emotions are experienced, processed, and symbolized will vary with each individual. This predictability is enhanced by attachment theory, the theory of relatedness that forms the basis of

EFT. So spouses who take an angry, pursuing, critical position in the interaction often access panic and insecurity
when the therapist directs them to explore their underlying
emotions. Attachment fears of abandonment and/or rejection
will surface. On the other hand, the partner taking a withdrawn position is more likely to access a sense of intimidation and incompetence related to being unable to please his
or her partner, as well as a paralyzing sense of helplessness.
This arises from not knowing how to respond to the partner
in a way that will elicit positive attachment responses, or at
least curtail the negative cycle.

INTERVENTIONS

As previously discussed, the nonverbal behaviors of the therapist are an essential part of accessing underlying emotions.
These behaviors convey acceptance and help to create a
secure base from which each partner can explore his or her
experience. They also either help or hinder the client's ability to focus on and process his or her experience. The power
of these nonverbal behaviors cannot be overemphasized.
They often make the difference between an effective and
noneffective intervention; between the client engaging in his
or her experience and simply labeling and/or avoiding it.
When an EFT therapist is eliciting underlying emotions, he
or she will usually take an open stance toward the partner,
often leaning forward and speaking in the manner described
as RISSSC on pages 109–110. In effect, the therapist models
an intense focus on a particular aspect of the partner's experience and invites the partner to follow and to emotionally
connect with the experience in a more intense way.

The interventions that the EFT therapist is most likely to
use at this point in therapy are:

1. Validation

Validation is crucial at this point in therapy. Reflection is
used and is a basic intervention in all steps, but in Step 3

it is more of a prelude to validation and evocative reflection and questions than a main intervention. The importance of the therapist's validation of emotional states becomes clear when one considers that a primary block to engagement with one's own emotional state is automatic self-critical cognitions about the unacceptable, inappropriate, and even dangerous nature of particular emotions. Expectations that certain emotions and their expression will be unacceptable to others also blocks such engagement. The message to be conveyed here is that the therapist sees each partner's emotions and responds to them as *valid, legitimate, understandable* human responses. This provides an antidote to the self-critical stance many clients take with regard to their emotions, and encourages deeper involvement in, and exploration of, them. The therapist's explicit valuing and acknowledgment of each partner's experience builds a secure base in therapy, allowing partners to express themselves more openly and risk the other partner's disapproval in the session. The EFT therapist will reflect a feeling and validate it as a first step in encouraging partners to enter more fully into their emotional experience.

Examples

1. **Therapist:** I hear that for you what Ellen calls your "constant gestapo questioning and analyzing" is like an urgent search—a search to try to find out why you never seem to get really close to her. As a scientist, it is a natural way for you to respond. You're trying to find the answer, trying to find the key to solve the problem that is torturing you: the problem of how lonely you feel in the relationship.

2. **Therapist:** It seems like it is somehow demeaning or embarrassing for you to talk about how you need comfort from Mark. You somehow seem to feel that this is something that you should not need, yes? It's hard for you to talk about that? Sometimes we are brought up to believe that being strong is not needing others, and then it makes it hard to admit when we find that

we do. It sounds like it takes a lot of courage for you to talk about this.

2. Evocative Reflections and Questions

These interventions are designed to open up and expand each partner's emotional experience of the relationship. The therapist follows the client's experience and focuses upon the partial, tentative, or "in-process" edges of this experience, which have a poignant and/or emerging quality. This intervention invites the client first to stay in contact with a particular experience, and second to process it further. As this occurs, new elements then emerge, which reorganize the experience. The therapist is a partner in this engagement, this processing and reprocessing, so that this experience unfolds and evolves in the session. As stated previously, the therapist may begin with a focus on a cue or stimulus, such as bodily response, or an impetus to action, or any awareness that arises spontaneously as part of the processing of that experience. The therapist may simply repeat certain phrases, offer an image or metaphor, or ask exploratory questions.

Examples
1. **Therapist:** What is happening to you, Jim, as your wife describes how she sees you and how disappointed she has been in this relationship?
2. **Therapist:** What is it like for you, Paul, to always be on shifting sand, careful, cautious, vigilant, on eggshells. How does that feel for you?
3. **Therapist:** What's happening for you, as you right now describe the "massacre," as you call it?
4. **Therapist:** What's happening for you as you throw up your hands and say, I can't comfort a raging bull.

3. Heightening

The therapist intensifies, crystallizes, and encourages the couple to enact key problematic as well as new, emerging emotional responses that organize interactional positions. Maintaining a consistent and persistent focus is also a way of heightening responses or interpersonal interactions and messages.

Example

> **Therapist:** Ted, you have said lots of things here but I guess the part that stood out for me was the phrase *it burns me*. It was when you were talking about Jenny's disapproval. It burns me. It's so painful for you not to be able to please her that it burns. Burns are unbearably painful. (Ted begins to cry)

4. Empathic Conjecture

In this intervention, the therapist encourages one of the partners to process his or her experience one step further by expanding on the present experience, using inferences drawn from the therapist's experience of this person, or his or her relational context, and incorporating the therapist's perspective on marital distress and intimate attachments. The therapist may offer a formulation of the person's experience that adds a new element, or put elements together in a new way, hopefully crystallizing this experience or symbolizing it in a new way. The more "in contact" with this person the therapist is and the more empathically immersed the client's experience, the more poignant and relevant such inferences will be to the client and the more likely he or she is to adopt and use them. The alliance in EFT is such that, if the therapist's comments are not useful or relevant, partners will usually correct the therapist or simply reject the formulation. In couple therapy, such inferences are open to immediate corrective feedback, either from the experiencing person, from the other spouse, or from the therapist's ongoing observation of the couple's relationship. Inferences that are too far away from the way clients frame their own experience will not be adopted, and, if offered continually, will damage the alliance, since partners feel misunderstood and discounted by the therapist. Ideally, these inferences are also offered in a tentative manner that encourages the client to correct them, and are only one short step ahead of the client's own awareness.

In EFT, these inferences are often used to crystallize partners' attachment insecurities and fears and to relate such fears to specific elements of the partner's behavior that act as triggers for such fears. These inferences are best made in a simple, concrete, and evocative way with the same nonverbal therapist responses suggested earlier.

Example

> **Therapist:** When you say: "I'm like a kid. I hate it, but I have to ask," and then stare at the floor, I get the sense that there's a shame in that for you, in asking? (Client nods) And a sadness perhaps?
>
> **Tim:** Yeah, oh yeah, I want not to ask and ask.
>
> **Therapist:** For her to come in and get you.
>
> **Tim:** Yeah, that's it. I really want that, but . . .
>
> **Therapist:** So it's hard to ask, and when you have to, you resent it?
>
> **Tim:** Right, so when I do ask, I guess I ask kind of pushy. I say "kiss me now."
>
> **Therapist:** You sort of feel small when you ask, so you make yourself bigger, pushier maybe?

5. Tracking and Reflecting Patterns and Cycles of Interaction

In both Steps 3 and 4, the therapist places each partner's emotional responses, as they are accessed, in the context of the other partner's behavior and the couple's cycle. This tends to validate each person's responses and begins to create a more process-oriented view of exactly what the problem is in the relationship. Step 2, the identification of the cycle, is then integrated into Steps 3 and 4.

As emotions are accessed, they are related to the cycle and to each person's attachment needs. The description of the cycle is, in turn, expanded to include each partner's compelling emotional responses. The context of the cycle stresses the legitimacy of each person's responses and feeds back into the further accessing and reprocessing of emotion.

In Step 4, the couple is ready to adopt the cycle and the newly accessed insecurities that feed into the cycle as *the problem.*

Example

> **Therapist:** So when he withdraws, like he did just now, when he went silent and turned away, that just makes you "go hot" as you put it. It's alarming. (She nods) You can't reach him, so usually now what would you do?
>
> **Helen:** I'd verbally clobber him. He can't ignore me.
>
> **Glen:** And then I'd withdraw more. It's the pattern we've been talking about. It's so hard to step out of.

6. Reframing of the Problem in Terms of Contexts and Cycles

This is both a general intervention in EFT that occurs throughout therapy (the problem is always placed in the context of the cycle) and a specific step in Step 4. Here the therapist summarizes the process of Steps 2 and 3 and explicitly formulates the problem as the positions the couple take in the pattern of interactions, the negative cycles that have taken over their relationship, and the compelling emotions that organize each person's responses. This replaces the general formulations of the problem that the couple came in with, such as "communication problems," or specific formulations that helped maintain marital distress, such as "the problem is that she thinks we have a problem."

Examples

1. **Therapist:** Yeah, the swing-and-run pattern is kind of running things right now, but I think you guys are starting to take it apart, bit by bit.

2. **Therapist:** So this pattern has kind of taken over your relationship. It gets in the way of all the closeness you used to have together and keeps everyone's emotions churning, so both of you are sensitive and raw. Is that it?

June: Yeah, and I understand how it keeps me hot and heavy, looking for trouble and pushing him away. So he hides more, but (to spouse) you get mad too.

Jim: I get most angry when I'm most afraid you'll leave. I think mostly we are both scared to death, and that throws everything off.

COUPLE PROCESS AND END STATE

The lack of open communication, particularly around attachment issues and emotional vulnerabilities, *constricts not only the couple's interactions, but also each partner's experiencing and processing of his or her own affect.* Distressed partners hide their vulnerabilities not only from each other, but from themselves as well in that even experiencing such feelings becomes problematic and/or foreign to them. Most partners therefore experience Step 3 of EFT as risky and anxiety provoking. They face at least four fears. These are:

1. The dragon of self-criticism, as in: "I hate this part of me, it's pathetic."
2. The dragon of testing out the process of revealing aspects of self that they are unsure of and uncomfortable with, as in: "I never felt this before, maybe I'm going crazy."
3. The dragon of facing the anticipated negative response of the other spouse, as in: "She'll laugh at me, worse still, she'll despise me. She won't want me to touch her."

4. The dragon of unpredictable change in a distressed but predictable relationship, as in: "I'm lost. I feel like I don't know you. Who have I been with all these years and what do I do now?"

The other side of the experience is that the partners find tremendous *relief* in being able to process and understand their own emotions and their relationship patterns, and a sense of *efficacy* when they begin to vividly experience how each person unwittingly creates the relationship cycle (as in, "If I created it, maybe I can make it different"). There is also relief in being able to acknowledge responsibility in a context where this does not incur a sense of shame or deficiency. Partners make comments such as, "I've never said this to anyone, hell, I've never even let myself feel this way before, but this is the way it is with me." The other partner's reaction to this is often puzzlement, disorientation, and disbelief, as in, "I don't believe this. I've never heard you speak like this before. I feel like I don't even know who you are."

In this process, the predictable support and direction of the therapist provide a secure base for continued exploration. For example, with a partner expressing the disbelief mentioned above, the therapist would reflect and validate such responses. This disbelief and even distrust and testing of the "new" partner is not seen as collusion, as in analytic models, but as a natural response to new and disconcerting perceptions of the spouse.

To maintain this secure base, the therapist has to be able to change focus rapidly from accessing one partner's feelings to exploring the impact of this on the other and supporting the other, or from helping the partner deepen his or her exploration of such emotions to processing the other partner's negative responses and including them in the process. For instance, when an observing spouse expresses skepticism, the therapist might state, "I see that this must be strange for you to hear this, different from how you have experienced your husband all these years. So it's a little difficult for you to take. Maybe you are too angry to hear what he is saying right now, but it seems important to me that he gets to say what is real for him. So I'm just going to help him do that for a moment, and then we will talk further about what it's like for you to hear this."

It is during Step 3 that each spouse's attachment issues emerge and begin to be clarified, and that these issues first become an explicit part of the dialogue between the couple. In Step 4, these issues and the interaction patterns that block emotional engagement are framed as the problem. *The couple adopts this frame and make it their own because it springs out of their immediate emotional experience. The negative cycle, not the other partner, becomes the enemy.*

The underlying emotional experiences are often different for male and female partners. Female partners more often identify lack of connection and deprivation of contact as the main factor in their distress, whereas male partners more often identify feelings of inadequacy and incompetence as the main element. In similar fashion, emotional distance in relationships has been found to be related to women's health status, whereas disagreements and overt aversiveness have been found to be related to men's health (Fisher et al., 1992).

This is also the time when attachment betrayals or crimes, that is, traumatic incidents that have damaged the nature of the attachment and actively influence the way the relationship is defined in the present, begin to be explored and clarified. For example, a small current incident in which one partner is disappointed may become an enormous issue because it evokes a key incident in the past, where one partner experienced traumatic abandonment, rejection, or betrayal at the hands of the other, or even another important attachment figure. As the emotions underlying interactional positions are processed, these incidents come alive in the session and begin to be dealt with in a constructive way. Chapter 12 discusses these attachment injuries in more detail.

As partners access and begin to reprocess their emotions, key cognitions, schemes, or working models concerning the perception and definition of self and other begin to surface in an alive and vivid way. This process continues and becomes more intense in Step 5. This is a process of discovery for the partners, rather than the disclosure of already formulated and familiar views. Fears about the unlovable nature of the self, for example, begin to be accessed in this step.

By the end of Step 4, the couple has formulated a coherent and meaningful picture and/or story of the patterns that define their relationship, as well as how they create them. This picture has been co-created with the therapist, but it is their story and they own it because it fits with their emotional experience. The self, as experienced in relation to the other, has already expanded, and the presentation of self begins to shift to be congruent with this experience. The withdrawn partner is now talking in the session about his or her paralysis in the face of the spouse's criticism, rather than just going numb and silent. The spouse is still angry, but not as actively hostile as before and is beginning to talk of his or her hurt.

This constitutes a *de-escalation*, one of the designated points of change in EFT. This is a first-order change (Watzlawick, Weakland & Fisch, 1974) in that the positions the partners take are somewhat more fluid, but the way the interactions are organized has not basically changed. The other designated points of change are when the withdrawn partner moves to a position of *reengagement* and asserts the terms of this reengagement, and when the previously hostile spouse allows a *softening*, and these will be described in a later chapter.

By this point in therapy, the perceptions of both partners have also begun to shift as each reveals more of him- or herself to the other. For example, the withdrawn partner is perhaps now perceived not so much as indifferent or uncaring, but rather as withdrawing to protect the self from the enormous impact of the other partner's actions. The therapist frames the negative cycle as the result of the enormous impact the partners have on each other and their attempts to cope with this. This is reassuring for partners and they are usually willing to adopt this frame, not only because they experience their partner differently in the session, but also because it is aversive to experience an attachment relationship as they have up to this point—that is, as one where they appear to have no emotional impact on the other partner. Withdrawers also usually react well to the discovery that their partner's hostility is not the result of random aggression, but is rather a desperate response to their own withdrawal.

The power of withdrawal seems to be a particularly novel idea to many partners. An attachment frame helps to elucidate the aversive impact of withdrawal, since, in this frame, withdrawal defines the person as inaccessible and unresponsive. The fact that the withdrawn partner seemingly cannot be reached or moved threatens the other's attachment security in a compelling way. In short, for both partners, the other now seems less dangerous and less difficult to influence than at the beginning of therapy. The more hostile partner's behavior might then be perceived less in terms of, "She is trying to destroy me" and more in terms of, "She will do anything to get me to respond to her."

This shift in perception is particularly enhanced by the fact that the therapist directs partners to interact on the basis of the newly accessed emotions. Thus a wife not only witnesses her partner elaborating on his emotional experience with the therapist, but also experiences him turning to her and sharing that experience, telling her, for example; "I'm so scared of disappointing you that I hide most of the time." This is not only new information of a powerful nature. It also redefines the relationship as one in which this kind of message or contact is possible and is, in and of itself, a new enactment, a new performance—a new form of emotional engagement—that changes the play.

By the end of Step 4, the partners are engaged in a new kind of dialogue about emotions, attachment issues, cycles, and how these all go together, and are beginning to be emotionally engaged with each other in the therapy sessions. With de-escalation completed, the therapy session is now a secure base where new and greater emotional risks can be taken and a new level of engagement initiated.

7

DEEPENING ENGAGEMENT

EFT: STEPS 5 AND 6

And she said, "I'm the maiden in the cave. Your fears—all this trust stuff—are like a dragon blocking your path to me. Am I worth fighting the dragon for. How can you turn away and let the dragon win?"

This chapter describes the beginning of Stage 2, restructuring key interactions—which the literature also titles changing interactional positions (Johnson & Denton, 2002). More specifically it describes Step 5, promoting identification of disowned attachment needs and aspects of self and integrating these into the relationship, and Step 6, promoting acceptance of the partner's experience and new ways of interacting. Step 5 is the most intrapsychically focused step in EFT. The experiential concept of changing in the process of therapy into more of what one is, rather than trying harder to be what one is not, is relevant here. As the self is experienced in a different way, the presentation of self changes, so the man who once cringed and placated now becomes angry and assertive. Step 6 involves the therapist helping the other partner to begin to accept and incorporate this new presentation into his or her view of the partner and to be responsive to the partner's new behavior in the interaction. The other partner needs considerable support to do this. As stated previously, distressed partners do not at first usually experience the other's shift from known adversary to unknown stranger as positive.

There is a sense in which Step 5 is a watershed in the therapy process. The first four steps lead up to Step 5; Steps 6 through 9 build on the processes inherent in Step 5, using these processes to restructure the partners' interaction. In research on the process of change in EFT (Johnson & Greenberg, 1988), the partners who allowed themselves to become intensely involved in their emotional experience were the ones whose relationship changed the most in therapy. This intense involvement is the essence of Step 5. The intense engagement with one's own emotions allows the therapist to begin to facilitate a new kind of emotional engagement with the other partner.

In Step 5, previously unformulated or avoided experience is encountered, claimed, and congruently expressed to the partner. This, in and of itself, expands each person's experience of the relationship. The withdrawn husband, who generally avoids the anxious feelings elicited by his wife's comments, and so ends up avoiding his wife most of the time, now fully experiences and states his fear of her criticism. In doing so he owns his strategies for dealing with this fear ("I hide and shut you out"). His revelation, to his wife and to himself, elicits new feelings in him as to his position in the relationship ("I don't want to be so afraid; I don't want to have to hide, I want to be accepted"), and presents a new image to his wife. This revised image then has the potential to evoke a new kind of response from her. Step 6 is, in fact, concerned with helping the partner deal in a constructive way with this new behavior (for example, revealing the self as afraid) and new image. Specifically, in Step 6 the therapist contains any effects of the initial discounting of the partner's new response by the distressed other, supporting the other in his or her confusion at encountering this "new" spouse. In effect, the therapist throws his or her weight behind the change in pattern.

The word *disowned* in the description of Step 5 is worth stressing. In Step 5, partners own and take possession of their emotional experience of the relationship, and this tends to *empower* the experiencing partner. How does this occur?

The process of Step 5 orients the individual to his or her needs in the relationship, and *newly accessed emotions also elicit new action tendencies.* For example, a withdrawn husband professes his fear and, in the process, accesses and expresses his unfulfilled need and longing for acceptance. This then also begins to elicit emotions that do not fit with his usual hiding and avoiding, such as anger; emotions that spark a longing to take a stand and state his desires.

In the description of Step 5, it is disowned needs that are referred to, rather than simply disowned emotions. The implication here is that accessing the emotions underlying interactional positions also accesses the attachment needs that are so often the referent for such emotions; for example, accessing a sense of abandonment panic also accesses the innate need for contact and reassurance from the attachment figure. *It is in Step 5 that attachment longings and desires begin to be clearly articulated.*

The description of Step 5 also refers to aspects of self, since the recognition of such primary emotions and needs is intricately connected to the definition of self. The most dramatic emotions that arise in Step 5 are connected to each partner's sense of self, particularly the lovableness and worthiness of self. The process of Step 5 can then be seen as one in which less known and accepted aspects of self are integrated into the person's experience and into the relationship. For example, allowing oneself to connect with, and expose to another, vulnerabilities that are usually denied or brushed aside, *expands the sense of self and the person's interactional position.* As a result of the powerful emotions that arise here, emotions that are intricately linked to the person's sense of identity and attachment security— core definitions of self and other—become available and open to modification. Such modification occurs through new interactional experiences with the therapist and, much more important, with the partner.

As Bowlby has suggested, emotional communication provides vital information for constructing and reconstructing working models of self (1988). However, if attachment theory is unfamiliar, one could also think of the links between self-definition and relationship definition in constructionistic terms—a perspective that is currently very much part of systemic therapies. According to this perspective, significant others are the principal agents in the maintenance of subjective reality, and particularly in the confirmation of that crucial element of reality called identity (Berger & Luckmann, 1979). Symbolizing and presenting a previously disowned aspect of self to a significant other, and then enacting that aspect of self in the relationship, expands and redefines the nature of self. This is particularly likely to occur if the other partner can accept these new aspects of his or her mate and if the effects of this enactment are positive for the relationship.

MARKERS

In Step 5, the therapist intervenes when:

1. The emotional responses accessed by a partner in Step 3 are experienced or referred to by the client in the session. These emotions are now more easily identified and symbolized by this person and related to his or her interactional position in the couple's cycle—such as when the therapist asks a withdrawing partner what is happening for him, and he replies in a congruent manner: "I just give up. I'll never make it with her, I feel small and scared. So then I back off, go away." The task here is to validate the emotion and the action it evokes, which is to withdraw and protect the self, and to help the partner further differentiate this experience and to own it.

These emotions are most often idiosyncratic versions of fear, helplessness, and despair. As this differentiation process continues, the way the emotion is experienced and understood, the experiencer's judgments about him- or herself for feeling this way, the view of the partner implied in the experience, and the usual way of coping with this experience, within the person and within the relationship, all become clear. This process is not an analysis or discussion of these elements. The person is immersed in the experience, and these elements emerge as the experience evolves.

2. A partner begins to explore, in a new and alive way, his or her underlying feelings, but is interrupted by the partner, or exits from the process into abstract cognition or general descriptive comments. The task is for the therapist to redirect the process and, if necessary, block the other partner's interference, thus encouraging a more intense involvement in the emotional experience.

In Step 6, the therapist intervenes when:

1. One of the partners, in Step 5, reaches a sense of closure or synthesis of his or her underlying emotion with the therapist and is able to clearly relate this experience to his or her habitual responses to the other partner. The therapist then requests that this person share this synthesis with the other partner and he or she does so, in an engaged manner. The focus in this sharing is on self, not other. The task in Step 6 is to support the other partner to hear, process, and respond to this sharing, so that this new experience can become part of, and begin to reshape, the couple's interactions. There is no reason why the observing spouse should be particularly open to, or trusting of, this shift in the way this partner presents him- or herself in the relationship. On the contrary, such partners have had years of disappointment and of negative experiences, which mediate against such responsiveness. If the therapist is not present, this lack of responsiveness to such sharing becomes a potentially aversive experience for the partner who is opening up. This results in a reinitiation of the negative cycle and a return by this partner to his or her more constricted

position in the interaction. From a systemic point of view, the therapist promotes and expands this shift in the pattern of interactions, this new kind of dialogue, so that it is not simply inundated by or subsumed in the more established pattern, but in fact begins to reorganize that pattern.

In general, the new responses of the risking partner elicit confusion and uncertainty, but at times the more blaming partner actually uses the situation where the other shows a new level of vulnerability as an opportunity to attack or discount this partner. The therapist has then to intervene in a way that we term *catching the bullet*. The therapist must modify the potential adversiveness of a negative response to the now vulnerable partner. So a blaming client might state, "That's ridiculous—I think you are just trying to look like the victim here. If you just want to play victim and look good—you should just get out of here." The therapist uses empathic conjecture and frames this response in terms of a new and confusing shift in the relationship dance that elicits a need to discount or disempower the partner. So the therapist might say, "This is hard for you to listen to. You really don't know how to take it when he says these things. It doesn't fit with how you see him. So you interpret his actions in a negative way. You get in your tank and fire, so as not to be taken in—is that it? It's hard for you to see that he is risking and reaching for you when he says . . ." (*Therapist seizes the chance to repeat the key comment of the risking spouse again and also validates the risking spouse*)

Step 6 almost always begins with the therapist asking the observing partner, "So what is it like, what happens for you, when your partner talks like this and says . . . ?"

INTERVENTIONS

Reflection and validation of emotional experience, and the interactional responses they evoke, are a constant part of the

EFT therapist's interventions and also operate here. At this point in therapy, however, other interventions come to the fore, and for this reason they are focused on here.

1. Evocative Responding

The therapist focuses upon the emerging but unformulated aspects of a partner's emotional experience and helps this partner to vividly grasp this experience, by unfolding and expanding it in the here and now of the session. The therapist uses vivid, specific, and concrete language, particularly images and metaphors, to assist the person in encapsulating his or her experience.

Examples

Expanding the felt sense of an emotional experience with questions and reflections is a key part of Step 5

1. **Therapist:** What is happening for you, Jim, as you look down and say, "It's scary, to tell her who I am."
2. **Therapist:** You're saying it's disappointing, Mary, is that right? (She nods) It's so painful to hope that he is going to be there and then, just when you need him most, you can't find him. You get that sinking feeling in the pit of your stomach that you spoke about (she nods) and then . . . What does it feel like?

Reflection and question come together here to put different elements of the person's experience together, in her own words, and then invite her to experience more of it.

Expanding the context, the cue for the emotional experience

Husband: Right about now I want to run and hide.

Therapist: This is scary, right now? (He nods). What happened? What did you see?

Husband: It's the look on her face. She isn't going to believe me, no matter what I say. I can't win.

Therapist: The look on her face?

Husband: Yes, her raised eyebrows, it's like, "Yeah right bud, tell me another one." Forget it.

Therapist: You were trying to reach her. Is that okay? (He nods, and she raises her eyebrows) And you feel . . . ?

Husband: Crushed.

Therapist: Crushed, crushed and defeated, like you want to run and hide.

Husband: Yeah.

Expanding the formulation/meaning of the experience and how it organizes the person's responses to the other

Wife: I can't bear it, I feel so sad. How dare you say these things to me. (*She exits from the sadness into anger at her partner, who has just told her that she doesn't accept the caring he offers*)

Therapist: You feel so sad about what he said, that the way he experiences it is that you can't accept his love.

Wife: (quieter) I don't know what he is talking about.

Therapist: Something happened here. Something happened that was "unbearable" for you, is that right?

Wife: It's like he's saying that it's my fault that I don't feel loved.

Therapist: Aha, you feel angry, like he is blaming you (she nods) for feeling so unloved (she starts to cry), so sad, so alone, and that's unbearable.

Wife: Yes, and I don't like that feeling, that sadness.

Therapist: How does it feel, that sadness?

Wife: Like I'm a little helpless kid, sniveling, I won't be spoken to like that (angry voice).

Therapist: Where did the sadness go? (She laughs) You sound angry now. (She nods) Does that feel better than feeling like a sad little unloved kid?

Wife: Yes. It feels safer to be angry. (She laughs) It's like then I don't feel so sad and helpless. It's better.

Therapist: You feel safer, bigger, being angry? So what happens to the sadness?

Wife: He doesn't see it, and it feels better.

Therapist: What would happen if you let yourself just feel sad?

Wife: I . . . I . . . might fall apart. I'd weep forever and he wouldn't like that.

The therapist then goes on to evoke and explore the grief and loss implicit in "I'd weep forever." The implications for the cycle are clear here: The wife's anger, as well as her need to protect herself from her own feelings of sadness and from her husband's feared rejection, narrow down her part of the interaction to angry complaining, which in turn evokes his withdrawal.

As can be seen from these examples, questions and reflections run together as the therapist tracks the person's experience and invites him or her to explore it. Simple techniques such as repetition also refocus the process on the more important elements, in this case the client's sadness. The therapist also replays the process, going back to the emotional experience and elaborating on it. Images that partners formulate in this process are particularly helpful and can be used in later sessions to evoke the emotional experience associated with them.

2. Heightening

The therapist heightens the emotional responses to make them more alive and present, and so facilitate the clients' engagement with them. The therapist also heightens the interactional position that reflects (and continually re-creates) these responses. Heightening is a way of helping partners fully experience and resonate with their emotions, and a way of creating a powerful experience in the session, which will then influence behavior outside the session.

Examples

1. Heightening emotion in Step 5

Wife: It's like I don't belong.

Therapist: You aren't part of the family, part of his life?

Wife: Right. I'm all by myself.

Therapist: All by yourself, there is no one beside you, no one to hold your hand, to support you.

Wife: (cries) I'm not important. We went on a walk and he was playing with the dog and he didn't even notice that I turned back and went into the house.

Therapist: He didn't notice that you had left. You weren't there. (She nods and cries) What did it feel like when you went into the house? You didn't matter, you were insignificant. (She nods)

Wife: Like I don't exist.

Therapist: Like you are invisible?

Wife: Yes, the invisible wife. (To partner) You don't see me.

Therapist: So it's like you're saying, after a while it gets so I feel like I don't exist here, I'm nothing to you.

There is a sense in which all the interventions in EFT heighten emotion, simply because of the focus on emotional responses and the validation of such responses. Here, however, there is a deliberate attempt by the therapist to make the experience more vivid and to capture the considerable significance it has for the person and the relationship. This does not just affect the experiencing partner, but has great impact on the other observing partner, who hears this partner not only saying new and different words, but actually being a different way— that is, experiencing deeply and in a manner that pulls for a more compassionate, caring response.

2. Heightening present and changing positions

This intervention encourages partners to own not just the emotions underlying their interactional positions, but also the positions themselves, which are reflections of these emotions and also ways of regulating them. A position that is consciously and actively taken and experienced as legitimate is already different from the exact same position, when it occurs as an automatic response to the other's actions in which the associated emotions are only dimly sensed.

As mentioned before, Step 5 is a watershed in the EFT process. It includes owning present experience and the problematic position that reflects that experience. It also lays the groundwork, by expanding emotional experience and expression, for new positions to emerge in Step 7.

3. Heightening the enactment of a present problematic position

> **Therapist:** Can you say that again, Pete: "I don't want to trust you, some part of me would rather die than ask for your help. I've promised myself I'd never give anyone the power to really hurt me again."

4. Heightening the enactment of an emerging new position

> **Therapist:** How did you feel about what you just did, Pete?
>
> **Pete:** You mean risking, risking showing her my softer side, my longings? (Therapist nods) Fine.
>
> **Therapist:** You feel strong enough to do that now, to take that step, to reach out to her. (He nods) Can you tell her what that was like for you, risking, going against the voice that tells you to protect yourself and reaching for her?

3. Empathic Conjecture

This is used in Steps 5 and 6 to expand and clarify experience in the former, as well as to frame any difficulties partners might have in responding to the emerging changes in their spouse in Step 6.

In Step 5, this intervention ascribes meaning or creates a contextual frame for the immediate, compelling emotional experience that is occurring in the session. If this frame does not fit exactly with the client's experience and enrich that experience, the client corrects the therapist and the therapist acknowledges and uses the correction. Often the therapist adds just one element to the formulation of the experience, or places it in the context of attachment needs and fears.

While insight might be part of this process as it evolves, this is not the goal of this intervention. The goal is to deepen the person's connection with his or her emotional experience and to allow this experience to further unfold.

Empathic conjecture is probably used more at this point in EFT than at any other. It is perhaps useful to state here that empathic conjecture is *not*:

- Replacing one set of cognitive labels with another.
- An abstract intellectual summary of experience.
- Instruction to the client as to a better way to be or view things.
- An attempt to create insight into self or other.

Correctly used, empathic conjecture arises from:

- The therapist's empathic immersion in the client's experience in the here and now.
- The therapist's sense of the relational context, the positions and patterns, and the intrapsychic experience that is usually associated with such positions and patterns.
- The theoretical framework of EFT, which assumes that attachment theory is a powerful framework for explicating adult intimacy.
- The therapist's own emotional processing, which provides clues as to how others might be experiencing a specific situation.

An ideal conjecture is respectful, tentative, specific, and just one step ahead of the experience of the client as the client is formulating it. It often focuses upon attachment fears, not just about others' responses, but also about the nature of self. This focus on fear makes sense when one considers that fear, in particular, constricts both inner emotional processing and interpersonal engagement, thus narrowing the range of interpersonal responses.

Examples

Empathic conjecture in Step 5

> **Therapist:** So, when you come home early, as you drive to the house, you have this image that you will find Walt making love to someone else? (Norma nods)
>
> **Norma:** I will catch him (angrily).
>
> **Therapist:** Betraying you. (Norma nods)
>
> **Walt:** I have never even thought of such a thing in all my life, why would you even think I could do such a thing?
>
> **Norma:** You are not making love to me!
>
> **Walt:** You won't let me anywhere near you. You frost me out. Otherwise I sure would. I love you. (Norma weeps)
>
> **Therapist:** What's happening right now, Norma? (She stares at the floor) Something touched you? You were angry and then you wept.
>
> **Walt:** Whenever I say I want her, love her, she weeps. There is a chink in the armor and then she goes silent.
>
> **Therapist:** Is that right, Norma? Is it hearing Walt say that he loves you that touches you?
>
> **Norma:** (edge in voice) I don't believe he wants me. (Walt sighs)
>
> **Therapist:** But just for a moment, what he said touched you?
>
> **Norma:** (defiant posture) I guess so.
>
> **Therapist:** It touched you to hear him say he wanted you, and you wept, part of you wants that, even

though another part doesn't believe him. (She nods) Would you like to believe him?

Norma: Of course, but it's never happened, never.

Therapist: It's never happened that someone has really wanted and valued and cherished you, and there is something really sad about that. It's worth crying for. (She nods) One part of you wants to believe him and one part tells you to give up, stop being stupid and protect yourself, look hard enough and you will find him betraying you, yes? He will let you down.

Norma: Yes, I don't want to want it . . . , to think . . . perhaps . . . , and then.

Therapist: To let yourself long for that love, only to have your hopes dashed again. You shut the longing down and stay tough, yeah?

Norma: I don't feel the longing, only the anger, I don't even care if I'm that important to him.

Therapist: Is that right? It's not worth crying about, being important to someone, being special enough for Walt to fight for?

Norma: I've never felt special to anyone. I've given up on it. Everyone lets you down.

Therapist: You can't trust anyone. (She nods) You won't give anyone the chance to let you down again. You're vigilant.

Norma: That's right, always watching, a voice says, "It will happen again, even with Walt, it will." (Clenches her fists)

Therapist: The voice says, don't even think of trusting him, it's a fool's game, right? Be on your guard. Come home early, who knows what you might find. You came home early to find what you are most afraid of?

Norma: (closes her eyes) The fear is so strong.

Empathic conjecture in Step 6

> **Therapist:** Walt, what is happening, as you listen to Norma talk like this?
>
> **Walt:** I feel lots. I think, it's not fair, I'm unjustly condemned, I can't prove to her that I'm not like that, it's futile. I don't deserve all this testing and suspicion.
>
> **Therapist:** Aha, you're indignant and hurt maybe. (He nods) Can your hear how difficult it is for Norma to even think of trusting you, of letting her guard down.
>
> **Walt:** I hear it.
>
> **Therapist:** What happens for you when you hear it?
>
> **Walt:** I feel sad. She's so wounded, and afraid . . . just like me!
>
> **Therapist:** Can you tell her?
>
> **Walt:** I see you're afraid. How can I show you that I won't betray you?
>
> **Therapist:** You want to know how you can help her be less afraid? (He nods) Ask her.

A special form of conjecture, a disquisition, is sometimes used in Step 6 to normalize any negative responses to the other's new experiencing and emerging new position.

Examples

Disquisition in Step 6

> **Therapist:** I understand that it is difficult for you to take such a risk and have Mary respond angrily, but for many partners who have been frustrated and hurt in the relationship, perhaps for a long time, it's very hard to respond when their partner begins to open up and take risks. Some people can't believe it, or are afraid to believe it. Some people want the other person to feel some of the same hurt they have felt over the years. It makes it hard for you to keep risking, but it's also really hard to take it in when our partner does something different. It's a whole new story, almost like

having a new partner, kind of strange, disconcerting.
But I don't know if any of this is relevant to you, Mary,
'cause you have your own feelings and realities.

As stated before, Step 5 is the most intrapersonally
oriented of the EFT treatment steps. Step 6 also focuses on
individual responses, so the more interpersonal interventions
are less prominent at this point in therapy. The reframing of
interactional responses in attachment terms is part of the
empathic conjecture intervention, but is used more as an
intrapsychic than interpersonal intervention here. The interpersonal intervention, restructuring interactions, does occur
in Steps 5 and 6, in that new experience that arises here is used
as the basis to create new kinds of interactions. This process
continues and is even more central in Step 7. It is interesting to note that even in the most intrapsychic steps of EFT,
inner experience is still related to and used to restructure
interactions. The EFT therapist is always standing on the
edge of inner and outer, and playing with how each reflects
and creates the other.

4. Restructuring Interactions

The therapist choreographs enactments of present positions
that are now more explicitly, consciously, and actively taken
and shapes those interactions to include new elements from
the newly synthesized experience arising in Step 5, thus
turning new emotional experience into new interactions. In
Step 6, the therapist monitors the responses of the other partner to this new experience or expression and, if necessary,
choreographs less constricting and/or more accepting
responses.

Examples
Step 5.

> **Therapist:** So can you tell him, Norma, "I am so afraid.
> I don't even let myself even hope, even long for your
> love anymore. I wrap my prickles (*Norma's word*)

around me and wait and search for evidence, for you to betray me. I only let myself touch that longing for a moment."

Step 6.

Therapist: Can you tell her, Bill, "I'm too angry to hear you right now. I'm not going to acknowledge the risks you're taking."

COUPLE PROCESS AND END STATE

What happens in Steps 5 and 6 from the couple's point of view? If therapy is going according to plan, many different elements are interacting on many different levels. Although one partner generally enters Step 5 before the other, both partners experience a similar process. This process is characterized by:

- An intensification and heightening of the emotional experience accessed in Step 3. This involves a process of differentiating and symbolizing this experience as it occurs. With this process comes recognition of the significance of this experience for the self in relation to the other—as in, "I have to protect myself. Who is going to take care of me? No one ever has and I gave up on it long ago. When we first got together, I hoped that you . . . but . . ."

- An owning of that experience as belonging to the self (not created by the other). As the person inhabits and lives out of the experience, he or she also owns the action tendencies, the impulses arising out of this experience, that have organized this person's interactional position and helped create the negative cycle in the relationship. For example, "I'm so scared. I guess if I do risk reaching for you, I do it in a kind of qualified, indirect sort of way and the minute it looks like it might go wrong, I run. Most of the time I guess I'm behind a wall. No wonder you can't find me."

• The expanded experiencing and owning of the experience and the person's position in the cycle also involve
the accessing of core self-concepts or models, which are
associated with the intense emotions that arise here.
These concepts seem to arise naturally in this kind of
emotionally loaded interpersonal situation where there
is also a therapist to provide safety. Experiencing the
pain of how one is negatively defined in an attachment
relationship accesses a partner's sense of self in a clear
and poignant fashion that allows for active exploration
and eventual reformulation, as in, "So I say to myself,
what do you expect? You're not good at this love stuff.
I feel about this big (making a small space between
thumb and forefinger). I can't even ask her anymore. I'm
some sort of freak in this emotional stuff, you know.
I know this, so when she starts to tell me she's
disappointed, as if I didn't know I was disappointing
her, I can't stand it. So I start yelling."

All of the above allows for a reprocessing of primary emotions related to the sense of self in relation to the other, and
in this process the experience of the connection with the
other develops and changes. Specifically, key wishes and
longings inherent in the emotion begin to emerge and to be
articulated. They can then be worked with in Step 7. Before
this stage, partners usually have difficulty articulating what
it is they want, perhaps because they do not feel entitled to
the response they need, or because their desires are not clear
to them or are too painful to hold in awareness. They are also
reluctant to ask, since asking would place them in a position
of vulnerability with their partner.

From an attachment point of view, attachment behaviors
begin to change at this point in therapy as the emotions that
organized them are reprocessed. A previously withdrawn
spouse becomes more accessible and also becomes more
assertive, taking some control over how the relationship is
defined and how he or she is defined within it. The models
of self and other, accessed as "hot cognitions" in this process,

are available for reformulation. Interactional positions are more actively taken and start to shift toward more accessibility and contact. Attachment fears and insecurities are reprocessed and become a recognized part of the interaction, rather than controlling the dance from behind the scenes.

In terms of change events, Step 5 is crucial. It forms the foundation for withdrawer reengagement for one partner, and softening for the other. These events are discussed in more detail in a later chapter.

What happens here from the point of view of the observing partner, who is often a step behind the other in the EFT process and observes the other as he or she goes ahead into the process of Step 5?

First, this partner sees his or her spouse being different. The word *being* is used deliberately in that this partner sees the spouse engaging in an intense exploration of his or her emotional experience, rather than simply acting differently. It is understandable that, when asked, couples identify a changed perception of their partner as the crucial change element in EFT. The way the spouse is perceived expands and becomes less rigidly organized. Old, set ways of viewing the other person are challenged by new experience. A partner who has never wept, cries, and a partner who is never angry, rages. This not only provides new information about this partner, but also fosters a sense of connection, a sense of shared common humanity between partners, which may have been lost in years of alienation and conflict. Partners speak of being touched, being moved in a new way, when witnessing their spouse's emotional reality. It may evoke compassion, or at the very least curiosity.

Second, this observing partner is also engaged by the other in a very new kind of dialogue. It may not necessarily be more comfortable, and at first it may even seem to be more dangerous than the usual negative, but predictable, cycles that the couple engages in. This new dialogue begins to not only impact the emotions, but also challenge the interactional position of this observing partner. On a very concrete level, the experiencing partner who is immersed in the Step 5 process may appear significantly less dangerous than before. Therefore, the need for strong defenses against him or her is suddenly less obvious. This other partner may also begin to take a more assertive position in the relationship, whereas before he or she had reacted in a passive manner. This can be frightening and/or very reassuring to the observing partner. In particular, the new dialogue contains the possibility of intimate contact, and the observing partner is then in the position of having to respond to this, usually finding that his or her response is ambivalent, at least at first, even if he or she has been struggling for such contact for years.

Third, the observing partner also hears the other take responsibility for the position he or she has taken in the relationship, and for his or her part in the way the relationship has evolved. This tends to undermine a blaming stance toward the other and encourages this observing partner to join in taking responsibility for how the relationship has evolved.

All of the above applies to whichever spouse leads in the process of therapy and enters Step 5 first. In a classic blame–withdraw cycle, the withdrawer will be encouraged to go first into Stage 5, but in a withdraw–withdraw cycle the most willing partner will usually go first. When the second partner also engages in the Step 5 process, it sets the stage for new bonding events, which usually occur when both partners are accessible and responsive—that is, as the second spouse engages in Step 7. As stated in chapter 1, the order and independence of the steps in the change process is exaggerated here, in the interest of clarity. The evolution of the increased responsiveness of the usually withdrawn partner and the increased openness of the usually critical partner are intertwined and reciprocally determining. The reduction in hostility of the critical partner invites the other's approach; the reduction in the distance of the withdrawn partner encourages the other to risk and ask for what he or she needs. This process occurs throughout therapy. In some couples, then, especially if distress is relatively minimal and not long standing, the partners may enter the steps almost simultaneously.

Step 6 involves the crucial evolution of a new kind of dialogue between the partners and requires that, as these partners go through this experience, the therapist stay with them, track their experience, and support them. A recording of these observing partners' reactions at this point might sound something like this: "Is this real? Can he really be feeling this? Why haven't I seen this before? He is playing games. I'm not sure if I can, or want to, trust this. He is sad, now I feel sad too. Should I let myself feel this way? I'm not going to let down my guard just like that. It feels good to know he isn't indifferent, but is he really scared? Perhaps he can open up and then, then what, am I going to risk it again? hope again? Not yet." If the relationship has been very adversarial, the first response is often some version of, "I don't believe this for a moment" or "Go tell someone who cares."

Step 6 has then an *intrapsychic component*, that is, helping the observing partner process his or her partner's new responses and respond to them, and an *interactional component*, that is, structuring a new dialogue, including the new elements now present in each partner's experience of the relationship. The observing partner is encouraged to explore any negative responses to his or her spouse and to express them directly—for instance, "I'm still too angry to hear you, and I'm not sure I want to believe you." As with the other steps, this step evolves over the course of several sessions, with the therapist fostering new and positive contact between the partners whenever possible. The experiencing partner may be framed as needing this observing partner's help in staying more engaged and risking more in the relationship.

As the experiencing partner stays out of the negative cycle and continues to construct a new position for him- or herself in the relationship, the other begins to be confronted with his or her own difficulties in becoming more accessible and responsive. It is often the case that the first partner entering Step 5 and then Step 7 evokes the other partner's insecurities and pulls this partner into the owning of his or her fears and insecurities; that is, into entering Step 5 for him- or herself. A now accessible and potentially responsive partner challenges reservations that this observing spouse may have about connecting with the other, confronting this spouse with his or her own unwillingness to risk and trust.

At this point, a certain amount of testing may be part of the therapy process and indeed may be necessary before this partner can begin to respond to the changing other. Such testing is reflected, validated, and placed in the context of the cycle. The therapist might reflect the need for testing and the anxiety behind it. Eventually, if it continues, the therapist may become more confrontative, as follows: "You are standing back and testing him again and again, asking him to prove that he loves you—that he has changed. This is so natural, given how much you have been hurt. But really, he can't prove to you that you should risk—give him the benefit of the doubt. He will make mistakes—he is learning too. It really boils down to whether you can risk—and begin to let him in when he knocks." The therapist then encourages both spouses to stay engaged and to tolerate the anxiety that a new way of interacting generates.

For the observing spouse, the process in Step 6 begins with a focus on the experiencing partner and evolves to a focus on his or her own ability to respond to this partner's new involvement in the relationship. For the experiencing spouse, Steps 5 and 6 expand this partner's emotional engagement in the relationship. This engagement then becomes an alternative to behaviors associated with the negative cycle, such as avoidance, withdrawal, or angry coerciveness. The second time through Step 6 is usually brief and uncomplicated, whether it involves the now reengaged, previously withdrawn partner responding to the softening of the more critical partner, or, as occurs less frequently and in less distressed couples, the softened critical partner responding to the increasing engagement of the withdrawn partner as this partner enters Step 5.

In the event that the observing spouse becomes so distressed by the emerging changes in the relationship that he or she escalates the negative cycle, and the usual ways of dealing with these reactions mentioned above do not seem to have the desired effect, an individual session for each partner can be initiated. This is discussed more fully in the clinical issues section, in chapter 10. Occasionally, key incidents in the history of the relationship, experienced as attachment traumas (described in chapter 12), reemerge in Step 6, blocking the observing spouse's ability to trust and respond to the other's new behaviors. An exploration of these critical attachment incidents or "crimes" can evoke the observing spouse's own deepest fears and hurts; that is, it can prime this person's own entry into the process of Step 5.

8

EMOTIONAL ENGAGEMENT: ENACTMENTS AND BONDING

EFT: STEP 7 AND CHANGE EVENTS

"It's hard for Piglet and Superwoman to be close."
"I need you to help me hold back the dark."

Jim (withdrawing spouse) [to partner Mary] beginning a transforming enactment: I want you to give me a chance—I want you to stop hammering me and help me learn to love you better. I can learn to love you better—I want to do that. I just got so used to hiding—but I don't want to do it anymore. Can you hear that?

Mary: Well—it's hard to take in—I'm not sure I believe you. But—you really want to learn to love me better?

Jane (blaming spouse) [to partner Paul] beginning a transforming enactment: I don't think—I do see you being more here for me—I do. But I don't think I can step out and meet you. Some part of me says that it's too risky—I have been hurt before. I am not sure I can do it. Maybe I am too scared to try now.

Paul: I think I did hurt you—but I want you to try and let me in.

This chapter deals with Step 7 of EFT, facilitating the expression of needs and wants and creating emotional engagement. Step 7 involves the last stage of the process in which new emotional experience and expression are used to change interactional positions and so restructure interactions. It is at this point in therapy that key change events associated with successful outcome in EFT occur. The completion of Step 7 for the less engaged partner results in the change event of withdrawer reengagement, and, for the other more critical partner, in a softening event, where this partner is able to ask for contact and comfort from a position of personal vulnerability. As discussed previously, withdrawer reengagement is usually established before softening events are completed. In addition, as the second partner, the blamer, reaches the end of this step and softens, resulting in both partners becoming accessible and responsive, powerful new bonding events can occur. These events then heighten the developing emotional engagement between the couple and construct a new positive bonding cycle. This cycle becomes as self-reinforcing as the original negative cycle, and fosters a more secure attachment between partners.

It is a matter of some controversy as to whether the erosion of marital satisfaction begins with negative conflictual interactions that erode positive sentiments or whether the absence of responsive intimate interactions that satisfy attachment needs erodes closeness and sparks more and more conflict and negativity (Roberts & Greenberg, 2002). Certainly secure bonding and the reciprocal loving responsiveness associated with such a bond allows partners to deal with differences and conflicts well. In any event, 20 years of practice and research in EFT suggest that once open, reciprocal responsiveness and emotional engagement occur, the couple experiences a new level of secure confidence in their relationship and can and do offer each other new levels of love and caring that appear to provide an antidote to previous hurts and to consolidate the gains made in the de-escalation phase of EFT.

For both partners, it is the processing of emotional experience in Step 5, and the subsequent interactional events in Step 6, that lead into the statement of needs and wants in Step 7. This statement, made as it is from an empowered, accessible position, constitutes a shift in interactional position that, in turn, challenges the other partner to engage in the same process and *pulls* this other toward the speaker. The processing of emotion in Step 5 leads naturally into a heightened awareness and expression of needs and wants, just as an awareness of hunger leads to a clear desire for food and an expression of that desire.

This formulation and expression of needs occur in the context of the person's interactional position. As the underlying emotion is engaged with and expanded, the position organized by the emotion also evolves and changes. So, for example, statements made in Step 5 that might be summarized as: "I feel small and inept with you, and live in fear of you really seeing this and leaving me, so I go numb and placate," evolve in Step 7 into, "I am tired of numbing out. I want to feel special to you. I want you to hold off on the criticism and quit threatening to leave. I'm not going to feel small in this relationship anymore." This partner now speaks from a position of increased efficacy, where he defines the relationship for himself, rather than reacting to the other's definitions. He is more engaged with his own emotional experience and speaks from an accessible rather than distant and inaccessible position. When his partner is able to join him here, not only do *new bonding events occur*, but the relationship also becomes redefined as a secure base. This redefinition then fosters the processes of Stage 3, consolidation and integration. This third stage includes Step 8, problem solving, and Step 9, the consolidation of new positions and more flexible interaction patterns.

As the two partners go through Step 7 in turn, they are able to stay engaged with their emotional experience and clearly state what it is they need in order to feel safe and connected in the relationship. The attachment needs elaborated in previous steps are now clear and can be expressed directly with a sense of legitimacy. The requests made are about key attachment needs for contact comfort, and about responses from the other that are crucial to each person's sense of safety and positive sense of self, rather than about instrumental roles or less emotionally central aspects of the relationship.

This kind of expression constitutes a new interactional stance on the part of the speaker that is more equal and more affiliative. These requests have the quality of a new and authentic attempt at engagement with the other partner, rather than a negotiation or proposed exchange of resources. The word *ask* is also important here. The requests are not expressed as demands on the other; nor are they stated in the context of blaming the other.

At this point, the person is also able to hold this position in a flexible manner, rather than being defensively organized and constricted in his or her responses, perhaps because this new position arises out of an integration of emotional experience, as well as a refined sense of how personal emotional experience and interactions with the partner are interconnected. When the other partner makes an accusation, for example, a reengaging withdrawer is usually able to hold his or her position and admit responsibility without withdrawing and evoking the negative cycle. A husband might say, "Yes, I did what I have done before. I'm so used to reacting that way. But I don't want you to decide now that I'm not trying and get so mad that I can't get anywhere near you. I'm going to work on me and us so that doesn't happen, and I want you to believe me."

The flowering of the Step 5 process is seen here in the way that the person enacts an expanded sense of self, a more differentiated working model of self and other. He or she begins from, for example, a withdrawn position of viewing the self as inadequate or unacceptable and the other as critical and dangerous in Steps 1 and 2, but comes to a position where frailties are viewed as part of being human and the self is worthy of care and has legitimate needs for such care. He or she is then willing to ask the other to meet those needs, as in "I am timid. But I can be strong too. You are not strong all the time either. It's hard to deal with my fears and find my strength, when you're yelling about how wimpy I am. And I want you to stop it. I want some respect. It's hard for Piglet and Superwoman to be close." The blaming partner's sense of self expands to include a clearer sense of attachment vulnerabilities and needs.

In Step 7, partners are able to present their specific requests in a manner that pulls the spouse toward them and maximizes the possibility that this spouse will be able to respond. The attachment signals are clear (Kobak, Ruckdeschel & Hazan, 1994). The nature of the requests made tends to confirm the other spouse's sense of being irreplaceable to, and having a powerful effect on, his or her partner. In attachment terms, this is very confirming and compelling. At this point, the spouse may make statements such as "I never knew that I was that important to you, that you needed me." These requests, in fact, implicitly address the deprivation and attachment needs of this listening spouse, and make it easier for him or her to respond to the speaker. Blocks to such responsiveness have also been addressed in the process of completing Step 6.

The process of Step 7 is essentially one in which the new emotional experience of Step 5, which has been integrated into relationship interactions in Step 6, is now used to restructure the relationship. The new emotional experience of a partner in Step 5 becomes in Step 7 a new interactional event that redefines the control and affiliation in the relationship.

MARKERS

The therapist intervenes when:

1. A partner reiterates or further expands the emotional experience encountered in Step 5, but does not

symbolize the needs and wants implicit in this experience. The task for the therapist is to help this partner formulate the needs and wants arising out of this experience, and to encourage the expression of these formulations to the other partner.

2. A partner spontaneously begins to state needs and wants to the therapist, but does not address these to the other partner, or exits from this process of sharing into a less pertinent or unfocused dialogue. The task for the therapist is to redirect the process of sharing toward the other partner, or back to a more pertinent focus, and support this person in sharing his or her desires with the other spouse.

3. The other partner either responds openly to the new behavior of the experiencing partner, or begins to discount this new behavior. In both cases, the therapist invites the experiencing spouse to continue to respond in an emotionally engaged manner, and state his or her own needs and preferences. The therapist may also need to reflect and validate the difficulties the other observing spouse is having in responding to the changes in his or her partner and in the interaction. On the other hand, if the other partner responds positively, the therapist acknowledges, heightens, and fosters this response.

INTERVENTIONS

As clients enter Step 7, they begin to take more and more initiative, and the therapist begins to hand the process over to them, becoming less active but encouraging and redirecting when necessary. The main task is to restructure interactions by tracking and heightening interactions, reframing interactions, and especially directing the creation of new interactions based on new emotional experience. Some of these new interactions will become new bonding events. More intrapsychic interventions, such as evocative responding and empathic conjecture, are used when blocks appear, or when people cannot move forward in the process. For example, when a partner suddenly finds it too difficult to ask for the response he or she needs, the therapist may help this person explore this difficulty.

Evocative Responding: Reflections and Questions

The therapist focuses upon the client's emerging experience to help him or her clarify wishes and longings, or to clarify difficulties with expressing such things to the partner.

Examples

1. **Therapist:** (to reengaging withdrawer) So, if I hear you correctly, you seem to be saying (*summarizes*) that the dread you have of her leaving, and her threats to do just that, leave you hanging, never on firm ground here, and that makes it difficult to let go and put yourself into the relationship, is that it?

   Tim: Yes, and then I close down, but it's not what I want to do. (He cups one hand in the other and holds them in front of him)

   Therapist: What you want is? (Tim does not respond, looking at his hands) Your hands are holding each other, like a little nest, a little basket. What is happening right now?

   Tim: I don't get to hold her like that. Her investment is mostly back home with her parents, if you see what I mean.

   Therapist: Yes. And what you want is?

   Tim: I want to hold her.

   Therapist: Keep her safe.

   Tim: Yes. I want her to put all her eggs in one basket, our basket, to stop running home.

   Therapist: To risk leaning on you. (He nods) Can you tell her that, please?

2. **Therapist:** It's too difficult for you to tell him about this?

Jane: I don't think I can. It's like, there's no point. He won't hear it (tears).

Therapist: How are you feeling as you say that, Jane?

Jane: I know what's going to happen. He'll get mad or make excuses.

Therapist: So it's like, you don't want to risk it.

Empathic Conjecture

It is sometimes necessary to help clients symbolize their longings, which they have often pushed aside to maintain the stability of the relationship, and to lessen their own sense of deprivation.

Example

Marion: This relationship has been so hard. I think I've buried any hope very deep.

Therapist: You're not sure you want to hope again?

Marion: Right. Sometimes it's okay to just go through the motions, live as chums.

Therapist: It's like all the longings, all the dreams you had when you first met Harry, are locked away now?

Marion: I guess. (Cries, then stops, pulls her head up, and flips her hair back with her hand; her face becomes tight)

Therapist: Help me understand? It almost feels like, "I won't long again, I won't dream and be disappointed"?

Marion: Exactly. (She tears again)

Therapist: But the tears . . . What are the tears for, Marion? What did you want so much and have to give up?

Marion: (bursting out) I wanted to be held, I wanted to be precious, just for a while, just to him. (Cries quietly)

> **Therapist:** And I guess some part of you still wants that? Yes? (She nods)

Tracking and Reflecting the Cycle

At this point in therapy, tracking and reflecting the cycle do not usually involve the negative cycle the couple came in with. It is more likely to involve reflecting changes to the negative cycle and the beginnings of a new, more positive cycle. More specifically, it often involves the tracking and reflection of minisequences that occur as inner and outer realities reflect and create each other. For example, in the session described above, the therapist might reflect and describe the process captured here in terms of how the wife allowed herself to express her longing but felt very apprehensive and so at the last minute qualified her statement, making it much more ambiguous, and therefore more difficult to respond to. The husband, also playing it safe, then responded only minimally. In reflecting this interaction, the therapist fosters an exploration of the process in which the wife's fears influenced her presentation of needs. This presentation then in turn influenced the husband's responses. The therapist can also replay the process to focus on and to explore a particular part of it.

The therapist also tracks and summarizes any new interactions that occur in Step 7. He or she highlights the risks taken by the experiencing spouse, the responses made by the other, and the attachment possibilities that such interactions hold.

Example

> **Therapist:** That's incredible, Terry, what you did just then. It takes a lot of courage to do that, to say to June, "Just quit telling me how to place my feet every minute and maybe we can dance together, I'd like to tango with you. If you'd just trust me a little, maybe I can figure out how to dance." And then June, you said something like, "Well maybe you can" and

laughed. That is pretty different from the first few sessions where the idea of trusting Terry to create this relationship was— (pause)

June: Intolerable. (Therapist nods) Now I guess I have the sense that he does want to dance.

Therapist: Aha, that makes all the difference. You are both finding new ways to be together, to build a relationship together, yeah?

Reframing

The difficulties that partners experience in stating their needs are placed in the frame of their experience of the negative cycle, and the expectations and vulnerabilities that arise as a result of that cycle.

Example

Therapist: I understand that for you it's like a death-defying risk to ask Graham this, after such a long time of feeling that you were not important to him. (She nods) It must be very scary. (She nods) He might . . . ?

Elisa: He might give me all the rational reasons why what I need is inappropriate, and then he'd turn away so that I feel small as well as alone. This is risky.

Therapist: To dare to ask for what you want in the face of such hurt and fear, to hope that he will respond, yeah? (She nods)

Restructuring Interactions

The most common intervention at this point in therapy, and sometimes the only intervention necessary, is the choreographing of a request and the heightening of a positive response. This choreographing of a specific move with congruent nonverbals in an ongoing interactional dance may require considerable, almost relentless focus and directiveness on the part of the therapist, however.

Example

> **Therapist:** So can you ask her, please, "I want you to start to get out of your tank. I want to be close."
>
> **Martin:** (to the therapist) Yes, I do want that. After all, then everything would be better—and the problems with her family would be . . .
>
> **Therapist:** Martin, can I interrupt you? Can you look at your wife and tell her that please—that you want her to get out of her tank and let you in?
>
> **Martin:** (turns to his wife and looks at her as he says) Yes, I want that—for you to let me in, and I'm not going anywhere. I want to be beside you, not in the next yard. I want some tenderness, and I want to give it back.
>
> **Therapist:** How does it feel to say that, Martin?
>
> **Martin:** It feels good, like it's real, and I feel taller for saying it. (Therapist nods and smiles)
>
> **Therapist:** What is it like for you to hear that, Susan?
>
> **Susan:** It's a bit scary, but, well, I think I like it, and (to her partner) I really like that you wanted to say it enough to risk it; it's different. It's more like when we were first together.

The therapist would then heighten this event and the possibilities it holds for a secure bond between the couple.

Rather than discussing couple process and end state in this chapter, it seems more appropriate to discuss change events, since the structuring of such change events is a crucial part of Steps 5 through 7 for each partner.

CHANGE EVENTS

The completion of Step 7 for a withdrawn partner is synonymous with the change event *withdrawer reengagement*, and the completion of Step 7 for a critical partner is synonymous with the change event called a *softening*.

After they have completed Step 7, both partners are more accessible and responsive and able to communicate directly about their attachment issues, so the therapist can then foster positive bonding events. Once this occurs, the last two steps of therapy, which include the process of termination, can begin.

The two change events mentioned above, reengagement and softening, have also been described in the original book on EFT (Greenberg & Johnson, 1988), and a transcript of a softening can be found in a book chapter already published (Johnson & Greenberg, 1995). However, the partners' progress through prototypical versions of these events is described here to help create a clearer picture of the step-by-step process.

Withdrawer Reengagement

This shift begins in Step 5, with the owning of emotions underlying the interactional position the person enacts in the relationship:

A usually withdrawn spouse experiences fully his real fear of contact, with all the weight and dread of his *catastrophic expectations*, as in, "She'll finally see how pathetic and inadequate I am." (The less engaged partner is often, but not always, male.)

He then processes this fear with the therapist, who directs him to share it with his partner. He does so congruently, that is, his verbal and nonverbal messages are clear and consistent. He might say, "I cannot let you see me. Sometimes I feel you must loathe me."

He then accesses more specific hurt that he is able to express directly to his spouse, as in, "I am not and can never be your wonderful, exciting first lover. I'm just me, and I can never make it with you. I feel so empty inside" (part of Step 5).

His spouse first responds with disbelief and cold detachment, but when validated by the therapist, she begins to struggle with her partner's message, as in, "You expect me to believe . . . I hope you do hurt . . . you never told me this . . .

I never expected this . . . It seems so sad . . . I didn't know I was hurting you . . ." (part of Step 6).

Supported by the therapist, the husband stays engaged and focused on his own reactions and the dialogue with his wife. His emotional experience begins to have implications for action, telling him clearly where he is and what he wants. He then feels entitled to his emotions and begins to verbalize these elements, as in, "I can't keep trying to prove I'm worth your caring. I won't spend my life that way, struggling up Everest, dealing with your criticism, and feeling too scared to try and get close. I'd rather sleep by myself and just accept being alone."

The therapist supports the partner to hear this and helps her deal with her anxiety.

The therapist encourages the husband to tell his wife his needs and wants. This includes what he can and cannot, will and will not, do in the relationship. He is now actively defining the relationship (the opposite of his previous behavior) and also himself, his role and desires, in it. He now states, "I want to feel desired, like I just might be someone you like to be with. I don't want to hide. I want you to help me learn about how to be close" (Step 7).

He now appears powerful rather than powerless, engaged with his emotions rather than avoiding them, present in the interaction rather than elusive, and seeking for rather than avoiding connection.

This sequence has been simplified to present clearly how this process evolves. Of course, there are various exits and distractions and points along the way where couples stall or become "stuck." After this change event occurs, there is also an integration of this experience into the person's sense of self and into the relationship. A partner will then come into the session and talk about him- or herself more positively, or be able to interact with the partner differently. He or she will also take pragmatic steps to change the structure of the relationship at home, such as making more decisions or being different with the children. He or she is moving into Steps 8 and 9. The pace of the process is unique to each individual.

In particular, it will take much longer and occur in smaller incremental steps if there has been a previous violation of human connection—that is, trauma has been inflicted by an attachment figure (Johnson, 2002). The therapist adapts the pace of the process to each person's style and history.

Softening

This shift begins in Step 5 and is often stimulated by the movement of the other partner to a more accessible position, as in the reengagement event.

Rather than focusing on the faults of the other, partners now begin to focus more on the self, accessing powerful attachment-related fears and/or experiences that organize their behavior in relation to their spouse. These fears and experiences are experienced intensely and processed anew in the session, and the relevance for the present interaction is heightened, as in, "I promised myself to never count on anyone again. Men will always betray you. You can't be that vulnerable. You might disintegrate. So I smack first and hold my soft sides in."

As a wife who is beginning the process tells her partner this, he is able to be more responsive than he was previously. This often enables her to continue to process her inner experience, and/or it allows the therapist to really focus on her immediate and clear reluctance to engage the other spouse. The wife, in this example, may access considerable grief, as she allows herself to touch the longing for, and the felt dangers of, connection with the other. Specific experiences in this and in other relationships, as well as specific hurts and key incidents, are accessed and reprocessed, as in "I have barbed wire around me, so he can't get in. I see the image of him smiling at another woman and turning his back on me and I go cold, cold, cold" (Step 5). The therapist then helps her share her experience directly with her spouse, as in, "I can't let you in," and helps the spouse respond in a caring manner (Step 6).

This partner's definitions of self and other become clear, as she expands and intensifies her engagement in her experience of connection and disconnection. The therapist helps her to explore these definitions and to engage emotionally with her partner whenever she can, as in, "The panic I feel when he blocks me off like that; I can't stand it. It's like a soft glove around my throat, suffocating me. I feel so naked, so helpless. I will do anything not to feel that." The therapist asks her to tell her partner about the panic, or perhaps to tell him, "I won't let you do this to me" (Step 5).

This partner's needs and longing now come to the fore, and the therapist helps her formulate them and share them with her partner: "I want you to hold me, to help me feel safe. I need you to help me hold back the dark" (Step 7).

As this partner addresses her attachment needs with her partner with a softer, more vulnerable stance, *the emotional contact between them is intense and authentic.* At this point, the therapist attempts to be as unobtrusive as possible and to support the couple as they take their first turn at a new dance of reaching, allowing oneself to be moved, and coming together in the beginnings of trust.

How quickly this takes hold outside of the session and is integrated into the relationship depends on the individual couple. This is also the work of the last two steps of therapy.

As a final note, it is important to mention a recent research study (Bradley & Furrow, 2004) that looked systematically at the process steps and the interventions used in successful softening events. This study found that the EFT therapist particularly uses evocative responding, heightening emotion and present and changing positions and interactional moves, validation and empathic interpretation focusing on placing responses, needs, and fears in an attachment frame in successful softening events. The study stressed the necessity for the therapist to focus on the more blaming partner's fears of reaching for the spouse and for the therapist to explicitly direct this partner to reach and risk in an enactment, asking for attachment needs to be met. The observations made in this study also identified interventions such as seeding attachment (see page 87) where the therapist, addressing a client's fear of reaching for the spouse, says some version of

"So you could never . . ." This intervention makes attachment longings and fears explicit and tangible. The researchers found six thematic shifts in the process of softening:

- a focus on possible blamer risking and reaching;
- addressing fears of reaching;
- supporting actual blamer reaching and stating attachment needs explicitly;
- supporting and validating the softening blamer;
- processing the event with the now engaged withdrawer; and
- supporting this partner to reach back and respond to the softening blamer.

The study found that the therapist would also return to a focus on fears of reaching if necessary. This focus included a focus on fears of how the other might respond (as in "He might just turn and walk away") and fears about self (as in "He will see I am not special enough—I'm too difficult"). This kind of research that dismantles and dissects key transforming events in therapy is crucial (Johnson, 2003) and has obvious relevance for enhancing the day-to-day practice of a model such as EFT.

9

THE CONSOLIDATION OF A SECURE BASE

EFT: STEPS 8 AND 9

"She's way more available. She holds my hand in bed."

"We still fight sometimes but she's not a stranger, and she's not the enemy."

"I can say when I'm insecure and that changes everything."

This chapter describes the termination phase of EFT: Step 8, facilitating the emergence of new solutions to old issues and problems, and Step 9, consolidating the new positions the partners take with each other. These new positions are more flexible and foster accessibility and responsiveness. The relationship now becomes *a secure base* from which to explore the world and deal with the problems it presents and a *safe haven* that provides shelter and protection.

STEP 8

The change events that have occurred in the previous steps now have a direct impact on the couple's ability to problem solve and cooperate as partners in their everyday life.

How does this impact occur? First, pragmatic instrumental concerns are no longer arenas for the couple's emotional struggles. *Issues become much simpler when they do not evoke attachment insecurities, power struggles, and battles over self and relationship definition.* For example, the problem of the family finances remains just that, rather than becoming the trigger for the negative interactional cycle, where one spouse blames and criticizes the other and the other gives up and refuses to talk. The process becomes one of addressing a common problem rather than conducting a negotiation with the enemy.

Second, the atmosphere of safety and trust that has begun to develop fosters the exploration of issues, as well as the ability of each partner to stay engaged in the process of discussion. Third, the couple spends less time and energy regulating their negative emotions and protecting their individual vulnerabilities. The partners then tend to use the problem-solving skills they have more effectively. Fourth, and perhaps most important, the nature and meaning of the problems that the partners face change, as a result of the change in the relationship context. Long hours at the office no longer mean that the husband is having an affair with his work; they mean that he has a demanding job. The partners define their relationship problems differently and face them together, as a unit, rather than alone, as isolated individuals.

Research on EFT has found that adding the teaching of communication or problem-solving skills did not improve EFT's effectiveness (James, 1991). In fact couples seem to be able to solve problems better after EFT, despite the fact that they have received no formal teaching in this area in therapy. This is not surprising in the context of the EFT model, which does not see such a lack of skill as crucial in the etiology and/or maintenance of marital distress. However, it is true that, as in all therapies, the couple learns new behaviors, even if they are not directly taught. In EFT, the therapist models new ways to speak to and reach each partner, simply by engaging in this process while the other observes. The process of therapy also shows, in a dramatic and alive manner, what partners can do and who they can be when they feel safe and their experience is validated. The therapist also responds to each partner in terms of his or her attachment insecurities, and so models this perspective for the other partner.

The process of addressing pragmatic issues more effectively often begins when the withdrawn partner reengages and begins to take initiative in redefining the relationship. A husband suggests, for example, that the chaotic state of the basement is no longer a problem, because, since he is now clear that he is not willing to clean it, and he understands that this is a long-standing source of frustration for his wife, he has just taken the initiative and hired someone to take care of it. However, larger, more significant issues are usually not resolved until both partners have gone through Step 7. Some issues may also involve life dilemmas that cannot be resolved in any absolute sense, but perhaps can be managed more effectively—the problem of caring for a chronically ill child, for example, or the problem of a career that makes difficult demands, such as frequent postings to new cities or countries.

MARKERS: STEP 8

In Step 8, the therapist intervenes when:

1. In the later part of the process of reengagement, a partner begins to own his or her part in, or perspective on, the pragmatic issues in the relationship. This perspective is now more proactive and opens up new possibilities for problem solving. For example, a husband states that he understands his wife's concerns over finances and is ready to take care of this, so he has arranged to deposit an amount of money each month in the family account. He then intends to run his business on his own terms, without his wife's interference. The task for the therapist is to support the reengaging partner's initiative, while helping the other spouse to be open and to respond to such actions. The therapist also helps the couple to articulate the effect this

problem-solving process has on the relationship and on the pattern of the couple's interactions.

2. When both partners have completed Step 7—that is, most often after the more critical partner has completed the softening process—the couple begins to discuss long-standing life dilemmas and/or decisions that in the past have been a source of alienation (such as whether to have another child). Such issues have not been resolved due to the conflict in the relationship, but also because the significance of certain issues is often intricately tied to the way in which the relationship is defined. For example, how much money to invest in a cottage may well be a very minor problem by the end of therapy, despite the fact that it has fueled many long arguments over the years. This is because the cottage no longer represents a valued refuge from the marriage for the wife, or a symbol of imminent separation for her husband. Very significant decisions, such as whether to have a child, are most often flooded with attachment significance. For example, a wife can let go of her defiant position and admit that in fact she does want to have a family only after working through her fears about relying on her husband and a previous incident in which she was ill, vulnerable, and did not experience him as responsive to her needs. The task for the therapist is to facilitate discussion and exploration while allowing the couple to find their own solutions. The therapist's focus is on how the dialogue about such issues can be a source of intimacy and contact, as well as on how to help the couple confront obstacles to positive responding.

STEP 9

Step 9 concerns the consolidation of the new, more responsive positions both partners now take in the interaction, and the integration of the changes made in therapy into the everyday life of the relationship and into each person's sense of self. As in beginning sessions, when the therapist was able to catch the couple in the midst of their negative cycle, to grasp the cycle in action and highlight it, so now the therapist can *catch the couple creating their new positive cycle* and being able to exit the old negative one. The power of capturing the moment is enormous. It is like stopping the complex dance of relating as it unfolds and holding it still so as to see how we piece it together.

In general, the therapist's main goal here is to identify and support healthy, constructive patterns of interaction. The therapist's concern is also to help the couple to construct an overview of the therapy process and to appreciate the changes they have made. The therapist helps the couple *construct a coherent and satisfying narrative, which captures their experience of the therapy process and their new understanding of the relationship.* In the attachment research of Main and Hesse (Hesse, 1999), the ability to create a coherent narrative about attachment experiences is a sign of secure attachment and is linked to contingent responding—that is, the ability to attune to the other. It is significant that couples are able to now create such narratives and the therapist supports this ability. In clinical practice, the creation of such a narrative not only seems to create a sense of closure for the therapy process, but also appears to reinforce the changes the couples have made.

This narrative or story can be used to validate and encourage the couple and can act as a positive reference point for the future. The story contains the differentiation of past ways of interacting and their emotional underpinnings, as well as the shift to current ways of interacting and how the couple journeyed from one to the other. In particular, the story focuses upon the ways they have found to exit from the negative cycle and create positive interactions. The therapist highlights the couple's courage, as well as the various times when they both took risks and made changes. The therapist also highlights the potential of the relationship to protect and nurture them in the future. At this stage in therapy, the therapist follows more than leads, commenting on the couple's process rather than directing it, as in earlier stages of therapy. The couple is encouraged to articulate future dreams and goals for the relationship.

When both partners have reached Step 9, termination issues are also addressed. Such issues usually include the expression of fears as to what will happen to the relationship without the therapy sessions, the discussion of the likelihood of relapse into the old cycle and how the couple will deal with that, and questions about how the process of marital distress or improvement evolved. The couple is encouraged to turn to each other, rather than the therapist, for support around these issues. Original issues also come up again here for review and emotional closure. *The goal is for the couple to leave therapy not only nondistressed, but also able to maintain an emotional engagement that will allow them to continue to strengthen the bond between them.* This then creates a secure base from which each partner can continue to develop his or her sense of self and efficacy in the world.

MARKERS: STEP 9

The therapist intervenes when:

1. The couple is able, in the session, to enact new positions and new positive cycles, as well as relate incidents of such cycles occurring outside of therapy. The contact between the couple is now obviously and tangibly different from the negative interactional pattern seen in the first sessions. The task for the therapist is to highlight these changes and to relate them to the security of the relationship, its future health, and the expanded sense of self of each of the partners. By symbolizing and heightening the changes the couple has made, the therapist helps the couple formulate these changes in palpable and concrete terms, thus enabling the couple to integrate them into their view of the relationship.

2. The couple suggests that they do not need the therapist anymore and are able to be specific about the
   changes they have each made, as well as how these
   changes have affected their relationship. They also
   express fears about not having the "safety net" of the
   therapy sessions. The task is to validate the couple's
   strengths and ability to sculpt their relationship to fit
   their evolving needs, as well as to reassure them and
   leave them equipped to deal with any reoccurrence of
   the negative cycle. The therapist also fosters their
   commitment to maintaining emotional engagement
   and a positive bond.

The therapist stresses that the changes that have been made
belong to the couple and actively discourages the attribution
of changes to his or her own knowledge and/or skill. The
possibility of booster sessions in the future is sometimes left
open, but framed as probably being unnecessary. When
necessary, such boosters usually consist of two or three
sessions after a particular crisis occurs—for example, when
the death of a child or an illness in one of the partners
severely impacts the relationship.

INTERVENTIONS: STEPS 8 AND 9

The therapist reflects the process of interaction between the
couple and validates the new emotions and responses they
share and enact. This is usually done with less therapist
direction and with less intensity than in previous sessions.
The therapist becomes most active when this process
begins to be derailed by a response from one of the partners. The therapist uses evocative responding to process
this partner's experience and to diffuse blocks to positive
responding. Empathic conjecture is, at this point in therapy,
largely unnecessary. If heightening occurs, it is the specific
changes made by the couple that are heightened. The
restructuring of the couple's interaction that has occurred

in therapy is made explicit by crystallizing present positions and cycles, by comparing them directly to the initial positions and cycles, and by heightening specific new responses. Throughout the final sessions, the therapist comments on the process from the metaperspective of attachment and the attachment process. Some examples of interventions follow.

Reflection and Validation of New Patterns and Responses

Example

> **Therapist:** I noticed there, Mike, that you were able to identify your impulse to run and hide, but then you just kept right on sharing and reaching for Mary. Do you know what I mean?
>
> **Mike:** Yes, I can do that now, but not all the time. It's 'cause she doesn't seem so dangerous anymore, and maybe I feel stronger?
>
> **Therapist:** Yes, it takes a lot of strength to do that, and it helped Mary stay with you and not get angry. Is that right, Mary?

Evocative Responding

Example

> **Therapist:** Can I just stop you for a minute, Jim. Things seemed to be going pretty well there for a moment (Jim nods), but then something happened that changed the dance. Do you know what I mean?
>
> **Jim:** Yes, she used that word *needy* and I freaked. That used to be a big put-down between us; she'd call me needy and I'd feel like I was some kind of defective idiot. That word is pretty loaded for me, so I got aggressive, like she was still the enemy.
>
> **Therapist:** Can you tell her about that feeling of being defective, Jim, and how it affects you and your ability to keep talking? Can you help her understand . . .

The therapist here redirects the interaction back toward a dialogue that is potentially intimate and constructive.

Reframing

The therapist frames new responses as alternatives to the old cycle and places old and new cycles in the context of intimate attachment. The therapist provides the frame for the couple's construction of the narratives "the way we used to be" and "the way we are now and can be in the future." The therapist, for example, may talk about how each partner now helps the other behave in a responsive and accessible manner and actively helps create attachment security for the other.

Example

> **Therapist:** So when David does this, tells you his fears, you feel really important to him and really connected. And that helps you stay out of the depression and stay more involved in the relationship, yes?

Restructuring Interactions

The therapist now consolidates the new positions the partners take with each other, by focusing and commenting explicitly on the nature of these responses. In a sense, the therapist summarizes the restructuring that has already occurred in previous sessions, or encourages the couple to create their own summary. The therapist also occasionally choreographs interactions that solidify new responses.

Example

> **Therapist:** You know, it really hit me just now, Carey, when you were discussing the incident at the party, how different you are with each other, compared to a few months ago.
>
> **Carey:** (laughs) A few months ago that would have been the start of World War III. And we can still have those conflagrations.

Therapist: Aha, those fights still happen sometimes, kind of like a relapse.

Carey: But we can get out of them now, and talk about them.

Therapist: How are you different, Carey, what has changed for you?

Carey: Well, my whole focus was to never let her get to me, you know, to numb out if I had to, and that would just fuel her rage.

COUPLE PROCESS AND END STATE

What does the couple look like at the end of therapy? At this point, when the therapist watches the interaction, it is difficult, or impossible, to identify fixed rigid positions. Both partners might withdraw for a moment; both can get angry and critical, but both take risks in the relationship and both are able to reveal their own vulnerabilities and respond to their partner in a caring way. In short, *negative interactions are more fluid and are processed differently, and they also have less impact on the way the relationship is defined.* On the other hand, positive interactions are more apparent and are also acknowledged and owned. The quality of the contact between partners has shifted toward safety, closeness, and trust. The way the partners talk about each other, the attributions they make, have taken on a more positive and compassionate tone, and in general the way the couple talks to each other has changed.

The quality of the interaction is perhaps best captured by the contrast between a dialogue where each person defends against the other and is concerned with regulating his or her own negative affect, and a dialogue where each partner is actively discovering the other, as well as the self, in relation to the other. Attachment theory suggests that in young children, exploration behaviors are fostered by a sense of safety and security; in adults, too, a sense of security seems to foster the curiosity and openness essential to adult intimacy.

Couple therapy does not always result in the creation of a more connected and intimate relationship. Occasionally, the process of clarifying the cycles of interaction and the underlying emotions results in the couple deciding to separate, or to live together in a parallel and relatively separate fashion. Then the picture at the end of therapy looks a little different. The negative cycle has been modified and the couple is no longer blaming each other or becoming stuck in painful impasses, where one tries to please while the other keeps his or her distance. In these cases, however, the positive cycles are much more constricted and result in calm effective negotiations, rather than intimate contact. For example, the couple may agree that they do not fit as spouses, but they have given each other much and wish to stay together for another three years to bring closure to their task as parents. They are clear that at that time they will both be free to pursue their own goals and other relationships.

If termination evokes great anxiety in one or both of the partners, the therapist uses evocative responding to help such partners explore their fears and directs them to discuss these fears with each other and ask for each other's help in dealing with them on a day-to-day basis. Generally, if the process of therapy has gone well, the partners face the end of the sessions with a certain trepidation, but they also feel more in control of their relationship than ever before. They are ready to leave the safe base of therapy and fly on their own.

The process of couple therapy may be relatively more intense and all-encompassing for some partners than for others. As people struggle with defining their intimate relationship, they also inevitably struggle with defining themselves, and sometimes events evolve into an existential crisis for one of the partners. The term *existential crisis* is used here as described in Yalom's text on existential psychotherapy (1980). Sometimes such partners are already in individual therapy, and the couple therapist can confer with the individual therapist to dovetail the two therapy processes. Sometimes the individual accesses real dilemmas and vivid choice points, in the process of couple therapy, that eluded him or her in individual therapy.

This process may be contained within the usual framework of EFT, or it may require a few individual sessions at some time in the process. In these cases, the end of therapy is usually more poignant or dramatic, since it involves not only the redefinition of the relationship, but also closure on an existential dilemma. For example, a 50-year-old man who has never been able to commit himself to a relationship, even with his children, struggles in therapy with all the very good reasons he has for his strict boundaries concerning close relationships and his fears concerning closeness. Couple therapy here involved a recognition of his longings for closeness and his fears of depending on another. The end of therapy also involved then a resolution of this individual's lifelong issue.

To summarize, at the end of therapy the following changes are usually apparent:

- **Emotional.** Negative affect has lessened and is processed and regulated differently. The couple can stay emotionally engaged and can use the relationship to regulate negative affect such as fears and insecurities. Positive affect has been evoked by more positive cycles of interaction. The partners are more engaged with their own emotional experience; they accept their own emotions more, and they can express these emotions in a way that helps their spouse respond to them.

- **Behavioral.** The couple behaves differently toward each other, being more accessible and responsive in the session and in their daily lives. As a result, each one experiences the relationship as more supportive. Behavior in interactions is generally less constricted and more responsive to the other's communications. Specific attachment behaviors change. For example, partners now ask for what they need, and they can ask in a way that helps their partner respond. Other behaviors not explicitly addressed in therapy also change, such as the amount and quality of the couple's sexual contact and their ability to problem solve.

- **Cognitive.** The partners perceive each other differently. They have had a new experience of the other in the sessions, and so they make different and more positive attributions about the other's responses. They have also included new elements in their definitions of the other partner and of themselves; in attachment terms, their specific models of the other, and of self in relation to the other, have been modified. They also have a different metaframework for relationships in general, since they have experienced their relationship through the therapist's attachment perspective.

- **Interpersonal.** Negative cycles are contained, and new positive cycles are enacted. The partners are now able to "unlatch" (Gottman, 1979) from self-reinforcing negative interactions, as well as initiate new responses that evoke more positive responses from the spouse and create more overall emotional engagement.

THE NURTURING AND MAINTENANCE OF A MORE SECURE BOND

In recent years, my colleagues and I have also found it useful to help couples focus more explicitly on how to maintain the gains they have made in therapy. For example, it is useful to ask partners how they intend to maintain the emotional connection they have worked so hard to create. Couples are encouraged to examine how they have structured their lives in ways that preclude the maintenance of a secure bond. One professional couple, for example, had evolved schedules that excluded any real togetherness. She arose at 6:00 and took care of family matters until she went to work. He arose at 8:30 and began work in his home office. After work, she drove her children to many different activities and then collapsed into bed around 9:00. He preferred to work until midnight. Weekends were totally dedicated to family activities and individual exercise routines. This routine evolved, at least in part, as a way of dealing with their lack of marital satisfaction, but it had become a way of life. Final sessions with this couple then involved a critical analysis of how to build their relationship into their life so that it could once again thrive. We refer to this as *scaffolding your life on your relationship* rather than leaving your relationship out of your life.

It is particularly useful to focus on attachment moments— moments of leaving, moments of reunion, moments of recognition and support, and ritual moments of connection. Couples are encouraged to explicitly decide on ritual patterns of greeting and leaving. They are also encouraged to make time to play together, apart from their time as parents and as employees. The return of a husband to a wife who has been at home all day with small children, for example, is often a setup for a sense of deprivation on the part of the wife. The husband is exhausted and needs to shut down for 20 minutes, but his wife then feels excluded. Partners are encouraged to discuss such key moments of differing needs and to also find ways to acknowledge and respond to each other's attachment needs. Ritual moments of connection, such as always having a private coffee together at the same place in the house at the same time of the day, also appear to be useful. Ritual times of sharing and holding at waking or at bedtime seem useful as well.

From the point of view of attachment, partners can sometimes begin to see their relationship as less of a background and more of a figural factor in their lives if they look through the lens of attachment, especially their attachment to their children. Most parents, for example, no matter how busy they are, deliberately say good night to their children and even spend a little focused time with them at bedtime. Most parents ask their children how their day was and offer support if necessary. Attachment relationships are framed as living entities, like plants perhaps. The couple's relationship is now healthy, but if never watered or fed, it will inevitably begin to wither and die. The attachment significance of specific behaviors can also be shared. For some partners, a good-bye hug and kiss is a more significant attachment signal than for others. Partners are encouraged then to explicitly share with their spouse the moments and responses that keep their bond alive and well and actively plan for the maintenance of the gains they have made in therapy.

10

KEY CLINICAL ISSUES AND SOLUTIONS

BECOMING AN EFT THERAPIST

In this chapter, clinical issues and questions that arise during the EFT training process are discussed. The kinds of issues addressed in this chapter are prognostic indicators for EFT, dealing with impasses in therapy, integrating EFT with other approaches, and the process of becoming an EFT therapist.

QUESTION: WHAT TYPES OF COUPLES AND/OR INDIVIDUALS IS EFT PARTICULARLY SUITED FOR AND, CONVERSELY, NOT SUITED FOR?

In general, EFT works best for couples who still have some emotional investment in their relationship, and some willingness to learn about how they may have each contributed to the problems in the relationship. This is probably true for all kinds of couple therapy. Being motivated to change, being willing to look at one's own behavior, and being willing to engage in the process of therapy, including taking emotional risks, are factors that have been generally associated with change in psychotherapy. There is also some research (Johnson & Talitman, 1995) that allows for more specific predictions as to who will benefit from EFT.

This research found that EFT worked best when the couple's alliance with the therapist was high. Presumably this is because the alliance enabled couples to participate fully in the process of therapy. The quality of this alliance was a much more powerful and general predictor of treatment success than initial distress level. What mattered most was the quality of the alliance—that is, the bond with the therapist, the sense of shared goals, and, in particular, the perceived relevance of the tasks presented by the therapist, rather than how distressed the partners were at the beginning of therapy. This perception of the relevance of the tasks that couples are asked to engage in could be a reflection of the skill of the therapist, who is able to tailor these tasks to each couple and to frame them in a way that is meaningful for them. It could also be a reflection of the general nature of EFT, that is, EFT may be particularly suited to couples who are lacking in intimacy and emotional connection and who see a focus on the quality of their attachment as relevant to their problems. It could also be, on a more general level, that EFT gets to the heart of the matter in relationship distress and so, at best, elicits a faith that this approach will lead to meaningful change and address clients' key emotions, their longings and fears. In general, in EFT research, there is exceptionally little problem with treatment drop-outs; clients do seem to resonate with this model and the attachment focus and the tasks implicit in it.

Even though experiential theory stresses the power of the alliance, the fact that in the research study mentioned above the quality of the alliance, rather than initial distress level, was so powerful in predicting outcome was surprising. In other studies using other therapy approaches, the couple's initial distress level has been overwhelmingly the best predictor of success in therapy. This implies that the central concern for the EFT therapist, particularly in the initial stages of therapy, must be to make a strong positive connection with each partner; to create a secure base from which each partner can explore the relationship. Stated differently, the central issue becomes whether a couple can engage in therapy, and how accessible they are to the therapist, rather than how large or intractable their problems appear to be.

Does engagement in EFT require that partners be particularly expressive or aware of their emotions? The answer from clinical practice is absolutely not, and the research referred to above found that a lack of expressiveness, or a reluctance to self-disclose, did not hamper progress in EFT. In fact, EFT seemed to be particularly powerful with male partners who were described by their wives as "inexpressive." This may be because when such partners do express themselves in the supportive environment of EFT, the results are often very compelling for themselves and for their partners. It is our experience that partners who have difficulty expressing emotion are moved and mesmerized by a process where they are seen and validated and where a therapist, as a trusted surrogate processor, walks around inside their world and helps them make sense of it. This research also provided evidence that men who are older (over 35) seem to be particularly responsive to EFT, perhaps because men tend to see issues of intimacy and attachment as more relevant as they get older.

For female partners, the variable that had the most impact on treatment success was the amount of faith they had that their spouse still cared for them. This was a powerful predictor of both partners' adjustment and intimacy at treatment termination and follow-up. In a culture where women have traditionally taken most of the responsibility for maintaining close bonds, this may represent some kind of bottom line, which can be expressed as: If the female partner still has some willingness to risk with, some trust in the other spouse, then couple therapy, at least this kind of couple therapy, has more chance of success. Conversely, if the female partner is truly unwilling to risk herself and engage emotionally with her partner, even in a supportive environment, then the possibilities for the relationship may be limited. This is then a crucial variable for the EFT therapist to attend to throughout therapy. A rigid lack of trust would seem to be an insurmountable obstacle to emotional engagement, and to marital happiness in general. Indeed, evidence is accumulating that *emotional disengagement*, rather than other elements such as the inability to resolve disagreements, is predictive of long-term unhappiness and instability in marriage (Gottman, 1994), and is also associated with a lack of success in various forms of marital therapy (Jacobson & Addis, 1993). Disengagement is associated with a lack of sexual contact, affection, and tenderness. It can be seen as an extremely insecure or damaged emotional bond, where emotional connection is experienced as too dangerous to be tolerated, or is no longer desired. In the latter case, such disengagement may signal the end of the process of protest, clinging, and depression, identified by Bowlby (1969), and the beginning of detachment and dissolution.

The level of traditionality in a couple's marriage does not seem to affect outcome in EFT. Couples where a very affiliative woman is married to an independence-oriented man, who would then most often be expected to display the classic criticize/pursue–stonewall/withdraw pattern identified as so deadly for marital happiness, seem to be able to make progress in EFT. In other marital therapies, this was not found to be the case (Jacobson, Follette & Pagel, 1986).

Another dimension that intuitively would seem to be important for the EFT therapist is that of rigidity versus flexibility. It is more difficult for the therapist to intervene effectively if a member of the couple has very constricted and rigid ways of processing his or her experience and of interacting with the other. The experience of pain tends to narrow human consciousness (Bruner, 1990), and for all couples part of the EFT process is to expand awareness and experience. However, there are some individuals with very rigidly held views of self and other, as well as very limited ways of regulating affect, for whom the expansion of such views and ways of processing is too high a price to pay for modifying their relationship. *In attachment terms, it is more difficult to intervene when working models are impermeable and thus unresponsive to new experience.* In the EFT process, this can result in either the less engaged partner refusing to become more involved or, more frequently, the more critical partner being unable or unwilling to complete the softening change event.

EFT has also been used to address a wider spectrum of problems than couple distress, which is sometimes only part of a broader clinical picture. For example, the role of relationship distress in the generation, promotion, and maintenance of depression has become clear and has been linked to an attachment perspective on close relationships (Whiffen & Johnson, 1998; Davila, 2001). The inability to create a sound connection to a loved one naturally evokes loss and a sense of vulnerability and powerlessness, as well as doubts about the innate worth of self. A lack of a supportive relationship also potentiates other stressors. EFT seems to work well with couples where the female partner is clinically depressed, alleviating the depression and the marital distress (Dessaulles, Johnson & Denton, 2003). It can be used in a shortened form to increase intimacy in mildly distressed or nondistressed spouses (Dandeneau & Johnson, 1994). It also appears to be effective with couples at high risk for divorce—for example, those experiencing chronic family stress and grief, such as the parents of chronically ill children. In a study with these couples, EFT improved not only marital adjustment, but also individual depression levels and the perceived stress involved in caring for the ill child (Walker et al., 1995). At two-year follow-up, these results remained stable (Clothier, Manion, Gordon, Walker & Johnson, 2002). Research tells us that in terms of psychiatric disorders, marital dissatisfaction is particularly associated not only with depression but also with anxiety disorders such as post-traumatic stress disorder. In numerous case studies (rather than in formal research studies), EFT has been successfully implemented as part of the treatment of traumatic stress in cases where one or both of the partners were suffering from post-traumatic stress disorder as a result of childhood physical and sexual abuse or as a result of traumatic experiences such as involvement in combat (Johnson, 2002). The main difference with traumatized couples (the spouse often suffers from secondary PTSD) is that the treatment process is longer (30 to 35 sessions is the norm). EFT is also used effectively (Makinen, 2004) and is able to renew trust with distressed couples who have experienced relationship traumas such as abandonment at crucial moments of need (see chapter 12).

The use of a systematic attachment-oriented couple intervention that focuses on the integration of emotion and the creation of a safe-haven marriage makes particular sense with traumatized couples. The most obvious reasons for this are the following:

- Traumatic experience floods us with helplessness, while secure attachment soothes and comforts us.
- Trauma colors the world dangerous and unpredictable; secure connection offers us a safe haven.
- Trauma creates overwhelming emotional chaos and assails a cohesive sense of self. A secure attachment relationship promotes affect regulation and an integrated sense of self, as well as a sense of confidence and trust in the self and others.

In fact, secure attachment appears to be the royal road to healing from all forms of trauma and to the promotion of resilience (van der Kolk, Macfarlane & Weisaeth, 1996).

WHEN IS EFT CONTRAINDICATED?

When is EFT not used? EFT is not generally used with couples who are clearly separating, where pragmatic negotiation or individual grief work may be more appropriate. (Still, a short form of therapy using EFT interventions has been used to help partners grieve and enhance emotional closure.) It is also not used with clearly abusive couples, where expressions of vulnerability are likely to be dysfunctional and place the abused partner more at risk. Abusive partners are referred to group or individual therapy to help them deal with their anger and control issues. They are only offered EFT after this process is complete and their partners no longer feel at risk. However, in practice the therapist has to sometimes make a judgment as to what is abusive. One abusive incident does not necessarily make an abusive relationship. The most useful guides here are the victim's experience of the abuse and the therapist's own observation of the couple's interaction. There are relationships in which no physical violence has ever occurred, but where verbal abuse in the form of threats, denigrating comments, and deliberate moves to hurt and intimidate the other occur on a frequent basis. The therapist has then to decide whether encouraging the victim of this abuse to move into Step 3, accessing underlying feelings, is functional or even ethical. If the therapist judges that EFT (and couple therapy in general) is not the best intervention at this point, he or she paints a diagnostic picture of the relationship and the cycles of interaction before outlining the choices the partners have open to them. To encourage the abusive spouse to go for treatment, the problem is often framed in terms of finding help to stop anger or violence from further taking over and destroying the relationship and the family. This kind of frame is similar to the externalizing interventions described by White and Epston (1990). From a more traditional dynamic point of view, it frames the violence as ego-dystonic or foreign to the abusive spouse's nature and well-being; it is then this person's enemy, an enemy that is able to create havoc in his or her family life and sense of self-esteem. This frame encourages the abusive partner to tackle the problem.

QUESTION: HOW DOES THE EFT THERAPIST DEAL WITH IMPASSES IN THERAPY?

The general answer to this question is that the therapist reflects the impasse, both in terms of specific interactions and specific emotional responses, and heightens the "stuckness" of the couple. As the couple enact the impasse again and again, different elements come to the fore and responses become more and more differentiated. The positions the partners take with each other become more and more vivid and immediate, as do their interactional consequences.

As the emotions inherent in these positions become reprocessed, new responses and perceptions begin to emerge. *Movement comes here not as a result of trying to do something different, but as a result of experiencing fully what it is that one does when threatened in the relationship, as well as how compelling and legitimate one's responses are.*

This dialogue itself also defines a new kind of contact between the couple, which opens the door for change. For example, it is more intimate and engaged (and therefore a step out of the impasse) to tell the spouse that you cannot and will not ask for love because, as you experience it, that is more excruciatingly demeaning, than it is to blame, justify your anger, and withdraw from the dialogue. At the very least, the therapist creates safety, maintains the focus of the session, and then simply blocks the exits the partners usually take, so that the impasse is confronted. The most common impasse encountered in EFT is when the second partner, usually the critical partner, enters Steps 5 through 7, and the opportunity for reciprocal emotional engagement presents itself. This most often presents as a crisis of trust, in that this partner sometimes has great difficulty confronting his or her hopes and fears and putting him- or herself in the other person's hands, even though this person now seems accessible and responsive. Often the therapist does not have to confront the couple concerning an impasse; the process itself confronts them. The therapist has simply to stay focused and support the client to struggle with his or her hopes and fears.

Are there different kinds and levels of impasses? It would appear so. In extreme impasses, the couple sometimes may not find a way through, but may actually integrate the impasse into their relationship, thus modifying the corrosive power of the problem. For example, one partner, who had been the victim of sexual abuse when young, had very clear limits and requirements around sex and physical affection. As a result of therapy, the husband was able to accept his wife's limits. The problem behavior remained, but did not now have the dire consequences it once had for the relationship. The husband's willingness to accept certain limits in the sexual area also strengthened the bond and increased the level of intimacy between the couple. This was possible largely because, by the end of therapy, these limits did not threaten the attachment bond between the partners.

In other extreme impasses, one partner may decide that he or she cannot do anything to create a difference that makes a difference and also cannot live in the relationship as it is. The couple may then decide to separate, or they will stay together with very modified expectations of the relationship. In such cases, the therapist presents diagnostic pictures of the impasse and outlines the choices open to the couple.

When dealing with impasses, it is helpful for the therapist to be able to step aside from the pressure to "fix" the problem and to recall that the goal of an experiential therapist is to help clients see, at times with excruciating and tangible clarity, the choices they are making and the choices that are open to them. It is one thing to intellectually discuss your unwillingness to trust another; it is quite another to hear yourself say, at the therapist's bidding, "I will never let you in. I will never let anyone in. I am alone with my fear." The "answer" to dilemmas in an experiential therapy is to grasp experience and how you create it with more and more awareness and clarity and to own it as an emotional reality. This reality often then begins to expand.

One kind of impasse that presents itself in EFT is what can be labeled the attachment "crime" or "trauma." This is a critical incident that captures the essence of, or symbolizes, the attachment betrayal or disappointment that has occurred in the relationship, and is accessed every time movement toward more contact occurs. These unresolved incidents effectively block risk taking and so the creation of new levels of emotional engagement. The disappointed partner uses this incident as a reference point for all the negative experience in the present relationship, while the other partner is continually frustrated and alienated by the reiteration of the incident. Such incidents are not "in the past," but are an alive and current part of the relationship. The EFT therapist helps the couple process this incident as it arises in the session, and reprocess the emotions inherent in the event. The attachment fears and losses associated with this critical incident or "crime" have often not been previously expressed, or even clearly formulated. What is expressed is usually blame and criticism of the other partner. Some attachment traumas from the individual person's past, such as childhood sexual abuse, may require individual therapy in addition to couple therapy. Often, however, the trauma occurred in the present relationship, and even if it evokes similar childhood experiences, it can be worked with in this context (see chapter 12).

QUESTION: HOW DOES THE EFT THERAPIST DEAL WITH PAST EXPERIENCES?

EFT does deal with past experiences inasmuch as they are enacted in present interactions. Intense affect, as it arises in present interactions, evokes past experiences that help the person construe, or make sense of, the present situation. In attachment terms, intense negative affect may call up old unresolved attachment hurts and losses and the working models that are associated with these experiences. The person moves from the present experience, "You betrayed me. I knew I couldn't trust you" to "I have never been able to trust anyone." The grief and pain of past hurts then infuse the present situation and help to determine how the person will regulate this affect, as in, "I will therefore shut you out and shut my longings down, like I did before." Past unresolved hurts and working models of attachment thus become part of the present; they are alive and accessible in the session. The EFT therapist will evocatively respond to such experience, helping the person reprocess such emotions and/or helping the spouse respond appropriately.

The EFT therapist also helps each partner construct a brief focused narrative of his or her attachment history, as it pertains to perceptions and responses in the present relationship. This helps to validate the way a particular partner experiences the present relationship; it also helps the other partner to see this person in a wider context. Indeed, in EFT *past experiences are referred to in order to validate and legitimize present responses, particularly ways of dealing with attachment needs and associated emotions.* For example, the therapist might validate a partner's fear of trusting her spouse in the light of the abandonment she experienced with her parents when her baby brother was born. This may also help her partner to see her withdrawal at certain times in the interaction in a more compassionate light.

In EFT, however, *the arena of change is the present relationship.* The client is not taken back to the past to gain insight and resolve past hurts; rather, the echoes of the past are dealt with where they are lived, in the present. *If the present relationship can be made more whole and secure, the past has been changed, in that its ramifications have been modified.* The past, in the form of personal sensitivities, is then integrated in a new way into the present. In addition, new experiences in the present challenge partners' working models, which are reflections of past experience, thus creating new expectations and new ways of regulating affect. Through the clearer, more coherent, and more complete processing of present attachment experiences, both the past and the present are then reorganized.

QUESTION: DOES THE EFT THERAPIST EVER CONTAIN EMOTION?

Emotion in EFT is experienced rather than discussed. It is felt rather than simply labeled, and can be intense and dramatic. Constriction of emotional experience and expression is also seen as a key part of relational problems. However, ventilation or expression for its own sake is not the goal in EFT. The experience and expression of emotion are powerful, and that power can be both positive and negative. The specter of uncontrolled emotion has been the rationale for individual and couple therapists keeping the expression of affect under tight control or avoiding it altogether (Mahoney, 1991). In experiential approaches to therapy, emotion has been viewed more positively (Johnson & Greenberg, 1994). Nevertheless, the EFT therapist also modulates the expression and experience of affect. If affect is viewed as the music of the dance, then there are times when the therapist needs to turn the music down, or vary the tune, just as there are times when he or she might turn the music up. When and how does the EFT therapist do this?

The therapist moves to contain affect that threatens to overwhelm either of the partners and his or her ability to stay coherently engaged with the experience or interaction. In a volatile attack–attack cycle, the therapist will reflect the emotions and the cycle; this tends to slow the cycle down and reduce reactivity. If necessary, the therapist will also actively block, divert, and refocus mutual blaming, as well as evoke softer feelings, perhaps of sadness or hurt.

On an individual level, the therapist will validate and support an individual in the midst of painful emotions. As in other experiential and dynamic therapies, the therapeutic relationship "holds" the client's emotional experience, making it safer for that client to confront that experience. The therapist's comfort and reassurance help the individual stay engaged with, but not be overwhelmed by, affective experience. *The therapist's ability to accurately reflect, accept, and crystallize such experience also helps the person regulate and organize the experience.* In general, making sense out of compelling experience makes it easier to deal with.

The more anxious a distressed partner is, the more chaotic his or her emotion appears to be. Trauma survivors, for example, who have been violated by the very people they loved and depended on may access terror, shame, grief, and rage almost in the same moment. The therapist then has to slow down the process of the session and name the emotions, linking each to the trauma and to the present interactions with the spouse. An example of this can be found in the literature on EFT (Johnson, 2002, chapter 6). In general, with such couples, EFT therapists find that grief and rage must be acknowledged but fear is the most useful primary focus, followed by an active focus on the shame that blocks a sense of entitlement and so prevents survivors asking for their attachment needs to be met.

In the general practice of EFT, the therapist will also routinely help the other partner attune to and respond to the person immersed in intense emotion in a manner that renders this emotion less burdensome. For example, anger is defused by the other's listening but exacerbated by the other's defensive withdrawal, just as fear is lessened by the other's expressed compassion.

On an interpersonal level, there are times when the therapist may interrupt expressions of negative affect, particularly secondary affect, such as reactive anger at the other partner. The therapist will redirect the process to the other partner's experience, or to the underlying experience of the blaming partner. The therapist may also reframe an expression of negative affect so that it can be useful rather than destructive in the therapy process, helping a partner move from "No one could trust you. You are so mean," to "I won't trust you. I'll show you that you can't control me."

The line between containment and the reprocessing of emotion, one of the central tasks in EFT, becomes murky here. *There is a sense in which the structured process of EFT, in itself, can be said to modulate and direct and, therefore, to contain emotion even though at times in therapy emotion is heightened and used to evoke new interactional responses.* The therapist also interrupts the expression of emotion when such expression is inconsistent with the present focus of the session, or seems to be a distraction, an exit, from the exploration of immediate primary feelings. The therapist will reflect the emotion expressed and validate the person's need to be heard on this topic, but will redirect the session back to the more pertinent experience.

QUESTION: DO INDIVIDUALS CHANGE
IN THE COURSE OF EFT?

If personality is viewed as a person's "lifelong style of relating to others, coping with problems and expressing emotions" (Million, 1994, p. 279), it would seem logical that a therapy that impacts how a person relates to significant others and expresses key emotions will likely impact an individual's personality.

In the first book on EFT (Greenberg & Johnson, 1988), there is a section on addressing individual symptomatology such as depression and phobias (pp. 189–193). Individual symptoms are viewed in that text as reflecting and constructing relationship rules and patterns of interaction. This seems particularly pertinent in relation to individual symptoms such as depression in women, since women tend to define themselves in the context of their interpersonal relationships and tend to be very negatively affected by the symptoms of relationship distress, such as the withdrawal of the male partner (Christensen & Heavey, 1990; Roberts & Krokoff, 1990). It can be argued that EFT, focusing as it does on emotional connection, may particularly address the needs that are most commonly expressed by women, making EFT a particularly appropriate intervention when the female partner is suffering from such symptoms and also experiencing marital distress.

However, even for partners who have no such symptoms, successful EFT involves an expansion and further differentiation of each partner's sense of self, focusing as it does on basic needs for security and connection, on how these are dealt with, and on how people are defined in interactions with significant others. Certainly there is evidence that, by the end of therapy, partners perceive each other differently (Greenberg et al., 1988) and respond differently to each other; thus partners get different feedback about who they are and tend to feel more accepted and acceptable. Each partner has also more fully experienced his or her emotional responses and attachment needs and has been encouraged to interact in new ways with the other. The unassertive man has risked being assertive, and the detached woman has risked asking for what she wants. This new experience changes the sense that people have of themselves and their abilities. *Rigid constricted interpersonal cycles narrow down the experience, presentation, and enactment of self. When these cycles are expanded, the sense of self also expands.*

As a couple therapist like myself, who was initially trained as an individual therapist, the power of couple interventions to call forth new aspects of each partner's individual personality is still surprising. It should not be, since the basic traditional underpinning of the whole psychotherapy enterprise is that new and different encounters with significant others, new kinds of relationships, allow people to change and evolve. Traditionally, such relationships were with therapists. In couple therapy, it is the already formed and powerfully significant relationship with the spouse that can be used to foster individual growth and to heal individual hurts. *Couple therapy can then be a crucial and necessary part of interventions that address individual issues, such as PTSD* (Johnson, 2002). Indeed, the literature on attachment and the implications this theory has for individual therapy and individual growth is growing (Sable, 2000; Siegel, 1999). This literature stresses that it are likely that primary emotional experience reveals both "how we know ourselves and how we connect to one another" (Siegal, 1999, p. 129).

In cases where an individual's interactional position and concomitant sense of self are very circumscribed and rigidly held, the couple therapy process may present this individual with a vivid existential crisis. A man who has played the part of a Don Juan all his life, for example, came to therapy mostly motivated by guilt, and confronted his inability to "let anyone in." This man, who had previously been in years of individual therapy and had a long history of brief idealized relationships, then accessed grief at the constricted relationships he had experienced with his parents, family, and lovers, as well as his enormous fear of placing himself in a position where anyone could abandon him. Past attachment experiences were touched and echoed forward into the therapy sessions. However, it was in enacting his refusal to connect with his present partner that his models of self and other and his attachment fears became accessible, and were able to be reviewed and expanded.

In couple therapy, human beings sometimes enact very basic human dilemmas that are difficult to evoke in individual therapy. This man explored all the ways he had of staying on the outside edge of his own emotional life and his relationships. He faced two dragons: the fear of dying alone, of never having connected with another; and the fear of being found wanting and, therefore, abandoned. His partner was able, with the therapist's support, to provide a secure base for him in the sessions, and he was able to face his dragons and make new choices. In such cases, couple therapy incorporates individual therapy. Both of the partners in the above case were seen in several individual sessions, and the process of couple therapy naturally potentiated the individual change process.

In general, there is growing evidence that actively treating individuals in their immediate social context makes sense, especially for problems such as depression and anxiety disorders such as agoraphobia, addictions, and obsessive-compulsive disorders (Baucom, Shoham, Mueser, Daiuto & Stickle, 1998). This is not surprising, given the pivotal role that relationships play in such disorders (Fincham & Beach, 1999; Davila, 2001; Whiffen & Johnson, 1998). From the attachment perspective, depression is a natural result of the inability to create a secure connection with a primary attachment figure on whom we depend. It is a natural move, then, for the EFT therapist to place depression into a couple's negative cycle of interaction and help the couple join together to defeat both the cycle and the depression. The inability to create a felt sense of security evokes loss and a sense of vulnerability and powerlessness, as well as doubts about the innate worth of the self, all of which are associated with the experience of depression. Lack of support can also potentiate other stressors. On the other hand, a more secure attachment potentiates resilience and is probably the best insurance against relapse in individual problems such as depression.

On a more general level, the ability to connect with our own feelings and with others is the basis of emotional intelligence, and emotional intelligence is synonymous with flexibility (Siegel & Hartzell, 2003). Flexibility is the sine qua non of individual adaptation and healthy functioning (Lewis, Beavers, Gossett & Phillips, 1976). To the extent that couple therapy enhances our emotional intelligence, it must then also enhance individual functioning and growth.

QUESTION: HOW DOES THE EFT THERAPIST KNOW WHICH EMOTION TO FOCUS ON?

There are a number of answers to this question. To be concise:

1. It's best to start where people are. At the beginning of therapy, the therapist focuses on and reflects the emotions, or even the lack of them, that the couple present. These are often secondary reactive responses, but the EFT therapist begins with the emotions that the partners spontaneously express. This is already a new experience, in that the partners are usually obsessively focused on the other's behavior, blaming or defending, rather than on the emotion itself, such as their anger and how they experience it.

2. The therapist follows the partners. As the couple feels more secure in the sessions, the therapist follows each partner to the edge of his or her emotional experience and then encourages exploration. He or she also structures interactional tasks that evoke new emotional experience and expression. The therapist focuses on whatever is most poignant for each partner, tracking each person's experience. It is therefore the experiencing person who lets the therapist know where to focus.

3. The therapist follows the maps provided by his or her own emotions and the drama of the client's relationship. The EFT therapist has different maps that suggest a particular focus at particular times in therapy. In experiential therapies, one map is the therapist's own sense of empathy, which

Guerney describes as a leap of imagination (1994). The therapist allows him- or herself to engage in the client's experience, to taste it and process it further, using his or her own emotional responses and empathy as a guide to the client's experience.

The second map is the drama of the positions that the couple takes in the interaction. *Each emotion has a "distinctive dramatic plot"* (Lazarus & Lazarus, 1994). Emotional realities are often connected with particular positions. Withdrawal, for example, is often associated with a sense of intimidation and helplessness, as well as with a sense of inadequacy or shame. We can then often predict a relationship stance from emotions, and inner emotions from relationship stances.

There are predictable common patterns in the way in which emotional experience organizes interactional responses. The therapist uses his or her knowledge of such patterns as clues to the underlying emotional experience of both partners, and as a guide to the new experiences that he or she might heighten to help partners change their positions. For example, the therapist senses that a husband fears his wife's rejection and therefore hides, but notes that if the husband could ever allow himself to express anger, this would empower him and revolutionize the way he interacts with his wife.

4. The therapist uses his or her theory of close relationships as a map. Attachment theory presents a context for the specific experiences of the partners, helping the therapist understand the client's experience at moments when the client may not, and giving the therapist a direction to move in. When the therapist cannot follow the client's experience, such a theoretical map helps the therapist to know where to focus. For example, attachment theory suggests that the only way some children have to maintain relationships with unavailable parents is to minimize their awareness of attachment needs and block out any longing for intimate contact. So when a partner says that he feels "nothing" in the face of very negative or very positive emotional responses presented by his spouse, this map suggests that it is useful to focus on his lack of response and the possible insecurity and inhibited longing that often organize such a response. On a more basic level, attachment theory tells the therapist that there is likely to be loss and desperation underneath a statement such as, "I am superfluous in this relationship—so I go on the Internet and flirt," no matter how cool and calm a manner the speaker uses.

QUESTION: HOW DOES EMOTIONAL EXPERIENCE EVOLVE IN EFT?

Engagement Expands Emotion

Generally, if one accepts that emotions that are threatening tend to be distorted, avoided, minimized, and constricted, on both experiential and expressive levels, engagement with, and acceptance of, one's emotions tend to clarify and expand them. Some emotions, such as fear and shame, seem to be so painful in and of themselves that a person's attention naturally moves to regulate these emotions, to contain the pain and reorganize the experience, rather than to engage with and process this emotion further. However, this reorganization (such as initial fear experienced and expressed as anger) often has negative side effects, such as further alienating one's partner.

Partners often also do not feel entitled to their emotions (Wile, 2002), or even feel ashamed of feeling them. A client might say, "If I feel this way, it means I am weak—pathetic." The shame-based meaning frame then blocks exploration of the emotion. The therapist's validation is the antidote for this. Partners also often move from acting out emotions, to naming and owning secondary emotions, to placing these in an attachment context and in the context of the cycle, to accessing primary emotions, to deepening these emotions and allowing these emotions to "move" them into new responses to the partner. With the therapist's help, a partner may move then from denigrating his wife, to naming his "rage" and owning it, to accessing the helplessness and grief underlying this rage, to accepting this helplessness without shame and integrating it into his sense of self and his view of close relationships, to asking for respect and comfort in a way that evokes caring in his spouse.

The expansion of key attachment emotion involves keeping this emotion in focus and processing it fully, rather than allowing it to be immediately reorganized in a way that protects the self. The adaptive action tendencies, crucial information about the self, and attachment needs implicit in the emotion are then available and can be used to organize interactional responses. The EFT therapist will move to block the reorganization of hurt into anger and instead will validate the hurt. This hurt can then evolve into a sense of helplessness and need for the other's reassurance and caring.

Another way of viewing this process is that engagement with emotions allows the person to experience conflicting emotional responses, such as a yearning for contact and a fear of such contact, and to create a more integrated response.

Specific Interactional Tasks Create New Experience and a New Story

The interactional tasks set by the therapist and the new responses made by the spouse also generate new emotional experience. For example, a spouse's offer of comfort and reassurance challenges his or her partner's sense of abandonment and evokes new emotional responses. The therapist helps the couple to construct a coherent unifying narrative of each person's emotional realities and how these realities define interactions. Couples leave therapy with a sense of how their emotional and interactional responses fit together and create their relationship; that is, they feel more able to create new and more positive emotional experience.

Emotional Processing Naturally Evolves and Has Its Own Pathways

In interactions with significant others, the experience of particular emotions seems to evolve naturally and in predictable ways. For example, in situations of insecurity or threat, a universal way of regulating hurt and shame is to "transform" such experience into secondary anger, or righteous rage, usually expressed in the form of blaming the person who has offended us (Pierce, 1994; Wile, 1994). The anger tends to protect the person from the sting of his or her own emotions and from possible anticipated harm from the other. If the primary response—the hurt underlying the anger—remains unprocessed, anger organizes inner and outer worlds, tending to evoke responses from the other that continue to fuel the angry response. This kind of anger is very different from the primary anger that arises when an intimidated spouse begins to contact his or her hurt and fear, which naturally evolves into expressed outrage at the partner's perceived lack of respect. The EFT therapist follows the natural pathways of such emotional processing. He or she is able to predict how this processing will evolve, and how he or she can heighten and use this process to shift interactional positions.

Particular emotions also evolve in particular ways. One especially problematic emotion is shame. Tears can bring people together and anger can be an impetus for assertiveness and respect, but shame by its nature hides and divides. Shame also appears to be such an aversive experience that it is seldom used to regulate other emotions in the manner described above (Pierce, 1994). Self-disgust, inadequacy, and a sense of worthlessness that create a model of the self as unlovable and undeserving of care make self-disclosure and the communication of needs and desires seem extremely hazardous. The most common ways of regulating shame seem to be to become angry at others or to generally numb emotion in attachment contexts, and withdraw from contact with others. The most common ways of regulating this painful emotion tend then to create interactions that again evoke the emotion itself, such as rejection from others. As shame is experienced and disclosed, sadness and grief naturally accompany it. If the other partner can respond in a reassuring way, the relief and comfort this acceptance provides act as antidotes to the shame experience.

Fear is the most pertinent and endemic emotion in distressed marriages. It evokes compelling fight-or-flight behavior, and constricts how partners perceive and interact with each other. Emotion has been described as an alarm system, a compelling automatic response that takes precedence over other responses; fear is perhaps the most obvious example. Various authors have identified the fears that typically arise in attachment relationships, such as fear of being left or abandoned, fear of being rejected or found unlovable, and fear of being controlled and helpless. Fear as a secondary response (given that it is more likely to be a primary response) is, in most cases, amenable to a therapy such as EFT; the therapist provides safety and support, and the partner is able to express anger, assert him- or herself, or express sadness. In EFT change events, it is usually fear, or attachment insecurity, that the person struggles with. In softening events, where a person risks reaching for the other and asking for his or her attachment needs to be met, anger or seeming detachment naturally gives way to powerful fears, which are encountered and processed in the session. These fears can then be regulated with the help of the spouse, who provides comfort.

Comment

Before going on to discuss the integration of EFT with other approaches, it is worth noting that there are clinical issues that are hard to address in written form. Learning to do therapy from a book can be compared to learning to sing a tune by looking at grooves in a record. Issues of timing, for example, are particularly difficult to address in this medium. This and other training issues are addressed in the original text on EFT (Greenberg & Johnson, 1988), which contains extensive examples of interventions and therapy sequences, and the by-now numerous transcripts of therapy printed elsewhere (see the Web site www.eft.ca for the many chapters and articles on EFT, most of which contain transcripts of the therapy process). There are also training videotapes of EFT (Johnson, 1993, and see the Web site) that show excerpts from a complete course of EFT, as given to one couple, and a consultation session. One of the very best ways to learn EFT is to make tapes of one's own therapy sessions and to replay such tapes, noting couple interactions and responses and the interventions made by the therapist. It is also useful to formulate different and improved interventions and hypothesize about what effects these would have on the process of therapy. The workbook written to accompany this volume should also aid in the learning of EFT.

QUESTION: CAN EFT BE INTEGRATED WITH OTHER CURRENT APPROACHES?

Since the conception of EFT, other approaches to couple and family therapy have evolved, specifically narrative- and solution-focused approaches. Both of these approaches are constructivist, viewing people's lives as shaped by the meaning they ascribe to their experience. In both, therapists take a nonpathologizing, empowering stance toward their clients, and in both these approaches, therapists take clients' statements at "face value" (O'Hanlon & Wilk, 1987); they believe what clients say, rather than searching for hidden motives. Hence, there are certain commonalities with EFT, especially with regard to these aspects. EFT, and other experiential interventions, also are constructivist, are nonpathologizing, and attempt to accept people as they are as a beginning point in therapy. The points of contact between narrative approaches and EFT are clearer, however, and a discussion of these points can perhaps elucidate EFT interventions further, as well as help readers familiar with narrative approaches to orient themselves to EFT interventions.

EFT and Narrative Approaches

Both EFT and narrative approaches view people as being actively involved in meaning making (Bruner, 1990)—that is, as constructing their experience and then using the meaning so constructed to orient themselves to the world and act upon it. Both view this construction as arising from, and constrained by, the reality of the social context. For both the EFT and the narrative therapist, objective reality is ultimately unknowable, and every way of seeing is also a way of not seeing. What you see depends on where you stand in the landscape.

Both EFT, with its roots in humanistic experiential approaches, and narrative approaches tend to view people in therapy as the experts on their own experience. The therapist is concerned with helping people construct that experience in a way that opens up more choices for them. Neither approach sees the therapist as having a privileged access to truth, but views the therapist as a guide in the "reauthoring" or, in EFT, reprocessing of life experience. Both approaches promote a therapeutic stance of faith in people's abilities to solve their problems, and both tend to minimize the differences between therapists and clients. Problems are seen as arising from a social context that would likely be problematic for the therapist, as it is for his or her client. Both approaches are also sensitive to the use of language to create new meaning, to reframe events and create a new context. Both tend to see expression as part of the organization of experience rather than simply a product.

In terms of interventions, there are also certain commonalities. As Minuchin and Nichols (1993) have pointed out, all therapists are storytellers. Many different kinds of therapists, including EFT therapists, also stress and use exceptions or new responses to problematic events (called unique outcomes in narrative approaches), to empower people and increase their sense of efficacy. Many therapists of different persuasions, including EFT therapists, also consciously create reframes to contradict or rename a dominant problematic pattern or "plot." However, the most unique and significant intervention in narrative approaches is that of externalizing the problem, rendering the taken-for-granted reality strange (White, 1993), and separating it from the person who experiences it. There is a significant commonality with EFT here in that, in EFT, the negative interactional cycle is externalized and both partners are framed as co-constructors and victims of this pattern, which has taken over the relationship.

The most common patterns identified in EFT are pursue–withdraw and attack–defend, although some couples may also display withdraw–withdraw or attack–attack patterns. These patterns have a life of their own and constrict the partners' interactions, precluding positive emotional engagement. In therapy, the partners learn how they help to evoke from each other the responses they find so distressing and so co-construct the pattern of interactions that defines their relationship. The couple can, therefore, close ranks against the pattern that is sabotaging their relationship. The problem is not "him" or "her" but the "dance we do together." The effects of this pattern on each person are elaborated, although this is done in a different manner in EFT and narrative approaches; narrative therapists are generally much more cognitive and discursive. In the beginning of EFT, this focus on the cycle provides a new context that allows the partners to take responsibility for their behavior, step aside from blaming, and begin to focus on how they share a common fate, rather than being stuck in victim and oppressor roles.

There are significant differences between EFT and narrative approaches, however. At many points in therapy, the EFT therapist "internalizes" responses. For example, rather than asking for a description of a husband's withdrawal and how it affects him in his life, as a narrative therapist might do, the therapist will ask in the here and now how it feels to withdraw, and what happens when he does this. The EFT therapist will then ask the wife how she feels when her husband withdraws. As the experience of withdrawal is expanded, new experiences and expressions arise that modify the withdrawer's position. The couple is not engaged, in EFT, in a process of fighting bad habits, as narrative therapists help couples to do (Zimmerman & Dickerson, 1993), but in reprocessing experience and expressing new aspects of that experience, in such a way as to undermine the problematic pattern. This then allows partners to experience alternative ways of being with the spouse.

EFT and narrative approaches also focus on the ongoing creation of identity. Narrative writers often speak of what the problem has told the person about him- or herself or what identity the problem has talked the person into. EFT therapists, on the other hand, listen for the self-definition that emerges in emotional experience and help the person articulate it. They attempt to expand this sense of self through new emotional experiences and new interactions with the most significant "audience" of all, the other spouse.

There are also times when stories and narratives are deliberately used by the EFT therapist. These are:

1. When the therapist summarizes and creates brief "stories" of each partner's attachment history as it relates to present interactions. The therapist uses the story to validate and legitimize the person's present perceptions and responses. This is done in front of the other spouse and places this partner's behavior in the context of his or her attachment history, often allowing the spouse to see his or her behavior as a reflection of this history, rather than simply a response to the present relationship. The more insecure the person's attachment style, the more inconsistent and incoherent his or her story about self in relation to others tends to be (Siegel, 1999). The therapist has then to support these clients more in the construction of their attachment story.

2. A disquisition (described more fully in chapter 4) is an intervention where the therapist tells the couple a story about couples in general, or about a fictional couple similar to themselves. The therapist tells the story of the couple's relationship as he or she understands it, including elements that the couple do not acknowledge but the therapist conjectures are present. The narrative reflects the therapist's sense of the couple's present reality, in a discursive nonpersonal manner, that elaborates on aspects of experience the couple seem to want to avoid or cannot articulate.

This intervention is less transparent and more indirect than other EFT interventions. The partners usually identify with some aspect of the story and begin to talk about their own experience in the light of the story. The aim of this intervention is to expand the partners' experience in the least threatening way possible, or to suggest an alternative way of understanding the relationship.

3. Later in the therapy process, the therapist and the couple construct the story of the therapy. This story summarizes the process the couple has been through and the changes they have made. This can be done to consolidate such changes or to highlight an impasse. As partners formulate and refine this story, crystallizing key change events and their part in creating them, the story becomes more integrated and creates a new model for the relationship, which the couple takes with them when they leave therapy.

The most striking difference between the narrative and EFT models is that EFT focuses upon emotional experience and the creation of new emotional experience in the session. This new emotional experience can then be integrated into a new story of the relationship. *The focus is less on the cognitive account or description of experience and more on the experience itself. Rather than attempting to "name the alternative plot" (White, 1993), the EFT therapist attempts to create it, and have the partners experience and enact it in the session.*

So questions such as "What actions would you be committing yourself to, if you were to more fully embrace this knowledge of who you are?" (White, 1993, p. 46) are replaced in EFT by a focus on the person's immediate emotional experience and an enactment of this new sense of self, as in the following example:

Therapist: What happens to you when your wife says this?

Husband: I get mad, but I stay silent.

Therapist: What is it like for you, to get mad and stay silent?

Husband: It's hard, I'd like to say . . . (pause), but I get anxious.

Therapist: It's scary, but you'd like to say . . . ?

Husband: Get off my back. Stop berating me.

Here, the therapist's focus on the emotional response evokes the action tendency implicit in the angry emotion. When the husband allows himself to feel and express his anger, he knows what he wants, and that is to set some limits for his spouse. He is then able to enact this in the session and so begin to create a new "plot" for interactions with his wife.

In EFT, experience and enactment tend to come before the synthesis of a new story. This is logical since EFT assumes that emotional experience is the key element in attachment "plots." As Bruner (1986) has suggested, there are always feelings and lived experience not encompassed by a person's dominant story or, in EFT terms, by a person's current awareness. The vulnerability of withdrawn partners, for example, is often left out of distressed couples' interactions and accounts of their relationship. EFT evokes such experience in the session and thus challenges the way the couple makes sense of their relationship.

The narrative therapist might ask partners to reflect on different elements of their experience, to discuss such elements, and to reason about their habits and beliefs in the light of this experience, for example, to identify and discuss unique outcomes. These are times when the problem did not occur or was handled differently. The EFT therapist is more likely *to create unique outcomes in the session*, or to heighten and expand those that occur naturally, than to discuss those that have occurred in the past or in other contexts. Strong negative affect also tends to predispose couples to discount and distrust unique responses from the partner. This makes such responses difficult to repeat, unless they occur in therapy where the therapist can support them.

EFT, perhaps, has more of the quality of a drama rather than a narrative. From an attachment point of view, if working models are taken as similar to a narrative, or a set of stories of relatedness, it may be difficult to expand such models or narratives without using emotionally oriented interventions to access such core cognitions and to evoke a corrective emotional experience.

EFT and Solution-Focused Approaches

It is easier to identify the differences between the solution-focused approach and EFT than the similarities, apart from the general parallel of both approaches sharing a constructivist and nonpathologizing orientation. Whenever possible, the EFT therapist also talks about and heightens and elaborates on what is going on right now between the couple, how they made that happen, and what such events mean for their relationship; however, to propose an extreme dichotomy, as some solution-focused therapists have done, between a solution and a problem orientation omits the focus of experiential approaches—the person. *EFT is neither solution nor problem oriented, but person oriented.* In experiential approaches, the person is always seen as larger than the problem, and as having the "solution" to the problem.

The alternative to being solution focused is then not necessarily to be immersed in the problematic, dominant story (Friedman, 1993), provided the therapist takes the stance that the person's personhood and experience are larger than the problem and the story of the problem. Immersion in experience does not, as some solution-focused therapists have suggested (Friedman & Langer, 1991), mire client and therapist in pathological thinking. In fact, immersion in experience, particularly emotional experience, is a direct road to new ways of seeing, new emotional responses, and new relationship stories. The person, from the experiential point of view, is not overwhelmed by a problem story, but by his or her way of processing experience and enacting the drama of attachment relationships.

From the EFT perspective, focusing only on exceptions to the problem is likely to discount the partners' pain and the significance of their struggle. In attachment contexts, negative emotion can become such an absorbing state that it is difficult to access meaningful exceptions, or to get partners to trust them and accept them as legitimate. This is particularly true if such exceptions open the floodgates of hope and fear, rendering the person vulnerable again to loss and disappointment. If a focus on exceptions does not work, then the solution-focused therapist might ask questions, such as asking a wife how she might respond differently to her husband if his "spiteful" behavior was due to hurt feelings. From the EFT vantage point, such insights or changes in perspective are more easily entertained when the wife has seen her husband experiencing hurt and when he has expressed this experience to her, and also when a therapist can help her process this. The EFT therapist would initiate this process and encourage the wife to respond differently in the here and now of the session. This new experience then becomes a key element in a new story of who her husband is and who he can be, in relation to her.

EFT and Bowenian Models

The question is often asked as to how EFT and EFFT relate to Bowen's model of couple and family therapy with its focus on differentiation of self. There are many differences between these models, especially in terms of how emotion and how needs for closeness with others are viewed.

One crucial difference between EFT and the Bowen model is the focus on corrective emotional experience in EFT, while Bowen tended to focus on a coaching model of therapy (Papero, 2002) that tries to generate increased rationality and insight, especially intergenerational insight and a stance of objectivity, as the main mechanism of change. Bowen's concern was to separate intellectual and emotional systems so that people do not become reactive and lose their "core" self in highly charged interactions. Experiential models such as EFT tend to focus on deepening and integrating primary emotion to go beyond reactivity, so that emotion can be used as a crucial guide for adaptive responses. The EFT and the Bowen therapist work to allow their clients to move beyond emotional reactivity, but the experiential and the attachment perspective views emotion as always being present and as basically adaptive so that separating thinking from feeling is not seen as feasible or as helpful if it were feasible. These latter perspectives do focus on the regulation of emotion; however, in contrast to Bowen's model, this focus on regulation often involves making emotion more available or articulated and using emotion to "move" clients into new relational stances.

EFT also focuses more on nurturance and connection and how this builds a coherent sense of self, while Bowen-oriented interventions tend to focus on boundaries, power, and control and the danger of losing the self or becoming "fused" with loved ones. Bowen particularly focused on these issues as they arise in three-way triangulated interactions between adolescents and their families (but not so much in dyadic couple relationships). EFT focuses on the generation of "effective dependency" (Weinfield, Sroufe, Egeland & Carlson, 1999) and sees dependency needs as adaptive survival strategies that can sometimes become rigid and constricting, whereas Bowen's approach focuses on more on independence and places dependency needs in a more problematic frame. Problems are framed in terms of insecurity in EFT, rather than as loss of self and fusion with another.

Both Bowen and EFT view emotional avoidance or "cut-off" and chronic anxiety as problematic in relationships, and both see a positive sense of connection as promoting flexibility and the tolerance of differences. However, processes of seeking love or support, seeking approval, and trying to please the other are often used as examples of a lack of differentiation in Bowen's model, whereas attachment-oriented approaches like EFT would view them as expressions of basic human needs that, if accepted, clearly expressed, and responded to are likely to lead to connection and so also to a stronger sense of self.

Both Bowen and Bowlby rejected psychoanalytic thinking, although Bowen-oriented writers still speak of processes such as family projection where intimates define each other and then enact the other's definitions. EFT therapists would tend to frame "projection" in terms of the circular self-reinforcing feedback loops in "stuck" and constrained close relationships. EFT also tends to stay with the present and maintain a safe empathic therapeutic relationship, whereas practitioners using Bowen's model often focus more on the past and inter-generational issues and on the therapist staying objective and separate from clients.

The central difference between EFT and Bowen's model, however, is clearly the orientation toward dependency. In the Bowen model, "fusion" with a loved one is a key part of dys-function. It is noteworthy that he first formulated his ideas when he was working with a schizophrenic population. Recent research on interactions between mother and child in fact suggests that there is no state of fusion from which dif-ferentiation then emerges (Stern, 1985). From the beginning, the human infant is wired for complex interactions with care-takers and has many capacities for self-regulation. Bowlby (1988), like many feminist writers, commented on the pathol-ogization of dependency and the glorification of so-called self-sufficiency and individualism. However, he also spoke of "efficient" and "inefficient" dependency. Efficient depend-ency involves an ability to construct a secure attachment with a partner and to use this connection as a source of com-fort, support, and nurturance. This connection is then inter-nalized and shapes a positive and competent model of self and a model of others as trustworthy. Efficient or secure dependency, which could also be termed mature interdepend-ence, is, in fact, in research studies associated with a more pos-itive, coherent, and articulated sense of self (Mikulincer, 1995). In attachment-oriented approaches, a strong secure emotional attachment to key others, where attachment needs can be expressed and met, and a strong and autonomous sense of self are seen as two sides of the same coin, rather than being on two opposing ends of a continuum. So the child who knows that the mother will be there when needed explores the environment more and takes more forays into the unknown. In adults, numerous studies have shown that a secure attachment to others promotes confidence and resilience in the face of stress. Secure attachment involves an inner representation of loved ones that we can use to comfort and support the self at times of stress, even when they are absent. Differentiation of self, if it is used in the general sense of being able to cope with the anxiety of being different and separate from others, is then part of attachment theory, but is best framed as differentiation *with* rather than differentiation *from*. Differentiation of self then is viewed in the context of relatedness to others, as part of connectedness not as a dichotomous or an opposing force (Fishbane, 2001).

In clinical terms, EFT as a humanistic experiential therapy can be viewed as promoting the construction of a strong "differentiated" sense of self in ways that also promote attunement to and emotional engagement with others. A few of these ways are summarized below:

- EFT is constructionist in orientation. It then focuses on how a person is active in generating and organizing his or her own experience and accompanying sense of self. For example, the therapist will promote awareness into the way a partner assigns a particular meaning to a relationship cue and then becomes absorbed in shame about the unworthiness of self and turns away from the other partner, even when this partner is offering validation and comfort.
- Experiential models of therapy and their view of the therapeutic alliance support individual growth and choice. The therapist is a collaborator, not an expert, and the client is afforded validation and respect. This, in and of itself, promotes the emergence of new and disowned aspects of self that can then be integrated and expressed in a relationship. So a partner begins to articulate his helplessness and to see this response as valid. He is then able to tell his partner about this, tell her how she helps

to evoke this helplessness and own his dysfunctional coping mechanisms. Experiential models assume that empathic responsiveness and validation do not create an "other-validated" or "reflected" and therefore less differentiated sense of self; quite the contrary, validation enhances and strengthens the self. The former perspective is reminiscent of the argument of the child-rearing expert Dr. Spock, who stated that the more you comforted and responded to a child, the more dependent and less self-reliant he or she would become. In fact, the research on attachment tells us that the opposite is true: The more accessible and responsive others are to our needs, the more sure of ourselves and integrated we become and the more we can soothe and validate ourselves.

• The goal of therapy is not to push clients into particular choices but to help them see the choices they already unwittingly make and the choices that are open to them. The therapist then stresses personal agency and helps them actively make and own their choices. So an EFT therapist might help a client state to her spouse, "I see you reaching for me—but I will not let you in right now. I want to keep you at a safe distance."

• The EFT therapist encourages clients to access, make sense of, and use their emotions to tell them what their needs and wants are and to assert those needs and wants to their partners. If the differentiation of self is used in the general sense of discriminating and owning elements of personal experience, then naming and asserting one's emotions can be seen as part of this process. Specifically, the validation and support offered in EFT help partners own their fears and assert their needs with the spouse. Their relational experience is then differentiated, owned, and expressed to the other in a way that reorganizes key interactions. This could be seen in terms of addressing what Bowen-oriented therapists might term boundary violations or attributions made by one partner concerning the other—for example, when a previously withdrawn spouse is aided to state to his partner, "I do want to be close. I do want to support you. But you have to stop smacking me and telling me I am not good enough and testing me all the time; that just drives me away. But I don't want to put up a wall between us. I want to help you trust me a little and I am sorry if I have let you down in the past."

- The EFT therapist helps clients make sense of, reflect on, and metacommunicate about their emotionally charged negative interaction cycles and build a coherent narrative about these cycles and how they impact each partner. This enhances clients' sense of agency and helps them to regulate their fears. It also helps clients step out of reactive arguments about competing definitions of the problem and blaming narratives and create together a coherent narrative that validates both partners. The Bowen and the EFT therapist would, I believe, appear to be most similar when this task of considering negative interactional cycles is occurring.

- In EFT change events, such as softenings, a vulnerable anxious partner is able to exit from emotional reactivity and defensiveness, articulate needs and fears, and stay engaged with his or her self and with the other. Once both partners are engaged, both are able to attune to the other and respond to this other while staying in contact with their own experience. They are at once more completely themselves and more completely connected with and responsive to the other. This is a picture of a coherent, well-articulated sense of self in action. It is also a picture of secure attachment, where both partners can regulate their emotions in such a way as to send the emotional cues that pull the partner closer and maintain connection.

Bowen's model, the experiential systemic framework, and attachment theory also have clear commonalities. First, they look at the couple in systemic terms, as caught in and creating circular patterns of interaction. All three focus on effective and ineffective ways to regulate fear and anxiety and how these ways can constrict interactions, and how the self is experienced and defined. What Bowen might view as emotional fusion, an EFT therapist would view as insecure anxious attachment, but both, I believe, would agree with Stern (1985) that "the sense of self is not a cognitive construct. It is an experiential integration" (p. 71). In the growing science of close relationships, interactions with others are more and more seen as an essential part of that integration, but perhaps attachment and experiential perspectives would adhere more to the view that "the differentiation process is inherently relational: this is not a solo journey" (Fishbane, 2001).

EFT and New Behavioral Approaches

In addition to the solution-focused and normative approaches, new versions of traditional approaches are emerging. For example, behavioral therapists have recently begun to integrate experiential interventions, which focus on emotional experience and the creation of acceptance between the partners (Dimidjian, Martell & Christensen, 2002). In these interventions, the therapist encourages the expression of feelings that are likely to foster compassionate responses from the partner; the problem can then become an opportunity for an intimate conversation, a chance to make contact. This version of behavioral marital therapy—influenced as it is by experiential concepts—focuses upon the pattern of interactions and emotional experience more than traditional behavioral approaches. Its originators make the point, however, that there is less emotional exploration and intrapersonal discovery than typically occurs in EFT. They speak instead about changing the stimulus control in the interaction; that is, changing how one partner expresses him- or herself, in order to change the other partner's response to a more accepting one. If they cannot be solved by traditional behavioral methods, problems can then be accepted and become less destructive to the relationship. A discussion of when such acceptance is possible can be found elsewhere (Johnson & Greenberg, 1994). It may be that such acceptance is only possible when the behavior that is to be accepted, rather than changed, does not constitute an attachment threat. For example, distance in certain specific situations might be accepted, whereas promiscuity might not. This work extends the behavioral troubleshooting intervention that does address emotional responses. However, from an EFT viewpoint, this technique tends to label emotional responses and to focus exclusively on their effects, rather than engaging in a reprocessing of such responses. In brief, this approach seems like an *outside-in* approach to change, rather than an *inside-out* approach, such as EFT. This approach does have some preliminary evidence as to its effectiveness (Johnson, 2003).

Summary

Traumatic experience is not traumatic simply because it is described that way (White, 1993), and attachment separation and loss are traumatic. Generally, the EFT perspective is that grief and fear cannot be "solved" or discussed out of existence. They can, however, be encountered in such a way as to evoke adaptive responses that enhance a partner's sense of self and the possibility of nurturing contact with intimate others. Focusing on such emotional responses is not seen, as it is by some narrative therapists, as "enlarging the client's view of the problem and intensifying his distress" (Friedman, 1992, p. 299), but as helping this person integrate such responses into his or her sense of self and relationship in a way that expands experience and generates new meaning frames. The EFT perspective is that new meaning and new behavior most powerfully arise from reprocessing experience with the therapist as a guide, rather than from a discussion of such experience. New labels and new ideas are seen as less powerful than new experience here, particularly experience that enhances a couple's ability to engage emotionally. The outcome data on EFT would seem to validate this. The research studies conducted on EFT not only offer evidence as to its effectiveness, but have also allowed the process of therapy to be studied and related to outcome and key change events to be delineated.

The strength of all these new approaches is that they add to the growing tendency in couple therapy to make therapy a relatively brief and respectful collaboration, where couples' resources are validated and their problems are seen as part of the human condition, rather than a reflection of personal deficits.

WHAT DO WE KNOW OF THE PROCESS OF BECOMING AN EFT THERAPIST?

At this point in time, we know many of the struggles involved in becoming an EFT therapist (Palmer & Johnson, 2002). A workbook of exercises for therapists who are learning to use EFT can also aid in this process (Johnson, Bradley, Furrow, Lee, Palmer & Tilley, in press). The therapist has to become truly comfortable with the basic premises of EFT, namely the nonpathologizing stance, the focus on process and how each experiential moment and interactional move is constructed, and the respect for people's dependency needs and the attachment perspective. The therapist has to be willing to refine his or her ability to empathically enter into the experience of each client and *discover* the shape and color of that experience. But most of all, the therapist has to become comfortable with engaging each client's emotional realities and joining them in processing this emotion in the present moment. The therapist learns to *trust the process of following, expanding, and integrating key emotions and using them to restructure couples' interactions.*

Some of the struggles that I and my colleagues have observed in couple therapists using EFT for the first time can be described as follows:

- Staying out of judging and blaming clients and framing the dance and the difficulties of processing attachment emotions as the problem.

- Building and monitoring the alliance. This can be particularly hard if clients become challenging or confrontative with the therapist. Therapists are encouraged to remain authentic and nondefensive and to be willing to learn from their clients.

- Maintaining the humanistic faith in people's ability to grow and make new choices even in the face of a multitude of complex problems. It is important to be able to tolerate ambiguity and complexity and to not become "impatient for simple answers to complex questions" (Mahoney, 1998).

- Resisting the tendency to become lost in content issues and staying with the *process* of how experience and interaction are constructed. From an EFT point of view, the problem is *never* about content issues, whether those issues are sex, money, parenting, or in-laws. The issue is always *how* the couple talks together and deals with key attachment needs and fears. The therapist has then to sort through content issues and move to the level of process. If and when the therapist loses track or becomes lost in content issues, he or she is encouraged to simply stop the process and request that everyone go back to the last comment that seemed clear and focused.

- Being able to move within and between. Therapists are often much more comfortable crystallizing clients' emotional experience or setting interactional tasks, but the EFT therapist has to do both. Often inexperienced EFT therapists are reluctant to invite clients to interact and create enactments, perhaps believing that they will lose control of the session if the couple becomes involved in an intense interaction. For most therapists, it seems easier to make intrapsychic interventions such as, "How does that feel for you when you say . . . ?" than interpersonal interventions such as "So can you tell her, please, I feel superfluous, unimportant. I don't know how to tell you—so I imply that I might have other lovers. But really I am just unsure of you and how important I am to you. Can you turn now and look up at her and tell her?"

- Being able to identify when the therapy process sparks the therapist's own attachment wounds or insecurities and seek the support and help of a colleague or supervisor. I can recall watching a therapy intake at a hospital clinic and realizing that I did not believe or accept anything the male client was saying—only to realize that he was vividly reminding me of a former spouse who had, from my point of view, betrayed me.

- Being able to be flexible and deal both with anxiously attached spouses who are overemotional and preoccupied with safety and with avoidant spouses who usually start off by having difficulty identifying any emotions and often make disparaging remarks about dependency. The therapist has to be able to deal with both exaggerated and disowned attachment needs and to contain emotion in one client while evoking it in the other.

- Learning to stay with and deepen emotion. As one therapist remarked, "I get them there and then I am not sure what to do with all the feelings." The standard EFT response is to reflect and validate. As the therapist reflects, he or she has the opportunity to "try on" the emotional experience and perhaps add an element to it, or organize it more coherently, or link it to the negative cycle or attachment needs. As the experience is presented again and again, the clients' engagement with it deepens and it begins to develop, as the features of a picture develop out of a photographer's tray. The therapist's use of vivid, specific, and concrete language and congruent nonverbals (RISSSC, as discussed on pages 109–10) encourages this engagement.

- Creating continuity and growth from session to session. This involves being aware of the steps the clients are in at any one time. If they have not de-escalated, it is a mistake to encourage them to take the kinds of risks that can be used to create more secure bonding later in therapy. It is also helpful to record key images, emotions, and statements of clients during or after sessions and glance at them before a session. A client's gradually emerging and deepening experience can then be evoked and made present in successive sessions. This also helps to stop premature interventions, such as structuring enactments before clients have clarified and engaged with their emotion, or encouraging blaming spouses to take large emotional risks with still-withdrawn spouses.

Supervision that is characterized by collaboration, mutuality, and respect is extremely helpful in learning EFT, as is the repeated observation of tapes of therapy sessions and the study of transcripts of EFT. The EFT certification process (see Training on the Web site www.eft.ca) involves the cognitive learning of the model, and group and individual supervision, as well as a summary presentation of a case example.

11

EFFT: EMOTIONALLY FOCUSED FAMILY THERAPY

RESTRUCTURING ATTACHMENT

The conviction that human beings have a need for connection with and confirmation from members of their family has been inherent in approaches to family therapy from the very beginning. However, family therapists usually focus on what occurs *between* individuals; emotions, viewed as occurring *within* individuals, are most often not addressed. Although there have been exceptions (Liddle, Dakof & Diamond, 1991), emotional responses have usually been considered unimportant or even subversive to systemic theory and therapeutic practice (Krause, 1993).

To a therapist who views emotion as a primary link between the biological and the social, the self and the system (Johnson & Greenberg, 1994, 1995), this seems unfortunate. Emotional experience and expression play a large part in organizing and regulating social interactions in families (Johnson, 1998), and can also play a significant part in reorganizing such interactions in therapy. Including emotionally focused change strategies in family therapy would address the concerns of authors who have suggested that current family therapies, focusing as they do on the conversational metaphor, neglect the experiential and the need for clients to experience themselves and their situation differently (Chang, 1993).

In the last few years, since the first edition of this book, the possible focus on emotion has also been placed more and more in the context of attachment and the perspective that attachment theory offers (Johnson & Whiffen, 2003). Attachment offers the family therapist a map to the intricate drama of family love and belonging. Theorists and researchers such as Moretti and Holland (2003) and Diamond and Stern (2003) are linking adolescent problems to attachment and formulating clear, explicit interventions that can be tested and systematically taught. This work also questions some of the old ideas about family transitions. For example, Moretti and Holland point out that in attachment terms a successful transition to adolescence does not mean that youth detach themselves from their parents. It is sustained connection that potentiates individuation. Attachment also forms the basis for tested infant–mother interventions (Cohen, Muir & Lojkasek, 2003). EFFT is part of this movement toward the integration of attachment theory and the music of the attachment dance, emotion, into the family therapy field.

BASIC GOALS AND TECHNIQUES

This chapter is a relatively brief outline of the use of emotionally focused experiential techniques with families. The focus of this book is couple therapy. However, since the perspective and techniques elaborated for couples here are also applicable to other family relationships, this chapter presents them in this context. The assumptions, goals, and processes of family therapy using emotionally focused interventions are essentially the same as in EFT. The therapist accesses key emotional responses that underlie the interaction patterns that define family relationships, particularly the relationship between the identified patient/client (IP) and the parents. As in EFT, the therapist uses new emotional experience and expression to modify such patterns. The assumption is that if such relationships change for the better, then the IP's problematic behaviors will also change, and this process will also impact how the IP is defined in the family and in his or her own inner world. The relational position of the IP in the family is viewed as helping to maintain this person's problems and/or preventing adaptation and change.

The goal here is to modify family relationships in the direction of increased accessibility and responsiveness, thus helping the family to create a secure base for children to grow in and leave from. From an attachment point of view, the more secure the relationships an adolescent has with his or her attachment figures, the easier it is for this person to act independently and confidently explore his or her environment. Secure attachment is characterized by the capacity to maintain close supportive relationships while also creating and maintaining personal autonomy. It is also associated with the ability to deal with environmental stressors and improved emotional adjustment, perhaps because secure corrections with others tend to have a positive effect on psychological factors such as self-efficacy (Bartholomew & Horowitz, 1991; Mikulincer, Florian & Wester, 1993).

Format

In this kind of family therapy, the general treatment format is that the family is seen all together for the first one or two sessions. This is to assess interactional positions and patterns and to identify problematic relationships and family cycles that appear to be related to the symptomology of the identified patient. After these sessions, family subsystems are invited to the following sessions; typically the parents/couple, the sibling subsystem, the IP and each parent, and the IP and both parents. This treatment involves a flexible combination of dyadic, triadic, and family group sessions.

The process of using the expression of newly processed emotions to create new interactions is essentially the same whether the session involves a client dyad or triad. However, dyadic sessions often encourage a sense of safety and focus, which allows for the creation of increased emotional engagement when this is desired. Changes made in the dyadic sessions are integrated in triadic sessions into the triangle of IP and both parents. Treatment is designed to take 10 to 15 sessions, and to be implemented by a single therapist or two cotherapists. Treatment usually ends with a session where all the family members are present and new patterns of interaction are consolidated.

Prerequisites and Contraindications

The prerequisite for this kind of family therapy is that the therapist be able to join with the family and individual members and to gain the family's trust and confidence, so that members actively engage in the therapy process.

This kind of intervention is not appropriate for abusive or violent families since the expression of vulnerability and a certain openness are fostered as part of the treatment process. Not only is this difficult to achieve in violent relationships, but it may even be inappropriate or put members at physical risk. Also, this kind of treatment may not be appropriate for families whose members now live very separate lives and who do not wish to examine or improve the contact between members.

FIRST SESSIONS (1–2)

These sessions combine treatment and assessment. The assessment focuses upon:

1. How family interactions are organized in the session— that is, who speaks, who is allied with whom, and who is excluded; how fixed the boundaries of various alliances are; how predictable and rigid the interactional patterns are in general; who is the most dominant and in control in the family; and how and what strategies members use to deal with conflict and the frustration of needs. How do members respond to

requests for support and comfort? Have particular events or crises occurred recently, or in the past, that seem to crystallize the way the family interacts and that they then enact as they talk about the event?

2. What is the emotional tone of the family in the session? What kinds of emotions are expressed, and by whom? Who seems to be in pain in the family, and how do they contain or express it? What are the family expectations about how emotions are dealt with? How do members respond to each other in the session?

3. How are patterns of accessibility and responsiveness perceived by the members of the family, and how do they hamper or help in the developmental tasks facing the family at this point in time?

4. What is the family's story? How did they get to therapy and what do they want from therapy? What is the attachment history of the couple and the manner in which the family evolved to its present state, including how crises occurred and how the problem evolved from various members' point of view? How do different members perceive the nature of the problem, right now? How is responsibility for the problem assigned?

5. What is the contract for therapy? How does the family view the therapy process? Can the therapist connect with the members and the family as a whole? How ready are individual members to engage in the therapy process—for example, to consider suggestions and to agree to try tasks set by the therapist in the session?

By the end of the assessment, the therapist should be able to identify key problematic cycles of interaction and to hypothesize about how they help to maintain the symptoms of the IP. The therapist also should be able to identify key relationships where attachment is problematic, and to have some sense of the emotional responses that prime interactional patterns. A clear sense then emerges of how relationships might be reorganized and attachment needs and fears addressed.

Working-Through Sessions

These sessions, which involve various family dyads and tri-ads, involve the same steps that have been identified in EFT in the working-through phase. They are:

- Accessing the unacknowledged feelings underlying interactional positions.
- Reframing the problem in terms of underlying feelings, attachment needs, and interactional patterns.
- Promoting identification with disowned needs and aspects of self and integrating them into relationship interactions.
- Promoting the acceptance of others' experience and new interactional responses.
- Facilitating the expression of needs and wants and creating emotional engagement.

As in EFT, these steps may describe the process in one session or across sessions and are often cycled through more than once, with different levels of engagement. To illustrate this part of the family therapy process a case example, and then a typical session from such a case, follows.

FIRST CASE EXAMPLE OF EFFT: MY DAUGHTER, I JUST WANT TO PROTECT YOU

The family consisted of a very traditional father, a mother, and three adolescent daughters. The oldest daughter was depressed and bulimic: she had dropped out of college. Father was highly educated and came from an ethnic background of extreme poverty and distant family relationships.

The father was seen as critical, controlling, and inaccessible by his wife and daughters, who all expressed anger at his habitual criticalness. He justified his actions in a painstakingly logical manner, stating that he was helping them. They dismissed and ignored his arguments. Mother portrayed the marriage as empty and lonely, and alternated between blaming her husband for all the family problems and taking them upon herself. She then would become very weepy and upset, and threaten to leave. The daughters all seemed careful around the parents, but they were visibly angry with the father.

The family pattern was that Father would criticize and lecture, Mother would try to intervene with no effect, and everyone would become very angry with Father. Mother would then become hysterical and say that everyone was driving her crazy and she was leaving the family. One of the girls would then get hysterical or sick and the family would calm down. Mother did occasionally leave the house during this sequence, but only for a few hours. After a short period of calm, the cycle would begin again. Overconcern and overprotectiveness coexisted in the family with a lack of contact (no one in the family ever touched the others) and security.

The oldest daughter, in particular, was trying to deal with her father's criticism and contagious fear of failure, as well as her mother's depression and need for support from her daughter. She had gone away to college but was terrified of leaving her mother lonely and depressed, and terrified that her parents would separate, or that she would disappoint them by failing. After six months of college, she had become suicidal and bulimic and returned home. To move out of this family and have a more separate life meant, for this young woman, facing all her fears of failing and thereby shaming her father and her family, and the possible loss and betrayal of her mother.

Sessions were held with the family, the couple (who presented as a dominant withdrawing husband and a depressed, enraged pursuing wife), the siblings, and the IP and each parent. By the end of therapy, the IP was in control of her bulimia and depression, and she had moved out to live with a friend. She had also applied to go back to college. The mother had begun to grieve the loss of her role as mother, and to confront and rebuild her "empty" life. She was deliberately less obsessed with her children's success, and less worried about them. She had taken steps not to intrude into the IP's life, and to reengage her husband in a marital relationship, as well as to formulate some goals for her own life. The sisters were also closer and more supportive of each other. The father seemed to accept his wife as more of an equal in the marriage, and to understand that his "worrying" and "advice-giving" behavior resulted in his family keeping him at a distance. He subsequently became more accessible to both his wife and daughters.

A Typical Session

What might one session of Emotionally Focused Family Therapy look like, with the family described above?

In a session with the father and daughter (Session 5), the therapist introduced the topic of the apparent distance between them. The father said that he was upset by this distance. The therapist helped him to expand and heighten this and to express his sense of loss to his daughter. With the therapist's help, his daughter told him that he drove her away with his critical lectures and constant advice about how she should be, if she was to be "successful." They then enacted their usual dance; with the father justifying his advice giving and blaming his daughter for not listening, while she withdrew.

The therapist then helped the daughter to access the compelling sense of sadness and helplessness that arose for her in this situation, and to express this to her father. The daughter explored her sense that in this relationship, she was defined as a failure and a disappointment. The therapist helped her to articulate how this undermined her confidence, and resulted in her spending most of her time warding off, running away from, and coping with the overwhelming panic that this evoked.

The therapist supported the father to stay focused in the dialogue and to respond directly to his daughter. The daughter went on to tell him how much she needed his approval (a Step 7 process). She also told him how desperate she was when she shut him out, and that she withdrew to protect herself and to avoid the panic she had described previously. The therapist then framed the father as trying to protect and give to his daughter by his advice giving, examining how this strategy unfortunately left both of them feeling helpless and afraid; he, because his daughter did not "listen" to his warnings, and she, because her father had "no faith in her."

Both were portrayed as the creators and victims of the cycle of critical advice giving and silent withdrawal. The father then stated that he did not know how to get close to his daughter or how to be a "good father." The therapist suggested that in this family, the daughter was the "expert" in showing warmth and approval and could perhaps help her father with this. He agreed that he would like to learn. The therapist also framed the father's approval as the key that could help the daughter manage her anxiety about going out into the world. The father, who had been marginalized in this family, was moved and encouraged by this frame, which was designed to act as an antidote to his sense of isolation and powerlessness, and his resulting coercive style.

In this session, the father and daughter found a way to "unlatch" from their usual pattern of interaction and create a new, emotionally engaged dialogue. At the end of the session, they were primed to begin to turn to each other to regulate their fears and anxieties, rather than triggering each other's fears. The daughter was also established as an expert in closeness, who could help the father learn about this, which moved her into a more equal and more adult relationship with him. This session reorganized the participants' interaction; this, in turn, impacted the family unit. It moved the father closer to his daughter and gave the daughter another potential source of support. The mother was then able to give up her mediator role, and to begin to change the nature of her involvement with the daughter.

This session involved a micro version of the process that occurs across many sessions in EFT. The goal here was to begin to modify the father's critical way of engaging with his daughter, since this seemed to be associated with her eating disorder and suicidal behaviors, and to foster interactions with him that would increase her sense of efficacy.

The interventions used here were as follows.

Reflection of experience

> **Therapist:** So, help me understand here, when your daughter called you and told you she was going skiing for the weekend, her first weekend at university, you felt this tightness, this tension. You felt you had to warn her that spending weekends this way might result in her failing. Is that right?

Reflection of pattern

> **Therapist:** What just happened here? Marsha, your dad was telling you how he says these things for your own good, to protect you, and you turned your head, and then your whole body, away from him.
>
> **Marsha:** I tune him out. I don't have to listen to this.
>
> **Therapist:** Aha, he's trying to protect you. But you're trying to protect you, from him, from what you hear in his voice?
>
> **Marsha:** Right. I hear, I'm going to blow it, I'll never make it, and anyway he knows what will make me happy better than I do.
>
> **Therapist:** So you get angry. Is that okay? (Marsha nods) You tune him out, and then you (to father) get even more tense and try harder to get her to hear you; you push more. Is that it? (He nods)

Validation

> 1. **Therapist:** So Marsha, when you left home you carried this weight on your back. Here you were going out into the world, which can be pretty terrifying just in itself, but you were also worried sick (*this is a deliberate frame, as she was bulimic*) that you would fail to please your parents, let the family down, let yourself down by failing to meet your "potential," right? (Marsha nods) Also you were worried that,

without you there to talk to, Mum would become more and more depressed, and then she might leave and the family would fall apart. Incredible weight to carry; so hard, I'm amazed that you made it through a whole term.

2. **Therapist:** It's so so important for you, Tom, to be a good father, to try to be, as you put it, the perfect dad. That's lots of pressure. And if Marsha starts to have difficulties, it sends you a message that you are deficient here. You should be able to prevent such things, yes?

Evocative Responding

1. **Therapist:** What is it like for you, Tom, to hear that your daughter becomes paralyzed by fear if she lets herself listen to your warnings and "lessons"?

2. **Therapist:** What happens for you, Tom, when your daughter talks of how much she needs your trust, needs you to believe in her, to approve of her?

Heightening

1. **Therapist:** Can you tell him again, Marsha, can you tell him, "I'm a disappointment to you, I know I am."

2. **Therapist:** So, can you tell her again, Tom, "I'm so afraid for you. It's so hard for me to see you walk out into the world, away from my roof, my shelter, and face the world that nearly destroyed me when I was young." Can you tell her, please.

Empathic Conjecture

Therapist: And with all this pressure, Marsha, you get worried sick, yes? (She nods) You try not to eat, to be slimmer, and to feel more in control. Then you get very hungry and scared and eat lots of food to comfort yourself. Yes? (She nods) But then you feel even more worried. It's like, you have lost control. You have failed, and all the weight of disappointing Dad and leaving Mum comes flooding in, and you throw up. Is that it, have I got it right?

Reframing

> **Therapist:** So, it's hard to get a hold of your fear and let your daughter find her own feet out there, Tom? It's hard just because she is so precious, yes? And because you feel your duty, as a good dad, is to protect her. For you, Marsha, all the warnings feed your own fears and part of you just gives up, gets paralyzed, yeah? Except when you get really angry at Dad and decide to stop trying, to kind of spite him, is that it?

Restructuring interactions

> **Therapist:** So can you tell him, Marsha, if I can try and summarize what you just said, "I need to know that I'm special to you and that you think that I can do it, that I can fly on my own. And that even if I crash, I need to know that everyone will survive and I'll still be special to you, even if I quit school." Is that it?

Termination Sessions

In these sessions, the focus is on highlighting changes from old patterns and responses, heightening the family's strengths and sense of self-efficacy, summarizing treatment gains, consolidating new interactional patterns, and supporting the family to formulate new solutions to old problems. Treatment ends with a family session with everyone present, where the collective family story of the problem, the therapy, and the present status of the family are summarized.

DIFFERENCES FROM EFT

In EFFT, there is a more intense focus on modifying specific interactions that appear to contribute to the IP's difficulties, and less focus, even in the couple sessions, on building intimacy per se. In the couple sessions, for example, the focus is on how the couple can help each other support the identified patient and actively create the kind of family life that they desire. The focus is then more circum-scribed than in EFT; it is the couple's relationship as it influences the larger system of the family. For example, the mother might describe how she turns to her oldest daugh-ter for help when she perceives her husband as unavailable. The session might then evolve around how each parent views the consequences of this for the oldest daughter, for the other siblings, and for the couple relationship, as well as addressing the blocks to emotional engagement between the partners.

Couple sessions might also focus on how the problems of the IP have impacted the parents' relationship and come between them as a couple. For example, when a wife accuses her husband of being ineffectual in tackling their daughter's problem, the therapist supports the husband to challenge his wife's viewpoint. He then is able to tell her how he would like to take care of his daughter and her, if only she will let go of the reins a little. He goes on to suggest that this would also allow the wife to step back from her intense power strug-gle with her daughter.

The couple is addressed as the architects of the family, not simply in terms of their own relationship. The EFFT thera-pist still attempts to increase safe emotional engagement between the couple and thus to improve marital satisfaction, but *the primary goal is to modify the interactional position of the IP in relation to the other members of the family*. If the couple wish to focus more intensely on their own rela-tionship, they may request couple sessions after family treat-ment has terminated.

The end of EFFT is usually characterized not by a soften-ing of the more hostile spouse, as in EFT, but by new responses on the part of the identified patient. These responses typically take the form of more assertive boundary definitions, including definitions of self, more clearly expressed attachment needs, and a more active definition of the relationship that he or she desires with other members of the family. There is a sense in which EFFT helps adoles-cents redefine the attachment relationship between parents and themselves into a more reciprocal, adult, and secure form, where difference and separateness can be tolerated. In many families, the children have to first connect before they can effectively leave.

In addition to the interventions used in EFT, this form of family therapy uses the assignment of some tasks and rituals to be completed outside of the therapy session. For example, the therapist might suggest that the siblings share an activity each week and so enhance the relationship between them. Structural systemic interventions have traditionally included the setting of such tasks (Minuchin & Fishman, 1981). However, in EFFT as well as in EFT, change is still generally viewed as occurring within the session rather than outside it.

If two therapists are involved with the family, then an intervention can occur where the two therapists enter into a brief dialogue with each other about the family, or the nature of the interactions happening in the session. This is similar to a reflecting team type of intervention, in that the family members become an audience witnessing a conversation that focuses on them and their relationships. In EFFT, however, this is usually a very brief discussion that is used for a specific purpose, rather than being a general and/or widely used intervention. It is, in fact, often a form of validation and/or conjecture, presented in a dialogue format. For example, one therapist might say to the other, "You know, I'm not sure I understand what is happening here, do you?" The other replies, "Well, I'm not quite clear whether Marsha [the daughter] is pleading for some acceptance from her mum, or if she is more interested in showing her mum that her mum can't control her; that Marsha can push her buttons by simply eating a large bag of potato chips." The therapists then turn to the family for clarification. This is only done when the session seems stalled in an impasse, or when the family is very reactive and emotionally volatile. It turns the family into an audience rather than participants for a moment, and introduces a more distant perspective for their consideration.

SECOND CASE EXAMPLE OF EFT:
HOLD ME TIGHT BEFORE I GO

This case was originally published in Johnson (1998) in the *Journal of Systemic Therapies, 17.**

Olga was tall, strikingly pretty, and articulate. She was 17, but could easily have passed for 20. She was diagnosed as bulimic and depressed, and had not responded to the group therapy for bulimics offered at the local hospital. She was also assessed as gifted, but had recently almost failed her grade in school. She was now entering her last year of high school.

Laura, Olga's mother, was 36 years old, small, pretty, and rather harried looking. She worked as a nurse. Olga's father had left the family when Olga was nine years old, and now lived in another city, maintaining very minimal contact with his daughter. Olga also had a small brother, Timmy, who was now five. Laura was dating Ted, a colleague at work. From the time Olga was five until she was eight years old, Laura had been extremely ill. She was diagnosed with lupus at one point, and was considered terminal. This illness had then gone into remission. Laura stated that she felt she had leaned on Olga too much during this time, and also when Olga's father had left her.

Olga had then experienced her mother being very ill, her father leaving, the arrival of Timmy (conceived by her mother in a brief liaison), and her mother recently initiating a new relationship. She had also recently broken up with her boyfriend at school. Olga said that she'd resented Timmy when he was born, but now liked being his big sister. She took care of him when her mother went out on dates with Ted, whom she "approved of."

The first session started with Laura striding into the room and, before she even introduced herself to me, announcing that she was not going to be "blamed and attacked" or "labeled" as the cause of Olga's problems. Olga muttered tearfully that she

*From "Listening to the Music: Emotion as a Natural Part of Systems Theory," by S. M. Johnson, 1998, *Journal of Systemic Therapies, 17,* pp. 11–15. Reprinted with permission of Guilford Press.

just wanted to improve her relationship with her mother. Laura and Olga then told the therapist their history and their views of the bulimia, which had started when Olga was 15, after a period of dieting. Laura admitted that with all the "comings and goings and ups and downs," Olga had had a hard time growing up. Laura spoke of her daughter as being very bright and independent, and had suggested Olga move out to live with a cousin for her last year of school. This would be good both for Olga and for herself, since Olga was now being very "difficult," refusing to help her in the house, and being "aggressive." Olga did criticize her mother in the session. She criticized her mother's parenting of Timmy, and her mother's "incompetence and weakness" in dealing with men. Laura would occasionally explode and strike back, but generally she stayed cool and removed, stating that it was time for Olga to start her own journey as an adult and stand on her own two feet.

The pattern of interactions between mother and daughter was clear. Olga criticized, complained, and became upset, while Laura was more removed and defended. She said that Olga should really be ready to move out on her own by now, as she had been at her age. Once this pattern was identified, it was accepted by both parties (Step 2 of EFT). Both were able to see how this pattern constrained their interactions and maintained their distress. Olga's critical complaints seemed to me to be primed by anger and an underlying sense of desperateness and sadness. I focused on, and expanded, Olga's comments to her mother, such as "you are so aloof," "you don't care if I leave and get sick," and "if I go to you with problems, you just push me away." As I reflected, validated, evoked, and heightened Olga's affective responses, she began to look sad and teary. With my help, Olga was able to formulate that she felt alone and abandoned by her mom (Step 3, formulating underlying emotions). I asked Olga to try to express these feelings directly to her mother, who then became very silent.

From an attachment point of view, Olga seemed to be insecure and protesting Laura's seeming unavailability (her boyfriend, job, and younger child did take up most of Laura's time). Olga's expressions of anger and defiance around chores primed Laura's withdrawal, while Laura's cool distance evoked Olga's desperateness and sadness. As I placed each one's emotional responses in the context of the cycle, Olga was able to tell her mom that she felt she was on the "outside" of her mom's life with Timmy and Ted. She had no sense of belonging in the family. This was exacerbated when her mother repeatedly suggested that it was time she left. My sense was that Olga needed to know she belonged before she could leave.

As Laura and Olga felt validated and heard in the sessions, the problem cycle began to de-escalate. Olga began to complete more chores at home, and arguments were fewer and less explosive. Laura also began to spend some time with her daughter. In the middle steps of EFT, new formulations of emotional responses are expressed by each person, which prime new responses in the other. The interaction expands to include new attachment behaviors that foster a more secure bond. Let's look at a snapshot that captures how Laura and Olga changed their interactional positions and so redefined their attachment relationship.

In Session 3, Laura begins to talk of the stresses in her life, how overwhelmed she is, and how Olga refuses to help in the house. Olga responds angrily by stating that she babysits Timmy and that's enough. I decide that, if possible, it is time to foster a shift to a more engaged stance for Laura.

> **Laura:** (to Olga) I know you had a hard time. Your dad left, and then I dated, and I had Timmy, and you were alone lots. But you are so aggressive. I don't understand why you are so angry at me. I have to bite my tongue all the time not to get into a big fight. (She tears)
>
> **Therapist:** How do you feel as you say this, Laura?
>
> **Laura:** What, Oh! I don't know.
>
> **Olga:** I can't say anything to you, I don't get to have any feelings at all. You just defend yourself.
>
> **Therapist:** Can we stop here just a minute?
>
> **Laura:** (looking out the window, speaking to Olga) You're always angry, that's the "feeling" I see.

Olga: No. You don't like it if I ask for caring either. It's like I shouldn't need it. You tell me I have to be independent.

Therapist: (stays focused on Laura and asks in a quiet voice) What is happening, Laura? What happens as you hear your daughter's anger and disappointment? (No reply) You are holding your arms across your chest, holding yourself, hm? (Laura turns her body away from her daughter and tears) What do you hear Olga saying to you in her anger?

Laura: She's attacking me. (Long pause; her voice begins to tremble) She's saying I'm a bad mom. (She swallows and looks out the window)

Therapist: (softly) That's what you hear in Olga's anger, her frustration, that you're a bad mom? And when you hear that you want to get away, to put distance between you and that message?

Laura: (turns and looks at me; her voice is resigned) Yes, it's always the same.

Therapist: What happens to you when you hear that message?

Laura: (long pause; she composes herself, her tone is now calm) I think it's really her dad she's angry at.

Therapist: (softly) What happens when you hear Olga's anger at you, Laura?

Laura: (she sighs, and her voice trembles) I think she's right. I haven't been a good mom. (Long pause) I was so sick when she was little and so unhappy with her dad. I tried to make her independent. If I was dying she had to be strong. I remember her saying, "Don't worry Mom, I'll take care of you." (She tears, covers her face in her hands) I wanted to make this perfect childhood for her and I couldn't do it. And I guess I'm still blowing it.

Therapist: That hurts, Laura, to say that? (She nods) It hurts to feel like you couldn't protect her and make everything okay.

Laura: (nods vigorously and stares at the floor) Olga calls me names sometimes, names like *bitch*. She was so mad when I got pregnant with Timmy. She said "How dare I do that." I split from Timmy's dad partly because of the way he was so distant with Olga. (She glances around the room, agitated, as if she's looking for an exit)

Therapist: Olga really has the power to upset you, throw you off balance, if you hear—

Laura: (interrupts and leans toward me) I'm a target, that's why I suggest she leave. I can't stand it, the tension. We'd have a better relationship if she moved out. If I go up to her room, I never know what's going to happen. I never know when she'll suddenly get mad.

Therapist: And you're afraid of her anger and hearing that message, that you disappointed her as a mom. (She nods) Sometimes you feel bad that maybe you don't think that you've been a good mom to Olga. It didn't work out the way you wanted it. (*This is an interpretation; I add a new element, fear, to her description of her experience*)

Laura: (leans toward me) Yes, yes, and I get so overwhelmed. Looking after everybody and never feeling good at it.

Therapist: Trying to look after everybody and never feeling that you're doing it right, that's hard. Can you tell your daughter, "I get so hurt by the idea that I disappointed you as a mom, I can't stay close and hear that message, I have to pull back." Can you tell her?

Olga: (leans forward; her voice has a very conciliatory tone) Mom, it was hard, but you did what you could, I don't feel like you've failed. You gave me lots. (She leans towards her mother) I just can't get close to you!

Laura: Well, I did fail, I was sick. I couldn't stop your dad leaving, and now you're throwing up. (Cries) Even if I try, I never say the right thing to you and then you get mad. I can't get it right. (*A Step 5 response, as this previously withdrawn mother accesses her deeper feelings. She weeps.*)

Therapist: It's so hard, so painful for you, this sense that you somehow aren't the mum you want to be. (Laura nods; I turn to Olga) Olga, can you hear how your anger opens this door for your mom, this door into all her fears that she somehow failed you as a mom?

Olga: (speaking very intently) Yes, but she didn't, that's not it. She gets all defensive, I just want her to comfort me, to help me with my feelings when I'm scared or upset. (*Stays engaged—a positive Step 6 response*)

Therapist: In fact, she's so important to you, her comfort and closeness is so important to you, that's what you're fighting for? (Olga nods emphatically) Because that contact with her has protected you, it has been a safe haven for you in the past. It has helped you to survive and now you can't find it, is that it?

Olga: (empathically) Yes. (She looks up at her mom)

Therapist: Can you tell her? (*I structure an enactment—motion with my hand toward Laura*)

Olga: (turns to her mother, in an intense pleading voice) Mom, I'm strong. You helped me be that way, but please don't push me away, not now. Growing up is scary, you know. I just need to know you're there. (*Responding to her mother's increased accessibility and engagement, Olga spontaneously softens and asks for her needs to be met*)

Laura: (tears and reaches over and holds her daughter) I am, I am. I want to be. I want to be close to you— sometimes I just don't know how—and I get scared of your anger— (*Step 7—withdrawer reengagement*)

In the process encapsulated here, Laura became more accessible and responsive to her daughter. She was able to articulate her sense of failure and get reassurance from her daughter. Olga then began to ask for reassurance and contact, rather than attacking her mother, and this continued in the following sessions. Olga was able to seek reassurance that her mother still needed and wanted the closeness with her; that moving out didn't mean losing her mom. This process positively influenced Olga's depression, and helped to bring her mother and Olga closer. I probed as to how the bulimic symptoms fit into the problem cycle. Olga was able to explore this topic and clarify that the cue for her throwing up was her feeling of being alone and unimportant in her family. This then elicited all her doubts about her own value.

Olga then began seeking out her mother or her best friend when she felt like bingeing and throwing up. She was also able to take her sadness about her dad's distance to her mom, and to have her mom listen and comfort her. For Laura, the discovery that she could help her daughter by her *presence*, that she did not have to solve Olga's problems or make reparation for the past, helped her stay connected with Olga. Laura specified her conditions for remaining open and involved. She put limits on Olga's expression of anger (for example, no name-calling), and insisted Olga express her needs rather than become aggressive.

Olga was able, in a more complete softening, to tell her mother of her need for reassurance and closeness, and acknowledge her hostile behavior. Laura also acknowledged that since Timmy was born she had neglected Olga, and Olga was able to accept this and understand some of her mother's stress. The relationship became safer, closer, and more equal. Both were able to confide in and support each other. After seven sessions, therapy ended, and a few months later Olga moved out to live with her cousin. She began to do well in school, and reported that her bulimia was no longer a problem. In the last session, I helped Laura ask her daughter to "Help me be the mom you want me to be." Olga was then able to express regret for her past aggression toward her mother. The fact that Olga was able to redefine the relationship as a safe attachment meant that she could now also move into more autonomy and independence. Therapy ended with mother and daughter being able to comfort and reassure each other; new emotional music had organized a new dance.

Bertalanffy (1968) has suggested that not all elements in a system are equal. There are "leading parts" that control other elements (p. 213). He went on to suggest that "a small change in leading parts can cause a large change in the total system." Clinical experience in EFT, and in using this model with families, has taught us that new information, and cognitive and behavioral shifts per se, are not as effective in creating this kind of general change. It does not seem to be true that restructuring any element will create systemic reorganization, although this was accepted systemic doctrine at one time. However, changing a "leading part" seems to create such a change, and create it efficiently and reliably, at least when the part in question is the emotion that organizes interaction.

PRESENT STATUS OF EFFT

At present, EFFT has not been systematically empirically validated in the way that EFT couple interventions have. There is, however, one promising outcome study with bulimic adolescents conducted at the Ottawa Hospital (Johnson, Maddeaux & Blouin, 1998). EFFT was found to be effective, with total remission of bingeing in 44 percent of adolescents and complete remission of vomiting in 67 percent of adolescents after a 10-session intervention. Significant reductions were also found on other variables such as depression and hostility. Armstrong and Roth (1989) found that 96 percent of adolescents with eating disorders evidence an anxious attachment style (compared to 24 percent of normal adolescents) with its concomitant sense of diminished self-worth. An attachment-oriented intervention may then be particularly relevant for this population. EFFT is also routinely used for depressed and suicidal adolescents (Johnson & Lee, 2000).

EFFT arose out of the realization that the change principles and strategies used in EFT could be applied to different contexts and different relationships; that is, to change inter-actions between father and daughter, or mother and daughter, as well as those that occur between distressed adult part-ners, and that changing such relationships then modified problematic family cycles of interaction.

This kind of family therapy addresses the concerns of those who are disturbed by "the disappearance of the individual into a systemic stew" (Merkel & Searight, 1992, p. 38) and attempts to extend systems theory by looking both within and between. Clinical experience with EFFT interventions suggests that distressed couples and distressed families are dealing with the same monster—disconnection and attach-ment insecurity—and that it can be defeated in much the same way.

12

RELATIONSHIP TRAUMAS: ADDRESSING ATTACHMENT INJURIES

FORGIVENESS AND RECONCILIATION

In the last few years, the study of impasses that block the completion of change events, such as blamer softening, that are a crucial part of creating a more secure bond, has led to the delineation of relationship traumas that EFT therapists have named attachment injuries (Johnson, Makinen & Millikin, 2001; see also Johnson, 2004). The delineation of these events has evolved in the context of attachment theory and the understanding of this theory as a theory of trauma—the trauma of separation and isolation in the face of overwhelming experience and vulnerability. The delineation of attachment injuries is an excellent example of how this theory can make sense of specific relationship-defining events and patterns and their impact on a relationship and so potentiate intervention. This work has also moved EFT interventions into the growing area of forgiveness and reconciliation (Coop, Gordon, Baucom & Snyder, 2000; Worthington & DiBlascio, 1990).

Attachment injuries are considered to be "violations of human connection" (Herman, 1992) that take the form of abandonments and betrayals at crucial moments of need. These violations then create or exacerbate insecurity in an attachment bond. They are considered traumatic in that they induce overwhelming fear and helplessness and, if not resolved and healed, severely limit trust and intimacy. The power of these events and their impact on couple relationships become particularly apparent when an EFT therapist asks a partner to risk and reach for the spouse in an engaged and open way. These incidents, which have been perhaps referred to before in previous sessions as a general hurt, then arise in the manner of a traumatic flashback and block engagement and risk taking. Injured partners describe how images and memories of these injuries are easily evoked and create a hypervigilance to possible reoccurrences or reminders. They also speak, in the way that echoes the general trauma literature, of numbing themselves in interactions with their spouse.

These incidents can appear, at first glance, to be relatively trivial; or they can be obvious in their compelling nature. A sense of being abandoned during childbirth or a miscarriage is one of the more obvious injuries. Finding a provocative picture of a co-worker in a partner's briefcase is hurtful but less obviously devastating, except when it becomes clear that this occurred at a time when the wife who found the picture was explicitly attempting to "prove" that she was a fulfilling sexual partner who would take risks to excite and please her spouse. Affairs can be attachment injuries or they may not be; this depends on the context of the affair and the attachment significance assigned to it. Whether the meaning of these events is immediately clear or not, partners speak of these events in life-and-death terms and move to a "never again" stance, where the main concern is to minimize risk rather than connect with the other spouse. The injury is used as a touchstone as to the dependability of the partner. The distressed couple is able to satisfactorily process the incident, and usually the offending partner has retreated to defensive position where he or she minimizes the incident or simply distances when it comes up.

Most couples have general hurts, but some have these kinds of traumatic wounds. These wounds must then be addressed if the couple is to move into less distress and a more secure attachment (Johnson, 2002). When a partner cries out for help in extreme need or is already massively vulnerable and is treated as insignificant by a loved one, the sense of basic trust in the partner is shattered. The attachment perspective and the framing of these incidents as relationship traumas helps the EFT therapist grasp them and move into helping the couple resolve them. A recent study that focused on couples with these kinds of injuries and significant marital distress (Makinen, 2004) found that 66 percent of distressed couples with these injuries could de-escalate, improve their satisfaction, and resolve their injuries in a 14-session course of EFT. These resolving couples significantly increased their marital satisfaction and their trust and forgiveness levels. Nonresolving couples tended to have more than one injury and lower trust levels at the beginning of therapy; offenders in these couples were also more avoidant. Even in these couples, there was less anxiety and pain at the end of therapy, but only minimal levels of forgiveness and no significant increase in marital satisfaction scores.

The observation of a number of cases prior to the above study led to a rational outline of the steps in the change process. This process is a Stage 2 process; the de-escalation stage of EFT has to already have been completed. After the injury has been resolved, the Stage 2 change events, reengagement and softening, seem to unfold in a natural fashion, and the couple can move on to consolidation. The steps in this process of forgiveness and the repair of an attachment injury are as follows:

1. The event is described with intense distress either as part of the general process of Stage 2 of therapy, or, more specifically, either as the therapist encourages the withdrawn spouse to risk engagement or, more commonly, the injured spouse to begin to risk connecting with her or his now more accessible partner. This spouse then begins to describe an incident in which he or she felt abandoned and helpless, experiencing a violation of trust that damaged his or her belief in the

relationship as a secure bond. This spouse speaks of this incident in a highly emotional, often disjointed manner. The incident is alive and present rather than a calm recollection. The partner either discounts, denies, or minimizes the incident and his partner's pain and moves to a defensive stance.

2. With the therapist's help, the injured spouse stays in touch with the injury and begins to articulate its impact and attachment significance. Anger and outrage now evolve into clear expressions of hurt, helplessness, fear, and shame. The connection of the injury to present negative cycles in the relationship becomes clear. For example, a spouse says, "I feel so raw still and so hopeless. I just scream and go hysterical to have some kind of impact on him. I want to tell him that he can't just wipe out my hurt like that. But he does it anyway."

3. The partner, supported by the therapist, begins to hear and understand the significance of the injurious event and to understand it in attachment terms as a reflection of his or her importance to the injured spouse, rather than as a reflection of his or her personal inadequacies or insensitivity. This partner then acknowledges the injured partner's pain and suffering and elaborates on how the event evolved for him or her. This is not so much a logical extensive explanation of the event as an account that makes this partner's actions predictable to the injured spouse.

4. The injured partner then tentatively moves toward a more integrated and complete articulation of the injury. He or she is able to express grief at the loss involved in it, and fear concerning the specific loss of the attachment bond. This partner allows the other to witness his or her vulnerability.

5. The other spouse becomes more emotionally engaged, acknowledges responsibility for his or her part in the attachment injury, and expresses empathy, regret, and/or remorse.

6. Aided by the therapist, the injured spouse then can risk asking for the comfort and caring from the partner that were unavailable at the time of the injurious event.

7. The other spouse now responds in a caring manner that acts as an antidote to the traumatic experience of the original injury. The partners are then able to construct together a new narrative of the event. This narrative is ordered and includes, for the injured spouse, a clear and acceptable sense of how the other came to respond in such a distressing manner during the event.

Once the attachment injury is resolved, the therapist can more effectively foster the growth of trust and the beginning of positive cycles of bonding and reconciliation. This process defines the relationship as a safe haven, fostering the resolution of other difficulties and pragmatic problems.

The concept of attachment injuries as relationship traumas has important implications for couple therapists. This perspective may explain why some couples have more difficulty responding to therapy. It seems logical that such events also need to be addressed and resolved to prevent relapse after therapy. The mapping of such events also allows for the formulation of a systematic set of interventions for their resolution. Some couples may be easier to assist in resolving these injuries than others. In general, those who endorse a more secure attachment style seem to cope better with trust violation episodes in their relationships (Mikulincer, 1998).

A brief snapshot of a typical process of resolution might appear as follows:

1. The wife, Helena, says, "No, no. I don't think I can ask him for caring. We are better together but . . . (She looks down and covers her eyes with her hand) I told myself I'd never . . . I think maybe we have gone far enough here—things are better. (She flushes red and her voice becomes monotone and soft) There I was, in labor. I was in labor and he asked the doc how long it would be. And the doc said all night, probably all night. So

he said he'd just go to the curling championship—he was the captain after all. And he'd be right back. And I cried. I didn't want him to go. But he went, and the baby was born. I don't know why I still go back to this. It's coming up a lot right now, when we are on the verge of retiring to this little village, away from all my friends and my family. (Her voice then changes and becomes sharp and she turns to her husband) But you won the match didn't you—that was what really mattered to you." The therapist says, "That was so painful for you—still is painful. And you learned not to count on Ted, not to put yourself in his hands, yes?" Helena says, "You bet I did." Ted responds, "Do let go of this, will you. It was eons ago and anyway you were fine. The doc said the labor was an easy one, and I was there the next time wasn't I?" Helena replies, "Only because there wasn't an important match on."

2. With the therapist's help, Helena stays with her long-held sense of outrage and begins to acknowledge the grief and despair that are still "alive" and remind her that she should not count on her husband. She is able to tell him how she had "hedged her bets" all through their marriage and turned to other members of her family instead of him, while "keeping the peace" with him. But now, ever since they bought this cottage for early retirement, she finds herself getting distant and irritable. Slowly, step by step she is able to access a "nausea" and a "sense of falling" when she thinks of how much she is going to need Ted in this new life. She begins to be able to speak of how much she had "given up" the night she bore her son alone. She weeps for her lost trust and connection and for the compromises she made through the years. She had decided that she could not "compete" with his fabulous career and his exciting sports life. She is now able to tell him, "I don't want to need you—I was so scared that night." The therapist says, "And you are scared now, Helena, yes—scared to put yourself in Ted's hands?" Helena weeps and agrees.

3. Ted, initially very dismissing of this "ancient event," begins to hear that his wife had felt abandoned and had been on guard all these years. He begins to resonate with his wife's grief and express regret that "maybe he had not been a very sensitive husband." He is able to tell her how "intimidated" he was—and still is—by the demands of being a husband. He only feels competent on the ice as a curler and in his office. He begins to be able to talk about how he sees his wife as an "expert at the feeling and loving thing" and that he feels now, as he had on the night of the birth of his first child, "often superfluous—on the edge of the family." He remembers that he did not know how to comfort and support her in the hospital so he turned to his "duty" as a captain of the team. He knew how to fulfill this role. In fact, he was always "scared" of losing Helena, when she "discovered" his inadequacies.

4. Helena now moves into truly grieving her disillusionment with her marriage as a safe haven and her loss of the hopes for her marriage. She also grieves the many years she never asked for connection with Ted but stayed "numb" and noted "every sign that I was not one of his priorities." She is able to tell him how much in fact she has longed to rest in his arms, how she needs his closeness and caring, and how terrified she now is to even talk about this.

5. Ted then opens up and weeps with remorse and regret for having let his wife down and for all the wasted opportunities for closeness over the years. With the therapist keeping him focused and heightening his engagement with his emotions, he validates her hurt on the night of the birth of their son and her subsequent decision to never turn to him or expect real connection. He acknowledges that he did not respond when she tried over the years to broach the subject of her need for him and her aloneness on that crucial night. He is able to say, "I did let you down. I did. And then I ran away and didn't want to deal with it.

I was always running away—proving myself at work. But now—now I do want to give you what you need— I do want to be close and have you count on me."

6. Helena then risks telling Ted about her fears of abandonment at the cottage, and her need for comfort and reassurance from him. She says, "I need to know that next time you get uncertain or scared, you will care enough to stay and learn how to be with me. I need to know I matter that much to you. Can you hold me tight?"

7. Ted responds with caring and relief and expresses his commitment to a new closeness with his wife. He also speaks of his own needs for her reassurance and support. The couple craft a coherent story of their marriage, the attachment injury, and its consequences. They also craft a clear image of future interactions and the responses that will keep their bond strong and secure. The process ends then not simply in forgiveness but in reconciliation and more secure bonding.

At the moment, the process of addressing attachment injuries is still being studied, but hopefully, as occurred with the softening event, the process of change will be even more clearly delineated and we will then study the key therapist interventions that reliably lead to the creation of trust and successful reconciliation after these violations of human connection. As stated above, preliminary evidence (Makinen, 2004) suggests that when a single attachment injury has occurred, a relatively brief EFT intervention lowers attachment anxiety, significantly increasing marital satisfaction and the level of trust in the relationship, as well as raising the level of forgiveness. The goal for the EFT therapist, when working with these injuries, is not just forgiveness but reconciliation and the ability to work through impasses to the creation of a more secure attachment.

The next two chapters will present two EFT sessions to allow the reader to "see" the process described in the preceding chapters.

13

THE PEANUT BUTTER INCIDENT: AN EFT SESSION

Husband: I tried to kiss you this morning, and you rejected me.

Wife: I had my mouth full of peanut butter at the time. I said, hold on, I'm busy.

Husband: So, I'm less important than peanut butter.

A professional couple in their late 40s came to the marital and family clinic in a large urban hospital. Paul and Elsa had been married for 20 years. They had two children approaching adolescence. At their assessment, they appeared to be a relatively sophisticated couple. He spoke in very intellectual terms with reasoned arguments and long digressions, while she wept. They stated the problem in terms of lack of intimacy. Elsa stated that Paul was a "stranger" to her and that she had given up trying to be close because she could "never do anything right, no matter what I try." Paul said that for him the relationship was in the "deep freeze." He was aware that he "pushed" for closeness, which was very much missing for him in the relationship—although he was also aware that he was a "workaholic" who spent most of his life deeply involved in his projects. Elsa stated that she felt continually analyzed and criticized and now avoided Paul by almost any means possible. Paul suggested that he was basically angry because she had "never turned up for this relationship." This couple's interaction followed a classic pursue/attack and withdraw/avoid pattern, with Paul being the pursuer and Elsa being the withdrawer. The couple were still relatively committed to the relationship, although each of them spoke of the possibility that it would end if things did not improve. Paul suggested that he might leave to find a more responsive partner, while Elsa spoke of leaving to avoid Paul's "constant criticism." At the beginning of therapy, the couple scored 82 on the Dyadic Adjustment Scale (Spanier, 1976). A score of approximately 100 is the cutoff point for marital distress on this commonly used measure; a score of 70 is typical of divorcing couples.

In this chapter a transcript of Session 11 is presented, together with comments on therapist interventions. This session is an example of how one incident can provide the structure for several sessions of therapy and be used as a microscope to explore crucial aspects of the couple's negative interaction pattern and underlying emotions. The episode presented here, the peanut butter incident, was used in Sessions 10 and 11 to access and expand Paul's experience of the relationship and to initiate the softening change event (as described in chapter 7) with him. This incident was chosen as a focus by the therapist because it vividly captured the responses that characterized key problematic interactions between the partners. It also clearly reflected the nature of the partners' attachment issues. The couple also completed an Interpersonal Process Recall procedure (IPR; Elliot et al., 1984) immediately following this particular session, as part of a pilot study for a research project. In this procedure, each partner views a videotape of the session with a researcher, who asks questions designed to elicit how this partner experienced the session. This chapter also contains a brief synopsis of these comments.

Before the session presented here, the couple had formed an excellent alliance with the therapist. The first few sessions, however, were challenging in that Elsa would weep and become very silent, while Paul would spin "fogs" (Elsa's label) out of words, taking the session into intellectual, tangential dead ends. As the therapist, I finally suggested that, since I was becoming very confused, I would touch the end of Paul's shoe when this occurred (he habitually placed one leg across his knee, so his shoe was easily accessible). This would then remind him to slow his mind down and allow the "fog" to clear a little. In these earlier sessions, the pursue–withdraw cycle went through a process of de-escalation and the couple began to spend some positive time together. Elsa also became much more engaged in the relationship. She was able to articulate her perception that she had been abandoned for Paul's work early in the relationship, and that now he was like "some stranger, who suddenly demands love and intimacy." She was also able to access and express her fear of Paul's criticism. As she experienced it, he was the judge and she was the criminal who was inevitably "condemned." She began to assert her needs in the relationship and to tell Paul that she was not going to be "destroyed" by his "fogs and arrows." She stated that she was not going to give, if her gifts were held up for judgment and labeled "inappropriate" (as was her Valentine's card).

In Session 10, the therapist began to focus upon accessing the insecurity that seemed to prime Paul's constant monitoring of Elsa's behavior and his critical analysis of that behavior. At this time, the couple recounted the peanut butter incident. This incident, where Paul had tried to make affectionate contact with Elsa, was for him an example of her "unattainability." It had occurred the day after their anniversary, which they had spent together in a relatively close way, and had then resulted in a reinitiation of the negative cycle. In this incident, Paul had tried to kiss Elsa when she was eating peanut butter and was "rebuffed." He then spent the whole day fuming and delving into dark, pessimistic scenarios about the relationship, and about the impossibility of connecting with anyone. Elsa, on the other hand, felt "coerced and trapped" and withdrew, although she did this to a lesser extent than before. Session 10 ended with Paul accessing some of his hurt and fear, but accusing Elsa of being unresponsive and withholding. Elsa became disoriented when Paul began to talk of his fears of being rebuffed, asking, "Who are we talking about?" I suggested that Elsa found it difficult to see Paul's sensitivity and pick up his attachment signals because she was not prepared for such messages from her partner, whom she saw as a "dangerous judge." I also suggested that Elsa did not understand these signals because Paul presented them "in disguise," as humorous and unimportant, to lessen the risk inherent in asking Elsa for a response. Let us now look at Session 11.

SESSION 11

Elsa: I wouldn't know how to describe this last week.

Paul: We had a bit of a tussle yesterday morning.

Elsa: We get off track. We need to know how to stay on track.

Paul: What is on track?

Elsa: When it's calm.

Therapist: Is "on track" the same as what happened on your anniversary, when you were together, and Elsa you felt close and Paul you felt that Elsa was "attainable"?

Paul: Yeah. But she's attainable such a small percentage of the time. Most of the time we're in neutral. There are high points, but then it's cut off, and then there's strong disagreements.

Therapist: Is it like you were talking about last time, Paul, on the anniversary, you had a great day together, and then the next morning you went to Elsa and asked her for a kiss, and her mouth was full, and you felt rebuffed. Then that broke the spell for you. There are moments when you are together, connected, and then something happens to break the spell, yeah?

The therapist creates focus by bringing in the incident, described in the last session, that interrupted a positive experience and reinitiated the negative cycle.

> **Paul:** Yeah. There is this habit we're in. It can be strong, like a whack. The other day (to Elsa), I tried to pinch your bum and you whacked me really hard.
>
> **Elsa:** I thought you were playing.
>
> **Therapist:** So this is the same. Something good is happening and you (to Paul) want to carry it on. You reach for Elsa somehow, and if she's not right there, right at that moment?
>
> **Paul:** Yeah. I can detect a certain level. It's like, she says, I'll give you a squeeze and then, Oh, time's up. It's time to move on to something else. I'm very much, I'm a little starved, and so for me it's like, heh, this is the beginning not the end.
>
> **Therapist:** You're hungry. You're starved. You want the contact and then, for you, it gets cut off.

Reflection. Evocative responding using Paul's image of deprivation.

> **Paul:** Yeah. There's no question it gets cut off. Clearly, that is what happens. I'm not working in her space in the right way to get beyond that.
>
> **Elsa:** I don't live it the way you do. I don't see it this way.
>
> **Therapist:** Well, in the last session (to Paul) we talked about you being hungry and that you have an incredible sensitivity, and when you reach for Elsa at these times, it's like having what you want just for a moment, and then losing it. Then you go off and say to yourself, "There you are, she's never going to connect with me. There you are, no one is ever going to connect with me." It becomes a catastrophe. Remember that stuff?

Reflection. Heightening.

> **Paul:** Yeah. That's it. I drag it out into the atomic
> bomb, and at an emotional level, that's what I'm feel-
> ing. Even when it's a joke, like we make it into a joke,
> both of us, there is something inside us that says, this
> is no joke.
>
> **Therapist:** It's not a joke. It's a bomb.
>
> **Paul:** Yeah, but if she decides . . .
>
> **Therapist:** It's like last time, where you talked about
> playing the game and Elsa making the rules?
>
> **Paul:** Oh, since day one. It's like Charlie Brown and
> the football, that's my complaint, whether it's valid
> or not, but you (to Elsa) feel like I set the rules.
> (Elsa nods) Well, you set the timetable in terms of
> intimacy.
>
> **Therapist:** And suddenly you feel cut off.

Evocative responding, focusing on the experience of loss.

> **Paul:** Yeah, it happens so often that you're right, I'm
> hypersensitive to it.
>
> **Therapist:** Elsa, you're looking puzzled, like in the
> last session, and I remember last session you said to
> Paul, "What are you talking about?"

*Paul is in Step 5 here, while Elsa is trying to accept his
new responses—that is, she is moving into Step 6 of the
therapy process.*

> **Elsa:** Yeah, Russian.
>
> **Therapist:** You said to Paul, you're talking in Russian.
> Right, it's like, I don't see this vulnerable person?
> (Elsa agrees) You see the person who sets the rules,
> the judge, the critic. You described it to me once as,
> I see fog and arrows.

Reflection of Elsa's experience of Paul.

> **Elsa:** I don't remember saying that, but I like it.
>
> **Therapist:** I'm hearing that you have been so busy here, protecting yourself from Paul's criticisms, from being "devastated" (*Elsa's word*), that for you to actually now get a sense of the fact that this dangerous critical person is in fact incredibly vulnerable and hungry for contact with you . . .
>
> **Elsa:** Yeah, it doesn't add up.
>
> **Paul:** I'm setting myself up here. She's content and I'm hunting around.
>
> **Therapist:** (to Paul) Could you tell her what's going on at those times? Could you say, I feel hurt, I wanted a kiss and you said no? (Paul pulls his head back and raises his eyebrows) You couldn't tell her?
>
> **Paul:** It's obvious in the action. I put my arm around her.
>
> **Therapist:** So she should know, know that you are trying to get some reassurance from her. Is that word all right for you, *reassurance*?

Interpretation/conjecture.

> **Paul:** Reassurance, acceptance. If she's attractive and I want to be close, and I do it. It's devastating to try, and oops, it doesn't work.
>
> **Therapist:** It's devastating to reach and you can't get her to respond.

Reflection.

> **Paul:** Yeah. The response is a joke. (He looks sad, near tears)
>
> **Therapist:** It's not a joke, is it, Paul? Because these times all add up to a sense that you're never going to get your

needs met here. It's deadly serious, right? All these little wounds add up to something deadly serious.

Heightening . . . conjecture.

Paul: Yeah. If Elsa laughs at me, and my melodrama, I laugh too. She pricks my balloons and I admire that in a sense.

Therapist: Some part of you says, Oh okay, she's pricking my balloon, isn't that funny, but another part doesn't think it's funny at all?

The therapist continues the heightening.

Paul: Not at all.

Therapist: The urbane scientist part of Paul would say, "Oh isn't that funny, she's just pricked my balloon." Then this other part would feel just devastated. This vulnerable side of Paul, that starts to feel that he's going to go hungry his whole life, that he's never going to be able to reach Elsa, to keep hold of that connection with her, is devastated.

Reflection and heightening. The therapist heightens the attachment significance of his experience.

Paul: Yeah, that's the problem, from my perspective anyway. You said it well.

Elsa: What balloon, what do I prick?

Paul: Maybe I'm blowing something up. I inflate this kind of incident into something big.

Therapist: (to Elsa) The way I understand it, the balloon is what happened on the anniversary day. It's when you two get together and Paul, you start to feel, my God, we're together, my God, this is it. She likes me. I'm connected, she is with me, here we are, it's happening. And there is this *hope*, this precious

tenuous feeling of connectedness, and the next day
you go to pat her on the bum, or to kiss her, and if
she doesn't respond, if she says, my mouth's full, or
anything . . . (pause)

*. . . Heightening, interpretation. Conjecture. The therapist
evokes an attachment drama of hope and loss. The therapist
also pauses to invite Paul to continue in this frame.*

Paul: Yeah (to Elsa), like the other day. I just reached
for your hand in the car, and you pulled away, like I
was a hot poker, you know?

*Paul brings up another example of these incidents. This
whole dialogue creates a new position for Paul in the relationship, which replaces his original detached judgmental
stance.*

Elsa: No, no, no, what was happening was . . . (to therapist) but finish the bit about the balloon.
Therapist: The sense I have is that you feel close and
it's good. The balloon is this incredible sense of hope,
that you two are going to be together, and Paul will
have his hunger for closeness satisfied.
Paul: And then, it doesn't happen.
Therapist: And then it gets *burst.* Do you understand
(to Elsa)?
Elsa: I guess I do. It's difficult for me to see why my
mouth being full of peanut butter and saying, just a
second, is piercing a balloon.
Paul: Yeah, but after that the dance doesn't continue.
The play changes. It's going in a different direction
afterward.
Therapist: Yeah. We did talk about that. The sense
I get is that you both recognized these incidents the
minute they happen. What you (to Elsa) said was

(*in Session 10*), "the minute I turn him down, I look at his face and I know he doesn't like it, and he's tense, and I know I've blown it. He's mad at me, and I feel trapped and so I withdraw," right? (Elsa agrees) And you (to Paul) say to yourself, "There you are you see, it happened again. I'm not going to do this anymore." And as you drive to work, this grows into, "This will never work, she will never be there." So something happens in that moment, and the two of you back off like mad. And you, Elsa, say, "He's pushing me, I've got to kiss him or he'll be mad," and Paul, you say, "She wasn't available for long, she's shut me out again."

The therapist paints a picture of this part of the cycle and its attendant emotional responses.

Paul: This is the balloon. In the face of these disappointments, I get into, do I really want the kiss (angry tone)?

Paul adds in the anger, the blaming element that dominated his part of the cycle at the beginning of therapy and that pushes Elsa away.

Therapist: If you can never trust that this connection is really going to be there, some part of you says, I'd rather not want it, right? I don't want to want this kiss.

Paul: Yes, it's a confused state, and thoughts and feelings come along that are very destructive and very judgmental and condemning. Like, you can keep your damn kisses.

Therapist: You can keep your damn kisses. Some part of you wants to say to Elsa, if you're going to suddenly shut me out, you can keep them, I don't want them, keep your kisses (all laugh).

Reflection and heightening. The therapist heightens this because it places Paul's hostile behavior in an attachment frame of disappointment and insecurity.

> **Elsa:** All because of a mouthful of peanut butter.
>
> **Paul:** No, so many thousand instances, you know. This was just one.
>
> **Elsa:** You know (to therapist), we were driving and he was trying to get my hand, you know, like a little guy, maybe going to hold his girlfriend's hand. So I moved it a quarter of an inch, and he couldn't grab it and I laughed. But he was so kidlike, so, I thought, he's playing. But now I realize, maybe he was not playing. I was the only one who was playing!
>
> **Paul:** I wasn't playing! I'm not playing at all. I'm trying to get a message across at these points when I come to you. You can characterize them as kidlike. When it comes to these things, I'm just not good at it. When I do make these little gestures and it appears funny to you, it might appear funny, but it's not funny.
>
> **Therapist:** (soft voice) Aha, it's not funny. It's you taking a risk and saying, are you still there? Do you still desire me? Tell me again, because I need to know that I'm really special to you, it's you doing that, right?

Conjecture using an attachment framework.

> **Paul:** (tears) Yeah. She does let me know sometimes. Last week, in the market, she said "I'd still pick you out of a crowd" and that made me feel good.

At this point, the therapist would normally ask Paul to tell Elsa that he needs reassurance that he is special to her and that he is very afraid that he is not. This is consciously not done here because in previous sessions this task proved to be excruciatingly difficult for Paul, and would result in many intellectual digressions. The therapist therefore chooses to keep the present focus and initiate this intervention at a later date.

> **Therapist:** You're a very intellectual person, Paul, but when you reach for Elsa at these times, it's a physical reaching. And it might look small, insignificant, playful, but in fact, it's serious. A serious attempt to find out if she's still there. (Paul nods) And if, for whatever reason, she isn't, and there might be incredibly good reasons, like your mouth is full (all giggle), somehow that bursts the balloon, dampens the hope, puts things back in neutral or worse.
>
> **Paul:** I am so sensitive. I know that sometimes Elsa can't do any right, you know. In bed this morning (to Elsa), you were trying to get extra space, maybe you were still asleep, and I made a move like that (to touch her) and you swatted me, like a fly, you know. I interpret that as rejection and I get angry.

Again the therapist chooses not to get Paul to express his feelings and needs directly to Elsa, but instead dramatizes his anger herself.

> **Therapist:** (to Elsa) Keep your kisses. (Paul nods) What's happening, Elsa, what's happening as Paul is talking about this?

The therapist switches the focus to the other partner, to keep her engaged and facilitate her own Step 6 process.

> **Elsa:** I was trying to understand. But when I say nice things, it doesn't count. It was the wrong place, or the wrong time. I think we both do it to both of us. He doesn't take it when I do tell him nice things. It's always the wrong time.
>
> **Therapist:** So, for you, there are times when you reach out to give, and Paul doesn't take what you have to offer?

Elsa: That's it. (Puts her hands up in front of her in a gesture of apparent helplessness)

Paul: It did make me feel good, when you said that, but I do qualify it. I guess, I put it in context. The context of all the other times she doesn't want to be there, that she prefers the TV or the dog.

Elsa: As soon as you qualify something, you don't take it as it is.

Paul: Well, it's when I'm vulnerable and we are alone that I want you to say those things, but I did like what you said when we were in the market, in a crowd.

Elsa: (agitated) Well, if you think that, when we are in bed, that I'm going to roll over and say take me, I'm yours, this isn't me. On this planet I'll never do this, this isn't me.

He qualifies her giving by saying that it occurred in the wrong place. This is the trigger for Elsa's irritation. She states her unwillingness to be controlled by Paul and his demands, which she had also asserted in earlier sessions. At this point, however, it seems like a detour, so the therapist moves to contain the detour. It is also a potentially negative stance here, where Elsa defines herself as someone who cannot or will not respond to Paul's needs, just as Paul is struggling to express then in a new way.

Therapist: I'm confused. I remember in Session 5 or 6 that you told Paul, I do want to give myself to you. Do you remember that? (She nods) And you said, "I try, and you don't accept my offer." So I have heard you say to Paul, I want to be with you.

The therapist wants Elsa to stay engaged at this point.

Elsa: Yes, I do, but not in this form, this, take me I'm yours, form.

Paul: It's not the form I care about, it's not the form. If I put my arm around you, I just want to be close to you. I just want you to respond.

The therapist decides to redirect the session.

Therapist: Let's go back to the mouthful of peanut butter. I like that one.

Elsa: (laughs) Yeah, you love that one.

Therapist: Yeah. I liked it. Elsa you said that you were busy, and Paul, you said to Elsa, you pay attention to the dog when you're busy, do you remember? (Paul laughs) It feels like a clear example of these incidents we are talking about. When you feel safer, you aren't feeling like Paul is about to judge you so much, you can be close, and Paul, you feel that she is there. Like she wants you. Kind of the opposite to what you said once, when you said that she'd never turned up for this relationship. You connect, and then Paul, you need to reassure yourself that you really did touch that closeness. You reach to find her again, to reassure yourself that it was real, right? (Both nod) And the timing is a little off, and Elsa, you can't quite respond in that moment, and then Paul, you're devastated, and the two of you withdraw and that negative cycle starts.

Conjecture built into a drama.

Paul: Yeah, and it's happening at a really subtle level.

Therapist: Right. But what isn't subtle is that then that negative pattern sets in. Paul, you get angry and critical, and Elsa, you shut him out and withdraw. So these little incidents throw all that good sense of connection off again.

Tracking and reflecting the cycle as it appears here.

Elsa: It sounds danger again.

Therapist: Right. Yeah, right. The alarm goes off again. It has been safe for a while and suddenly the alarm goes off. And then Elsa, you say, "I'll never do it right, why try," and Paul, you say, "I didn't want her kisses anyway" and get angry.

Paul: Yeah, we're laughing a little about it now, we can see it now, but when it happens . . . (turns to Elsa) I notice you don't cry so much in these sessions now.

Elsa: Well, the sessions are not so difficult.

Therapist: Yeah, in the first sessions, Elsa, you talked about your pain in the relationship, but then you came out and drew some lines about Paul's criticism, but now (to Paul) we are talking about your hurts in the relationship.

Paul: I'm still critical now. I'm no different.

Therapist: Feels pretty different to me.

Elsa: It's not as negative, the tone is different.

Paul: I'm still complaining, but maybe with less voltage.

Elsa: It's not like it used to be. If it happens, I can ignore it now.

Paul: Why would you do that?

The therapist decides to refocus the session again from what seems like a detour initiated by Paul.

Therapist: The relationship is safer for you? (To Elsa, who nods) Now we are talking about when you, Paul, feel vulnerable in this relationship. When you are out there, searching for this reassurance, that's hard.

Paul: Yeah, it's a much harder topic for me. That's for sure.

Therapist: It's hard for you to talk about that?

Paul: Elsa can open up, she can emote.

Therapist: It's harder for you to show Elsa the emotional side of you. (Paul nods) So it would be really hard for you in those situations that prick the balloon to let Elsa know how devastated you feel, when you cannot reach her again. To show the part that gets hungry and scared that you've lost her again, and that she's gone back to being unattainable.

Repetition of attachment themes.

Paul: (very still and quiet) She sees that.

At this point the therapist again chooses not to ask him to tell Elsa how hard it is for him to be vulnerable with her.

Therapist: Does she? In the last session she said quite clearly that she didn't see it.

Elsa: I never saw it this way. I always saw it as a joke.

Paul: I speak in irony, with humor, that's my style.

Elsa: When you reached like that, it was so clumsy, it couldn't have been any clumsier, honest to God.

Paul: Maybe I present it as a joke.

Therapist: (reflectively, slowly) It was clumsy. Paul is a very sophisticated person, the opposite of clumsy. Suddenly here is this different person, suddenly he is clumsy, and you say to yourself, "This is a joke." (Elsa nods) But it is not a joke, is it, Paul? Most of us, if we get scared and we are right on the edge of the cliff and facing something we long for very much and are scared that we are never going to grasp, we don't look cool and sophisticated. We fumble, we miss, we don't read the clues right. We get clumsy, we are so terrified that what we want so much is not going to happen.

Validation, heightening. A brief general conjecture to provide a context for Paul's behavior.

Elsa: (to Paul) I didn't see it like that.

Therapist: There is no reason why you should see it. You are used to seeing Paul as this supercompetent scientist, this powerful person. Perhaps you are not prepared for this other side of Paul. (She nods) And Paul, in the last session you talked very movingly about how Elsa is still beautiful for you. (He nods) You talked for a moment in the voice of a young man who has just fallen in love, who might be clumsy. I guess, I am struck by this word *clumsy*. At these points when you're reaching for Elsa, you're not cool and in control. You are the Paul who is vulnerable, more unsure of yourself, reaching for something you're not sure is there? (Paul agrees) And Elsa, you look, and you see urbane Paul, who can shoot you down with a single arrow, and you say to yourself, "Oh, he is joking." (Elsa nods)

The therapist uses the word clumsy *to heighten the sense of Paul's vulnerability.*

Paul: Under these clumsy moments there is a real fear. A fear that this is all going to fall apart. Maybe it was never solid, maybe the connection was never there, and why don't I just accept that. It's loaded.

This is the first time that Paul has openly acknowledged fear.

Therapist: Maybe it was never there?

Paul: Yeah, maybe it was an illusion. Those little gestures are ways of saying, hey, let's not go down that path.

Therapist: The path that leads to the loss of the relationship, right?

Paul: Right. But maybe, maybe, it's too needy, that part. It's not attractive, there are attractive and unattractive elements . . .

The therapist notes this and will go back to this in the next session. What the therapist hears here is the working model of self, in this case a model of the dependent self defined as unlovable. This arises very frequently at this point in the process. For now, however, the therapist decides to refocus the session.

> **Therapist:** So what are you trying to say to Elsa when you reach for her, Paul? You're trying to say . . . ?

Now the therapist invites him to take the risk and express his need.

> **Paul:** (long pause, laughs) Let's get married! (Elsa laughs)
>
> **Therapist:** Let's get married. So in that little touch is, let's get married. Come and be with me, or, are you going to be with me or not? (Paul smiles and nods) It's a proposal in disguise. It's done in a way that you're not so naked, so vulnerable, yes?

The therapist heightens Paul's response and accepts the level of risk he is ready for at this time.

> **Paul:** So when she doesn't respond, when I don't get reassured, it's like I'm less important than peanut butter.

At the end of the session I validate how Paul is taking risks and how Elsa is struggling to see, as I put it, a "brand-new Paul." I then end the session by talking about how strong and how sensitive they both are and how much impact they have on each other. My goal for the next session is to continue the softening process, and to request that Paul state his fears and needs directly to Elsa. This would then move him into Step 7 of the therapy process. In contrast to the first few sessions, Paul brings more and more of himself into the interaction and is more and more accessible, and Elsa is engaged and available.

Couple Process

After this session, each partner was shown a videotape of the session and encouraged to comment on the process. This was done with the understanding that each partner's comments would not be shared with the other partner or the therapist. Such sharing only occurred later, when the couple agreed to allow the information to be used in this volume. The interviewer asked process-oriented questions, such as, "What was happening for you here?" Both partners assessed the session as productive, assigning it an 8 on a 10-point scale, and both explicitly stated that they trusted the process of therapy, even if they were not always clear as to where it was going, and they trusted the therapist.

Paul's Perspective

Paul commented that the therapist put "her finger on how he was feeling. She tuned in to me." He particularly noted that it moved him when the therapist recognized how vulnerable he was. Paul felt dismayed when his wife stated that she did not see the vulnerable side of him and sensed that the therapist was emphasizing this to help Elsa see it.

Paul wanted Elsa to be more involved in the session, to say more instead of "hesitating," because, as he stated, "the only thing that really counts is Elsa's reassurance to me that she wants to be with me. I need to hear that from her." As well as recalling how he experienced the session at the time, when he watched the video he stated that he could observe himself "bullying the relationship" and "playing a negative record" by criticizing Elsa. He stated that this probably set things up not to work.

Elsa's Perspective

Elsa thought that the session was a good one because she was hearing things from Paul that she had never heard before, and this was "very revealing." She felt that they were "discovering things that were buried. We are on the right path." She also experienced Paul as less blaming and accusing in this session. She saw him as taking a risk and "being scared of my reactions, that I might think he was a wimp." She suggested that "if we keep going this way, I'll understand better and I'll be there better. As opposed to being in a fog, being lost and shutting him out." For Elsa, Paul's speedy, intellectual, and ever-changing comments and asides confused and overwhelmed her to the point that she would just stop listening. In this session the "fog had lifted."

Elsa also stated that she didn't want to say too much in the session and interrupt the process of Paul expressing himself. She wanted to give him space and hear what he had to say, so she stayed quiet. She felt that the session had been not only "an eye opener, but an ear opener." Even though she was quiet, she felt included in the session. She recognized that in the first sessions she had often been the focus of attention and she had felt "understood" by the therapist, and that now it was Paul's turn. Elsa mentioned that she felt good when the therapist redirected the session after her comment "to say, take me I'm yours, that is just not me." She felt that this comment was a "dead end." She also felt "put on the spot" by Paul here and felt like resisting his pressure. Paul, on the other hand, felt a little cut off here by the therapist, but commented that, if he had kept going in this vein, Elsa would probably have "frozen" on him.

In the next session, Session 12, Paul talked more openly about how his vigilance and monitoring of Elsa's responses reflected his "fear," specifically the fear of losing the relationship. He also spoke of his sense of being "invisible" and not having an impact on Elsa. Elsa responded that she could not read his mind and was "bound to fail" if he could not show himself more. I suggested that he help Elsa with this, and Paul spoke of his anxiety about showing his vulnerability to Elsa, because she might "jump all over him." At the end of the session he stated, "It's fearful for me to feel how much I need you, to feel my dependence. That I can sing in the shower or not because of you, that my happiness relies on your acceptance." He then asked her, "Do you really feel okay about me being dependent and needing reassurance?" Elsa told him that this was not a problem for her, although she still felt a little hesitant, because she still viewed him as "a little dangerous."

Session 12 continued the process of the softening that Paul began in Session 10 and continued in the session transcribed above. In these sessions, Paul moved between Steps 5 and 7 of the EFT process, while Elsa moved slowly and surely through Step 6, accepting new aspects of Paul and coming to trust them. Every couple is different, and this couple was very aware (even before the IPR procedure) of the process of therapy. In previous sessions, Paul had sometimes asked me, "What are you doing here?" I would then tell him. For example, at one point I replied, "I am blocking your exits and trying to slow you down, so you can stay right here, in this place for a while, because I think that right here is very important." The process of therapy was therefore more transparent than usual because the couple wanted it that way.

Later in therapy Paul was able to talk openly about his "deep longing" for closeness with Elsa, and a sense of being "wanted" by her. Elsa was then able to respond positively to this. She attributed her increased engagement in, and satisfaction with, the relationship to the fact that she now "had more of a voice here," and she could "stand up more." At the end of therapy this couple scored 107 on the Dyadic Adjustment Scale, placing them in the nondistressed range on this instrument.

14

A STAGE 2 EFT SESSION

"We go our own ways—there is a wall between us—or is it a war?"

"Whatever it is we are both dying of loneliness in the same bed."

Jon came to see me with a referral from his doctor. This referral told me that Jon was very depressed due to stress at work and to distress in his marriage; the latter problem Jon had agreed to discuss with me. Jon told me that he and his wife, Beatrice, had married young and 10 years ago had emigrated to Canada from Europe. He had found work in a very specialized part of the banking industry; work that he hated but that had allowed him and his partner to survive and have two children, the younger of whom was now two years old. He stated that he felt "completely alone" in his marriage and also "trapped" in that his desire to leave his profession was greatly discouraged by his wife. Beatrice had agreed to couple sessions. Since I had seen him, I requested that she come to see me once by herself, and then we would begin joint sessions. Beatrice expressed much anger at her partner, stating that since the birth of their second child, there had been little affection or sexuality and that she believed her husband expected her to "make him happy," which she resented. She had, in the last few months, "given up" and started to go "cold" when he did approach her. She said, "It is hard for me to show emotion. He says I am critical, and he sees me as the enemy. But I am

297

wanting love too." She spoke of missing her family in the old country and her fear about her partner's depression and his desire to leave his profession, since she only had a part-time job with a law firm. Both partners were easy for me to create an alliance with, and both stated that they wanted to repair the relationship, if such repair was possible.

Beatrice and Jon's negative cycle seemed to vacillate between withdraw–withdraw and a blame/attack followed by defend/withdraw pattern, with Jon being the defending withdrawer. This mutual withdraw pattern seemed to fit with Beatrice's descriptions of having recently "given up" and "put up a wall." This pattern is common when more critical pursuing partners begin to grieve the relationship and move into detachment. The couple's cycle was exacerbated by Jon's clinical depression, for which he was placed on medication by his physician. He spoke of never being sure about how she felt about him and so being too terrified to risk asking for attention, while she spoke of being uncomfortable depending on anyone and wanting connection, but not feeling valued by Jon. If we consider this couple in terms of attachment styles, Jon seemed to have an anxious attachment, overlaid by his depression, and Beatrice seemed to have a fearful avoidant style. She confided that any sign of "weakness" or dependency was punished and treated with derision in her family of origin. To give a sense of where this couple started from in the process of therapy, an example of a piece of uninterrupted dialogue from an early Stage 1 session follows.

> **Beatrice:** Well, I am completely discouraged. He just accuses me of being angry all the time! But he wants me to take care of him—like I am his mother or something.
>
> **Jon:** (very quietly) You are angry all the time. You called me "the devil" the other day.
>
> **Beatrice:** You just shut me out like I don't matter— that's it—I just don't matter to you.
>
> **Jon:** After the last session I asked you to come and hug me—don't you remember that—I asked.

Beatrice: Yes—yes—I suppose you did—after all these months—well I just don't trust it. We are too trapped in our old ways of coping.

Jon: I just get hammered, judged and hammered—no matter what I do. Don't you see I am depressed? Can't you give me a kind word now and again?

Beatrice: Huh—depressed—You are just grumpy—or behind a wall. You shut me out.

Jon: The other night—I tried. I moved my knee—I touched your knee. (He begins to tear) But then (he throws up his hands)—you moved away.

Beatrice: (in a flat voice—staring at the floor) I do move away now—You think I should just be there waiting for your every touch? (Jon shakes his head and turns away)

Jon: If I do show you I need you—you don't respond anyway. What's the point?

Beatrice: You never show you need me—not really. I am irrelevant. I am the maid. I am air.

In Stage 1 of therapy, this couple was able to share that they both felt alone and desperate—fearing the marriage was on the edge of breaking up and feeling helpless to prevent it. They were also both able to talk about how sensitive they were to being judged by the other, and how they both felt that they got caught up in trading criticisms and getting caught in who was most at fault in the relationship. Jon was able to talk about how anxious he was and how he tried to be very careful to avoid Beatrice's anger and "rejection." He was able to acknowledge that his withdrawal left them both feeling alone and deprived. Both partners were able to see how the depression and Jon's feelings about being trapped in his job were putting pressure on the marriage. Beatrice was able to see how her anger was part of the cycle they both were caught in and that now her "coldness," when Jon did take very small risks in reaching for her, kept them both hurting and terrified. Both were able to explore how they had never been able to create a really secure connection, and Beatrice was able to disclose that she had never experienced secure attachment, as I described it to her. She described her parents as distant and punitive. Both agreed that "trust was hard." Beatrice in one session accessed much grief and shame at her apparent "worthlessness" as reflected in the responses of those she loved. Jon then tried to comfort her. And both agreed that it was "scary to have those needs for soft touch and caring." Jon was able to tell his wife that "I am overwhelmed by your anger, but I just can't lose you—I will fight for you" and she began to hear him. The relationship improved and we had de-escalation. The couple felt, after seven sessions, "more connected." One session involved Jon being able to talk to his wife about his depression and her being able to be supportive. The task now was to move into Stage 2, focusing on helping Jon become more engaged and Beatrice to continue to process her fear and begin to trust his increasing engagement. Both partners showed great courage, integrity, and willingness to look at how they became caught in the cycle of mutual blame and distance.

STAGE 2 SESSION

(This session is given here unedited and was observed and taped in a live session at an EFT externship.) The therapist's goal here was to encourage more engagement for Jon and to continue to help Beatrice open up and deal with her attachment needs and fears so that she could then soften and connect with her partner.

After a few minutes of introductory discussion and settling in, Jon was able to discuss how he had confided in his wife the previous evening that he believed that he had a learning disability, like his daughter, and that this was one of the reasons he found his tasks at work so difficult. She appreciated his being able and willing to do this.

Therapist: So you were able to break out of the old "both behind a wall" or "hammer and defend" patterns and have a real discussion. (They both nod agreement) You were able to step out of what we have been dealing with in this relationship. The pattern—as you have described it—is that Jon, you end up feeling hopeless and overwhelmed, and then you get irritable, or you shut down and numb out—yes? (he nods), when really you need soothing and comfort but it is so hard to ask Beatrice for that. And then Beatrice, you understand what is happening as that you don't matter to Jon, and you get angry and try to "hammer" a response out of him. (She nods agreement) But more recently you just try to shut down too—'cause it's too hard to need someone who is so distant—yes? (She agrees) Then the two of you feel alone—and scared. Dying of loneliness in the same bed, as you said in the last session.

The therapist gives a summary of the cycle and the underlying feelings accessed in previous sessions.

Jon: Yes—and then when I do get up my courage and try—just a little—a tiny step to connect— (He throws up his hands)

Therapist: Beatrice is unsure—she doesn't trust you—your reaching—so she moves away.

Beatrice: We are not emotionally connected—so when he risks a little—there is no reaction.

Therapist: You don't feel safe enough to respond—so you play it safe and stay behind your wall? (She agrees) But last night—things are changing a little because Jon was able to confide in you about how hard he finds his work. He took a risk—and you felt like he was "letting you in" and you appreciated this.

Beatrice: Yes—It was a risk. He took a risk—'cause he could be criticized as having a weakness—a learning problem.

Therapist: He let you in and you saw that and were able to respond. You appreciated him taking that risk.

The therapist heightens and highlights an exception to the cycle—responsiveness.

Jon: (to Beatrice) Yeah. You listened and you didn't start blaming me or criticizing.

Beatrice: Why should I blame you?

Jon: (Puts his head in his hands and bursts into deep sobs)

Therapist: (pauses—leans forward—hands Jon a tissue—waits, and then says softly) You were really really worried about that, right? You were really scared. (He nods) You feel bad that you have never fit in this job—and you were so scared that Beatrice was going to judge you and tell you that you were disappointing—yes? (He nods and weeps) (Turning to Beatrice) Did you know how big a risk it was for Jon to do that—to confide like that?

Beatrice: (beginning to tear)—Well—yes—I guess so— I realize now—I guess he was scared.

Therapist: (to Jon) What was your worst fantasy, Jon? What was she going to say—the worst catastrophe? When you risked—she would say—?

Evocative question to elicit fears.

Jon: (cries) She would say—no wonder our kid can't read—there is something wrong with you.

Therapist: That took so much courage—so scary— (*Validation*)

Jon: I guess I had no other choice.

Therapist: Oh, you did have other choices—to shut down and avoid or to get irritable. But you found your courage and you invested in the connection with your wife. You reached for what you needed even though you were scared. (*Validation*)

Beatrice: (shrugs) We connect by talking about the kid—that is always the way.

Therapist: Aha—it's easier to talk about your kid. But Jon—you were vigilant for—ready for—dreading—terrified of hearing from Beatrice that she disapproves of you—finds you wanting—and you still reached for her—in spite of your fear of seeing—?

The therapist stays focused on his reaching and his fear. Heightens fear and validates courage.

Jon: (very quietly—almost inaudible) Contempt—yes— (long silence) Contempt or something like that.

Therapist: That if you reach, the fear is that she will respond with contempt—with the message that you are failing with her—somehow not good enough— (He tears and nods) So that keeps you treading water here. (*This is his image from the last session*) And that is part of the depression—it's so hard for you to accept that this job is very hard for you—you maybe are not that suited for it. You fight failure at work every day—and you are scared that Beatrice will not be able to accept this and then—when you come home and want to reach for her—you fear her judgment—her contempt.

The therapist integrates his work dilemma, his depression, and his fear of his wife's contempt. As therapist and client walk again through the scene—the picture develops further.

Beatrice: (to Jon) I am in a role here with you—I am not your tyrant father, you know!

Jon: Why is my father suddenly in the picture?

Therapist: We have talked about the cultures you both grew up in and that you both have these raw places—sensitive spots—especially about being judged and told you are somehow unlovable. (Both nod) And these sore spots—they get sparked off right here— with each other. Then—when you need comfort—it is so hard to reach for each other. And this is a time when you are struggling with the whole career thing and you desperately need Beatrice's support—Jon— Yes? (He nods) (*Refocus on vulnerabilities—and his high need and present sensitivity*) So it is so hard for you to share with her—reach for her. (Soft voice) You are so afraid that you will look into her face and see that you have disappointed her—that she is judging you as not good enough— (He weeps) And that keeps you holding back—numbing out. (*Links fears to stance in relationship dance*) But then Beatrice can't find you either and—as she said in the last session, she can't find you—she begins to believe that she is "not important to you—not worth the effort"— (*Connect fear and withdrawal to cycle*)

Beatrice: It's a vicious cycle—

Jon: Yes, its a circle—and we get stuck.

Therapist: But you are getting out of it. It's risky— hard. But you know how to struggle. (*Validation*) You came here to Canada together—left all you knew and struggled to survive. But you need each other's sup- port—right? (Both nod) Jon, do you think Beatrice understands how afraid you are to talk to her about these things? And how you shut down and numb out (*repeating images from last few sessions*)—when you get so afraid she will judge you—show contempt—? (*Return, refocus, repeat*) (He weeps) And that holds you back—from reaching for her. (Turns to Beatrice) And then you say to yourself, as you told us last time—"I'm not important to him at all—I'm not worth the effort." (Beatrice nods emphatically) But—in fact—he holds back because he is so afraid to reach for you—confide in you—because you and what you think of him is so desperately important. (*Reframe*)

Beatrice: Oh—oh— (She looks at Jon and turns and tilts her head on one side—furrows her brow in surprise as people often do when they encounter a new way of seeing things and are "trying it on." We call this response "dog listening to recorder.") Hum—yes—Hum—I never think of it like that. Well, it's a vicious circle.

Therapist: But you are getting out of it—it is not defeating you. Do you think, Jon, that Beatrice really understands how afraid you are to reach—to talk—to tell her your issues and fears and longings?

Jon: Well—this is a milestone—the other night and sessions like this. (Turns to Beatrice, and becomes agitated) Before I'd try to talk and you'd swipe it away (makes a large swipe action with his hand), and you'd say—"Well, just try harder at work—and fix it—you fix it—what is wrong with you." But I can't "just fix it." I can't. (He tears again)

Beatrice: (soft voice) I don't think I said that—not like that. But I didn't understand, Jon—I had no idea. You just looked irritated and—

Therapist: (to Beatrice) You are saying—maybe I didn't understand—but then maybe you didn't let me in— (She agrees) So I didn't see your pain. Is that right?

Beatrice: Yes—I'd offer what I thought was practical advice.

Therapist: When maybe what Jon was longing for was soothing and emotional reassurance and comfort.

Jon: (very quietly) That just wasn't there—it was totally lacking—

Therapist: (to Jon) And you didn't know how to ask for this support. You needed a safe place—and it has been so hard for you to tell Beatrice how hopeless and helpless you felt at work. You didn't feel confident and in charge anywhere— (*Repeating his words from a previous session*)

Jon: Well—she is trying to listen now—but—

Therapist: Can you turn your chair and look at her? (He does this) Can you help her understand how you feel right now—what this fear feels like—your fear of her judging you—how it holds you back—paralyzes you—can you? (*Structure an enactment—evocative images*)

Jon: It's so very hard to tell you— (Long pause) (Very softly) Imagine—when I go to work—for the last few years—I get stomachache—shivers—I feel nauseated— I take longer than everyone else to do my job—it's— it's—degrading—

Beatrice: (leans forward) Degrading?

Jon: (cries) Like I am stupid—

Therapist: You judge yourself Jon—yes?—You think you should be able to do this—and you fear her judgment too—?

Jon: I shouldn't be there really—I don't fit—

Therapist: Aha—and when you feel small and "degraded"—like you are failing—it must be so hard to ask for special help and comfort from your wife—?

Jon: Yes—yes—like how can I ask—when—when . . .

Therapist: When I don't deserve it even—when I am failing— (He nods and cries)

Beatrice: But—then I don't know—you leave me out. I don't get the chance to help—

Therapist: You'd like to help. (She nods) Do you hear her, Jon?—It's so hard to ask Beatrice to see your pain when you yourself can hardly accept that this job had become so hard for you— (*Reflect lack of entitlement—his own self-blame. Repeat.*)

Jon: Yes—I can't. (Long pause) So I tell her a list of solutions—ideas for a new career—and she just gets mad. I hear the contempt in her voice—and I just get smaller and smaller—

Beatrice: I only got mad when you said you wanted to be a salesman.

Therapist: (*maintain focus*) What you are telling Beatrice is that you shut down because it is terrifying to talk about this—and risk her contempt—that part of you even thinks maybe you deserve? (He nods) You are not entitled to ask—hum? (He nods) And you need it so desperately— (*Reflection, empathic conjecture*)

Jon: I cannot do it without her—I cannot— (weeps)

Therapist: Can you tell her? (*Set up enactment*)

Jon: (Shakes his head—stares at the floor)

Therapist: It so hard to tell her. You need her help so much—you are in pain—you have your back to the wall and you need your wife to come and stand beside you—yes? (He nods and looks up at her pleadingly) And you are terrified to ask. (*Using RISSSC nonverbals to heighten*) Can you hear him, Beatrice—what happens to you when he says that he needs your help?

Beatrice: I feel—I feel— (looks up at the wall—pause) encouraged—like this is a way for us to get close again—to share again—yes—I have felt so shut out for so long now.

Therapist: It's affirming—reassuring for you to know that you are important to him—that he can risk even if he is afraid—that he needs you?—

Jon: (looks up at Beatrice) I want to reach for you—need your caring—Maybe then we can build—

Therapist: Heh, Jon—you are reaching—even though it is so hard—you are risking—reaching for your wife— (*Validation*) (He smiles) What is it like for you to tell her this?

Jon: (smiles) Encouraging—

Therapist: Beatrice—I think I hear you saying to Jon— I want to be there for you—is that right? (She nods)

So—can you tell her, Jon—what would help you—
what do you need? (*Evocative reflection and set up
enactment*)

Beatrice: (to Jon) I feel closer when you share your
feelings—

Therapist: That is precious for you—because then you
feel important to him—and not so alone—yes?
(*Empathic conjecture. Heightening.*)

Beatrice: No one in our families ever shared feelings.
It is so strange for us—

Therapist: (turns back to Jon) Is this reassuring to you,
Jon—to risk like this and to not have your worst fantasies come true? She isn't judging you—instead her
face goes soft—and she says she feels closer and she
wants to be there for you. (She nods vigorously)
Can you hear her, Jon? What is happening for you?
(*Evocative questions—responding. Reflect process—
heighten process.*)

Jon: (leans toward his wife—very soft voice) Yes—it's
wonderful—it's what I need. It makes such a difference—I have been alone too—we both have—

Beatrice: Yes—both our parents would have got all
judgmental and in our families no one does this. You
couldn't tell your mum anything like this—and I
think if you had had a different upbringing—

Therapist: (*stop and refocus*) Can I stop you for a
moment, Beatrice—I would like to stay here a
minute—So Jon—Can you tell Beatrice what you need
from her? We have talked about how you feel raw
when you come home and how you numb out—and
then all Beatrice sees is a distant snappy man—so she
now shuts down too— (*Reflect cycle, set up enactment*) Can you tell her—?

Jon: Yes. (Turns to her) I am afraid to talk—I might
break down—so I build a wall around the bad
feelings—to cope—

Therapist: And then all she sees is the wall— (He nods) But if you did reach for her help—her support— when you came home—how could she help you? What do you long for, Jon—at that moment? If you could show Beatrice how much she matters to you— how much you need her? (*Evocative questions. Heightening.*) You are fighting so hard—fighting a job that makes you sick—a depression—fighting for your relationship—that is huge—What might you ask for? (*Validation, set up enactment*) (Therapist gestures toward her)

Jon: (very slowly) I think—a real hug—that would do it—maybe—

Therapist: Being held?

Jon: Yes—yes—if we hug now it's a brush-off. But a real hug—where I feel she wants to hug me—she means it—a real hug would really comfort me—yes—

Beatrice: But—I am not superwoman, you know—I am not a supernurturer—it's not my nature—there has to be some connection—I need help here—

Therapist: Yes—right. He has to be able to ask—to tell you what he needs—

Beatrice: Some women can do this—they just radiate nurturing.

Therapist: Oh—do they really? Oh—well maybe—but I always assume that partners have to be able to take a risk and ask for caring—and also ask in a clear way—not a hidden or ambiguous way. It's too hard to guess—and you have felt very shut out too. (She nods and tears) (*Validate*) So Jon—you are saying that you need to be held—to feel safe and soothed by your wife—to know she is with you—yes?

Jon: Yes—we have all these tasks and chores—and she works in the evening—but some sign that she wants to spend time with me—but then I have been pretty distant—

Therapist: (*refocus*) Can I go back here? Can you ask her for a hug, Jon?

Jon: It's difficult. Suppose she doesn't feel like it? (He throws up his hands)

Therapist: So can you tell her please—it is very very hard for me to come and ask to be held—to feel I deserve it—to feel it—risk it with you—risk you responding to me with contempt. (*Evocative reflection/integration of his position—set up enactment*)

Jon: (turns to her, with a more assertive tone) It is so hard for me to ask—'cause I say to myself—I'll be shown a cold face—brushed off—it's very scary. I'd rather it just happens.

Therapist: (soft tone) If only I didn't have to ask. (All laugh) Maybe we would all like that—but— (pause) What was it like to tell her that? (*Evocative question*)

Jon: Well—it wasn't so hard—maybe it's not so bad— (He smiles)

Therapist: (to Beatrice) Do you believe him? 'Cause other times I have seen Jon take a risk and you have said—"I don't believe you"—yes?

Beatrice: Yes—yes I do believe him. I see he is afraid to be refused. I see that—and I have given him the cold shoulder—

Jon: Right—yes—So then I say to myself, why should I try? Why should I even show signs? Even now—my head says—forget it.

Therapist: Aha—'cause if we are vulnerable—and we reach and the other person can't respond—isn't there—we feel even worse. (Jon—Yes, yes) So it is easier to shut down—protect yourself, and so hard to risk and ask for that hug when you come home (*validate*)—to ask for her reassurance and comfort.

Jon: I can try—now maybe I can try—

Therapist: Aha—What happens to you, Beatrice, when you hear that? What happens to you when Jon tells

you that he'd like to be able to come and say—
"Beatrice, I am so sacred to reach for you—I have been
in this battle all day and I just need for you to put your
arms around me and hold me"—What happens for you
when you hear how much he needs you and that he
is so afraid to ask? (She stares at the floor) Can you
look at him right now, Beatrice? (He is staring at her
intently with tears in his eyes) (*Heightening, evocation
of Jon's reaching—engagement. Evocative question.*)

Beatrice: (looks at him—long pause) It's sad—it's so
sad.

Jon: (very very softly) This fear is based on experience, Beatrice—I have been rejected over and over
and over—

Beatrice: (tears—also very soft voice) Yes—I know—
but I have felt so left out—so shut out. I got angry—
I gave up.

Jon: (reaches for her hand) I know—I know—I didn't
understand.

Therapist: Beatrice—you would end up feeling so
unimportant—so not included in his life—so when he
did make little signs that he needed you—you would
be so hurt and so upset—you couldn't see them—trust
them—You couldn't respond—and then Jon—you
would feel rejected. (*Validate, reflect minicycle of
rejection—this has actually occurred in previous
sessions*) So now, when he asks here—you feel sad.
You would like him to be able to ask? (*Reflection,
evocative question*)

Beatrice: Yes—I'd like him to not close up—to be
open—

Therapist: You are saying—if you risk and stay open
that helps me respond—but when I feel shut out then
I do protect myself and go "cold"—am I getting it?
(*Reflect the process—the steps in the attachment
dance*)

Beatrice: Yes—exactly—that is what I observe with me—

Therapist: Can you tell him about your sadness when he tells you "I get so scared to reach for you when I need you"? (*Evocative responding—set up enactment*)

Beatrice: (turns to Jon) It's sad—it is so sad. That you are scared to reach for me—so I can't comfort you—I need that too, you know—of course I do.

Jon: (smiles at her—leans forward) Well—we were not able to—maybe now—

Therapist: (to Beatrice) You'd like to comfort him (Beatrice agrees) and you'd like to go to him for comfort too? Yes? (She agrees and smiles at him) In all this dance of depression and jobs that don't fit anymore and relationship uncertainty you lost each other for a moment—yes—you both got scared—you fought—and then you shut down and protected yourselves— (*Reflect, integrate, summarize problem situation— emotional responses*)

Beatrice: Yes—I feel like a bug lying on my back—feet in the air—unable to move. I don't know how to move.

Therapist: Hum—yes—and Jon you are nudging her— by asking her—risking—trying to get closer—trying to flip her over—help her flip so she can move—Yes? (*Use image to heighten drama of dance. Note image for future sessions.*) (They both laugh) But that is a real image of how you have felt in this cycle—yes? Helplessness, stuck.

Beatrice: I do need to be nudged—I do.

Therapist: So we are talking about how you can both help each other out of this cycle—this cycle that has kept you so sad and alone. Beatrice—you are saying— "Don't leave me alone and helpless—on my back— cold and stuck—reach for me." And Jon, you are saying, "When I am drowning—I want to reach for you and get reassurance— (They both agree) Both of you need reassurance and comfort. (*Evocative summary of positions if voice of primary emotions heard*)

Beatrice: Yes, yes, yes. I shut down so much that I didn't dare ask a question. He'd see it as an attack even if it wasn't. So I stopped asking. So then we were both alone, I guess.

Therapist: Right—Everyone was on guard. So you are saying to Jon, if he was able to tell you—"It was so hard today and I need you—I need a hug"—that would help. You are telling him—he does need to ask, that would feel good and reassure you that you are special to him—yes? (*Reflect possible scenario of safe connection and reflect and validate her feelings*)

Beatrice: Yes—I want it to grow—the openness. I need the emotional closeness.

Jon: Maybe we can build it now—

Therapist: Well—you guys *are* building it. You have come so so so far since the first sessions. You are so much more open and much softer with each other. (*Validate*)

Jon: She smiles a lot more.

Beatrice: (smiles at him) Yes—and if I feel closer, it is easier to give hugs. Men think first the hug and then the closeness—but—

Jon: So—let's meet in between.

Therapist: We are talking about a very special kind of hug here—a hug that helps you both feel safer and begin to trust again—Jon is telling you he needs your arms around him.

Jon: Yes—when I feel all alone—it just puts the depression through the roof.

Therapist: So, Jon—you are telling your wife—when I come home I need to touch and feel you close to me in a hug— (He nods) Can you tell her please? (*Set up enactment*)

Jon: (to Beatrice) When I come home, I need closeness. I long for that—that would help me so much. (He tears)

Therapist: Can you hear him, Beatrice?

Beatrice: Yes. It is like cracking a nutshell. He's opening up to me and to himself.

Therapist: And that takes so much courage. (*Validate*)

Beatrice: Yes—so he can face the problems at work—and that helps us too.

Therapist: So you respect his opening up and risking—? Can you tell him?

Beatrice: I respect this very much. How you are willing to look inside and to risk with me. Being able to ask is important—and I respect you for struggling with a sense of feeling not good enough and not fitting in at work too.

Therapist: You are both doing so well. I think we have to stop. I would like you to talk about the session at least twice during the week—for 20 minutes or so—if you can. I appreciate how hard you worked and how much you let me in here in this session. You both show such commitment and courage. Thank you for working so hard with me.

Change events, such as this withdrawer reengagement session, are usually the most intensely focused and directive of all EFT sessions. They also usually contain more enactments, and the enactments are more significant. This couple, though very distressed when they came in, were also particularly allied with the therapist and motivated to prevent the loss of their marriage.

After this session, however, Beatrice decided that she could not really trust Jon. She noted that "I know I get mad and I slam the door on him and won't respond to his knocking. But I don't believe in his bids for closeness." He said he was "dodging bullets again," but he was able to tell her—"Don't give up on us, Beatrice—I am fighting for the relationship." Gradually Beatrice began her own journey through Steps 5 and 7 of EFT and through a crisis of trust. She was able to access the risk of being hurt again and also to explore her sense that to be vulnerable in her family of origin was to be instantly punished and despised. She began to be able to ask him for reassurance.

As a result of their progress as a couple, Jon was able to make some decisions at work and explore the options of lateral moves that allowed him to work at tasks that were more comfortable for him. Beatrice then began to explore further the lack of a secure attachment in her family of origin and how love was always tied to performance. Her tendency to judge and set high expectations for herself and Jon was then explored. Jon was able to comfort and reassure her when she grieved the lack of nurturing attachment in her youth, but it was very difficult for her to let him do this. He was able to make statements like, "Your pain is my pain—I want you to let me support and comfort you—Let me in and I will care for you." She would reply, "But it is hard to take your armor off—not sure how to live without it." A key moment in her "softening" process came when she spoke of the "voice of caution" that bade her keep Jon out. I then expanded on the description she had given in response to my probing about whether she had ever experienced a loving, secure attachment, as I described it to her. She replied that for a short time she had such a relationship with her grandmother, who was "her angel." We then spoke about her grandmother and her relationship with Beatrice for a few minutes, to make it tangible and present. I then asked her what her grandmother would tell her, if she listened to her grandmother's voice, about this dilemma as to whether to trust Jon. What would this voice say about whether to let him closer and let herself, against all her family and cultural dictates, depend on him? With much emotion, Beatrice replied, "She'd say, 'Trust him—try it—he's soft—he won't hurt you or take advantage.'" This seemed to be a turning point in her softening process.

In the next session, the couple began the session by sharing how they had been able to hold each other at night and felt much "safer and closer." They also spoke of being confident enough to reach for each other and ask for closeness. My sense that they were now moving into the consolidation phase of EFT was confirmed when they began to talk about the "negative blip" they had experienced. Jon had experienced Beatrice as suddenly becoming "cold and demanding," and rather than withdraw he had decided to express his feelings of being blamed and the fear that came up for him that he "blew it somehow and will never get it right." He began the process of expressing this by sending her an e-mail and then continued in face-to-face dialogue. Beatrice at first saw this as a "power struggle—he wants the right to go and do what he wants to do—to take time for fun. Doesn't matter about me—again I don't matter." But then, rather than stay in this place, she began to hear how upset and helpless he felt, and recognized that this made her very anxious. She was able to decide to tell him that she was "afraid." She expanded on this and articulated that she feared his depression was returning and that he would then withdraw from her again; he might give up trying to repair their relationship.

She then stated that this moment—when she went to Jon and expressed how afraid she was ("I told him—I was trembling")—was like a "switch that changed everything." He was able to comfort and soothe her, and they were then able to talk about what happened and be close. She experienced this as a "miracle." She continued, "His armor disappeared and he was soft." Jon agreed that seeing her fear "turned off" his anxiety and evoked the desire to care for and protect her. They also spoke of how their actions here went against all their cultural training to never reveal weakness to another. We spoke of the power of being able to express vulnerabilities and pull your partner closer.

I then validated their ability to deal in a new way with their attachment fears and to exit from their usual cycle. We articulated how a very brief incident—a single brushstroke—had become a whole picture, expanded as it was by their anxieties, their vigilance for danger signs, and their past "stuckness" in the negative cycle. I also heightened and validated their ability to move out of this cycle and reach for each other in a way that created connection. The couple agreed to continue to actively build safety in their relationship, to hold each other and confide any moments of connection and of fearfulness that came up during the day. The growing security and connection between them was tangible and continued to grow over the next few sessions of the consolidation phase.

This couple worked with intensity and focus. The process above occurred in 12 sessions. This is not possible with every couple; some couples need to go at a slower and more diffused pace. They were on the edge of a precipice in their relationship, and this was very motivating. His depression and job issues heightened the marital issues, but also heightened their motivation to deal with them. This couple was also interesting because they came from a very traditional and authoritarian culture where the values were antithetical to those implicit in the creation of secure attachment, and this had to be recognized and worked with in therapy. Although secure attachment was unfamiliar territory (except for Beatrice's relationship with her grandmother), they described themselves as accessible and responsive to their own children, and their own attachment longings and fears, wired in by evolution, were still accessible as a guide in the renewal of their own relationship. Jon's depression also improved. The above session is a particularly good example of a very focused session and of the use of enactments in change events in EFT.

EPILOGUE

The first edition of this book was written in the hope that it would "contribute to the evolving field of marital and family therapy." And indeed this field has evolved; the utilization of couple interventions, in particular, has increased enormously in the last decade (Johnson & Lebow, 2000). In the seven years since that first edition, EFT has also evolved. It has become better known and has continued to develop and to be applied to more diverse populations. It has also, I believe, contributed to the field. EFT is now included in the professional exams of many mental heath disciplines and has become more and more an accepted part of the mainstream in couple therapy. In part, this is because couple and family therapy have changed and become more consonant with the experiential philosophy of EFT. The couple therapy field has become more collaborative, and it has also become more open to working with emotion and to the growing research on adult love and attachment. The field has also become more integrative (Lebow, 1997), so that a systemic perspective is no longer seen as necessarily excluding a focus on inner experience.

EFT has also entered the mainstream of the couple therapy field because this field has begun to embrace research and the need to show empirical support for interventions, rather than to see empiricism as a modernist enemy that must always be resisted. In the discipline of understanding and repairing complex family relationships, we need all the help we can garner from case studies, clinical observation, and research studies that focus on the process of change and the impact of specifically described interventions. This field has, of necessity, begun to embrace and reconcile both art and empiricism (Johnson, 2003d).

This second edition, like the first, was written for novice therapists, one of whom once told me, "I know how to touch people's emotions, but I don't know what to do with them when I get there." It is again my hope that such therapists will, after reading this book, have a clear sense of how to access and shape emotions, and how to use them in enactments to change key patterns of interaction in intimate relationships. This book was also written for more seasoned therapists, who hopefully will find that EFT will hone and refine their own wisdom and enhance their interventions. This book hopefully speaks to the therapist who sees therapy as an art, as well as the therapist who sees therapy as a science.

Like the field of couple and family therapy, and our understanding and study of attachment relationships, EFT and EFFT are still growing and evolving. Two very exciting growth points in EFT are the continued study of the process of change and the application of EFT to new and diverse populations. It has been the dream of couple and family therapists since the field began to be able to describe change processes and events, show that they significantly impact key relationship variables, and then to be able to state exactly what the therapist does to create this change. We are finally getting there.

The application of interventions to different populations is also key to the growth of the field. EFT is being used in clinical practice with and studied in relation to many different kinds of couples—for example, older couples, gay couples, couples struggling with cancer or chronic illness, and couples struggling with PTSD and with depression. EFT is also taught and used across different cultures, including Finland, Australia, and Taiwan and China. Such diversity of application is possible perhaps because this approach addresses universals such as emotion and the bonds of attachment, and because the method of intervention is respectful and collaborative. It can then be easily adjusted to take account of individual differences. In relation to this, it is interesting to note that in the epilogue of the first edition I stressed the power of validation as an intervention and the fact that to be seen and affirmed, first by the therapist, and then by one's partner, is often a transforming change event in and of itself. This stance of trust in the client's intentions and abilities and the willingness of the therapist to be a student of, rather than an expert on, partners' construction of their relational experience allows the EFT therapist to adjust to different clients and to different worldviews.

What makes EFT a powerful intervention? The two key elements that were definitely present, but less articulated and understood when EFT was first formulated in 1982, are the focus on emotional experience and on attachment. To me, it has always made ultimate sense that in a therapy modality focused on the most powerful emotional bonds we ever make, new emotional experience is a primary, direct, and particularly salient route to change. It is often, in fact, the only route to lasting change—to creating differences that make a difference. After 20 years of practice, the power of tapping into emotional processes and using them to shape new interactional positions still surprises and enthralls me. This makes ultimate sense when we consider that emotional signals organize our relational reality and our dance with our most significant other. This focus on emotion is problematic, however, to those who tend to see emotion only as a dangerous or even iatrogenic factor. In general, it seems that the mental health disciplines and therapy practitioners are more and more intrigued by and open to the transforming power of emotion and the positive power and knowledge associated with it. The use of emotion in psychotherapy is also becoming more and more delineated.

The area of adult attachment is the area where the most transforming growth has taken place in the last decade. This growth in conceptualization and in empirical support has taken adult attachment from the margins of psychology into a front-and-center position. This growth has, to a greater and greater extent, offered the couple and family therapist a map to love and belonging that can potentiate intervention (Erdman & Caffery, 2003; Johnson & Whiffen, 2003). The power of EFT is not only that it engages people and engages their emotions; it is also that it focuses on the dynamic of bonding and the creation of more secure bonds, bonds that enhance individual growth, coping, and health, and create stable, resilient families. In a culture obsessed with the individual, a perspective that emphasizes that the dangers of isolation and our need for significant others can, like feminist models that take the same view, be seen as subversive. Whatever the political ramifications, this new understanding of love will, I believe, shape the field of couple and family therapy in years to come and continue to guide the EFT therapist toward interventions of more and more specificity and more and more potency.

REFERENCES

Ainsworth, M. D. S., Blehar, M. C., Waters, E., & Wall, S. (1978). *Patterns of attachment: A study of the Strange Situation.* Hillsdale, NJ: Erlbaum.

Alexander, F. (1948). *Fundamentals of psychoanalysis.* New York: Norton.

Alexander, J. F., Holtzworth-Munroe, A., & Jameson, P. (1994). The process and outcome of marital and family therapy: Research review and evaluation. In A. Bergin and S. Garfield (Eds.), *Handbook of psychotherapy and behavior change* (pp. 595–607). New York: Wiley.

Alexander, P. C. (1993). Application of attachment theory to the study of sexual abuse. *Journal of Consulting and Clinical Psychology, 60,* 185–195.

Anderson, H. (1997). *Conversation, language and possibilities.* New York: Basic Books.

Armstrong, J. G., & Roth, D. M. (1989). Attachment and separation difficulties: A preliminary investigation. *International Journal of Eating Disorders, 8,* 141–155.

Arnold, M. B. (1960). *Emotion and personality.* New York: Columbia Press.

Baker Miller, J., & Pierce Stiver, I. (1997). *The healing connection: How women form relationships in therapy and in life.* Boston: Beacon Press.

Bartholomew, K., & Horowitz, L. (1991). Attachment styles among young adults. *Journal of Personality and Social Psychology, 61,* 226–244.

Baucom, D., Shoham, V., Mueser, K., Daiuto, A., & Stickle, T. (1998). Empirically supported couple and family interventions for marital distress and adult mental health problems. *Journal of Consulting and Clinical Psychology, 66,* 53–88.

Berscheid, E. (1999). The greening of relationship science. *American Psychologist, 54,* 260–266.

Bertalanffy, L. (1968). *General system theory.* New York: George Braziller.

Beutler, L. (2002). The dodo bird is extinct. *Clinical Psychology: Science and Practice, 9,* 30–34.

Bograd, M., & Mederos, F. (1999). Battering and couples therapy: Universal screening and selection of treatment modality. *Journal of Marital and Family Therapy, 25,* 291–312.

Bohart, A. C., & Greenberg, L. S. (1997) Empathy reconsidered: New directions in psychotherapy. Washington, DC: APA Press.

Bordin, E. (1994). Theory and research on the therapeutic working alliance: New directions. In A. O. Horvath & L. S. Greenberg (Eds.), *The working alliance: Theory research and practice* (pp. 13–37). New York: Wiley.

Bowlby, J. (1969). *Attachment and loss: Vol. 1. Attachment.* New York: Basic Books.

Bowlby, J. (1973). *Attachment and loss: Vol. 2. Separation.* New York: Basic Books.

Bowlby, J. (1979). *The making and breaking of affectional bonds.* London: Tavistock.

Bowlby, J. (1980). *Attachment and loss: Vol. 3. Loss.* New York: Basic Books.

Bowlby, J. (1988). *A secure base.* New York: Basic Books.

Bradley, B., & Furrow, J. (2004). Toward a mini-theory of the blamer softening event: Tracking the moment by moment process. *Journal of Marital and Family Therapy, 30,* 233–246.

Bradley, J. M., & Palmer, G. (2003). Attachment in later life: Implications for intervention with older adults. In S. M. Johnson & V. Whiffen (Eds.), *Attachment processes in couple and family therapy* (pp. 281–299). New York: Guilford Press.

Brennen, K. A., & Shaver, P. R. (1995). Dimensions of adult attachment, affect regulation and romantic relationship functioning. *Personality and Social Psychology Bulletin, 21,* 267–283.

Bretherton, I. (1990). Open communication and internal working models: Their role in the development of attachment relationships. In R. Dienstbier and R. Thompson (Eds.), *Socioemotional Development: Nebraska Symposium on Motivation* (pp. 57–114). Lincoln: University of Nebraska Press.

Bretherton, I., & Munholland, K. A. (1999). Internal working models in attachment relationships. In J. Cassidy & P. Shaver (Eds.), *Handbook of attachment: Theory, research and clinical applications* (pp. 89–111). New York: Guilford Press.

Bruner, J. (1986). *Actual minds, possible worlds.* Cambridge, MA: Harvard University Press.

Bruner, J. (1990). *Acts of meaning.* Cambridge, MA: Harvard University Press.

Burman, B., & Margolin, G. (1992). Analysis of the association between marital relationships and health problems: An interactional perspective. *Psychological Bulletin, 112,* 39–63.

Cain, D. (2002). Defining characteristics, history and evolution of humanistic psychotherapies. In D. Cain & J. Seeman (Eds.), *Humanistic psychotherapies* (pp. 3–54). Washington, DC: APA Press.

Cain, D., & Seeman, J. (2002). *Humanistic psychotherapies.* Washington, DC: APA Press.

Chang, J. (1993). Commentary. In S. Gilligan & R. Price (Eds.), *Therapeutic conversations* (pp. 304–306). New York: Norton.

Christensen, A., & Heavey, C. L. (1990). Gender and social structure in the demand/withdraw pattern of marital conflict. *Journal of Personality and Social Psychology, 59,* 73–81.

Clothier, P., Manion, I., Gordon Walker, J., & Johnson, S. (2001). Emotionally focused interventions for couples with chronically ill children: A two year follow-up. *Journal of Marital and Family Therapy, 28,* 391–399.

Cohen, N. J., Muir, E., & Lojkasek, M. (2003). The first couple: Using Wait, Watch and Wonder to change troubled infant-mother relationships. In S. M. Johnson & V. Whiffen (Eds.), *Attachment processes in couple and family therapy* (pp. 215–233). New York: Guilford Press.

Collins, N.,& Read, S. (1994). Cognitive representations of attachment: The structure and function of working models. In

K. Bartholomew & D. Perlman (Eds.), *Attachment processes in adulthood* (pp. 53–92). London, PA: Jessica Kingsley.

Coop Gordon, K., Baucom, D. S., Snyder, D. K. (2000). The use of forgiveness in marital therapy. In M. McCullough, K. I. Pargament, & C. E. Thoresen (Eds.), *Forgiveness: Theory, research and practice* (pp. 203–227). New York: Guilford Press.

Cummings, E. M., & Davis, P. (1994). *Children and marital conflict.* New York: Guilford Press.

Damasio, A. R. (1994). *Decartes' error: Emotion, reason and the human brain.* New York: Putnam.

Dandeneau, M., & Johnson, S. M. (1994). Facilitating intimacy: A comparative outcome study of emotionally focused and cognitive interventions. *Journal of Marital and Family Therapy, 20,* 17–33.

Davila, J. (2001). Paths to unhappiness: Overlapping courses of depression and romantic dysfunciton. In S. R. H. Beach (Ed.), *Marital and family processes in depression: A scientific foundation for clinical practice* (pp. 71–87). Washington, DC: APA Press.

Davila, J., Karney, B., & Bradbury, T. N. (1999). Attachment change processes in the early years of marriage. *Journal of Personality and Social Psychology, 76,* 783–802.

Dessaulles, A., Johnson, S. M., & Denton, W. H. (2003). Emotion focused therapy for couples in the treatment of depression: A pilot study. *American Journal of Family Therapy, 31,* 345–353.

Diamond, G. S., & Stern, R. (2003). Attachment based family therapy for depressed adolescents: Repairing attachment failures. In S. M. Johnson & V. Whiffen (Eds.), *Attachment processes in couple and family therapy* (pp. 191–214). New York: Guilford Press.

Dimidjian, S., Martell, C. R., & Christensen, A. (2002). Integrative behavioral couple therapy. A. S. Gurman & N. S. Jacobson (Eds.), *Clinical handbook of couple therapy* (pp. 251–280). New York: Guilford Press.

Douherty, W. J. (2001). *Take back your marriage.* New York: Guilford Press.

Dunn, R. L., & Schwebel, A. I. (1995). Meta-analytic review of marital therapy outcome research. *Journal of Family Psychology, 9,* 58–68.

Erdman, P., & Caffery, T. (Eds.) (2002). *Attachment and family systems: Conceptual, empirical and therapeutic relatedness.* New York: Brunner-Routledge.

Ekman, P. (1992). An argument for basic emotions. *Cognition and Emotion, 6,* 169–200.

Ekman, P., & Friesen, W. (1975). *Unmasking the face.* Englewood Cliffs, NJ: Prentice Hall.

Elliott, R. (1984). A discovery oriented approach to significant events in psychotherapy: Interpersonal process recall and comprehensive process analysis. In L. Rice and L. S. Greenberg (Eds.), Patterns of change (pp. 249–286). New York: Guilford Press.

Elliot, R. (2002). The effectiveness of humanistic therapies: A meta-analysis. In D. Cain & Seeman, J. (Eds.), *Humanistic psychotherapies: Handbook of research and practice* (pp. 57–82). Washington, DC: APA Press.

Feeney, J. A. (1994). Attachment style, communication patterns and satisfaction across the life cycle of marriage. *Personal Relationships, 4,* 333–348.

Feeney, J. A. (1999). Adult romantic attachment and couple relationships. In J. Cassidy & P. Shaver (Eds.), *Handbook of attachment* (pp. 355–377). New York: Guilford Press.

Fincham, F., & Beach, S. (1999). Conflict in marriage. *Annual Review of Psychology, 50,* 47–78.

Fishbane, M. (2001). Relational narratives of the self. *Family Process, 40,* 273–291.

Fisher, L., Nakell, L. L., Terry Howard, E., & Ransom, D. C. (1992). The California Family Health Project: III. *Family Emotion Management and Adult Health Family Process, 31,* 269–287.

Fonagy, P., & Target, M. (1997) Attachment and reflective function: Their role in self-organization. *Development and Psychopathology, 9,* 679–700.

Fraley, C. R., & Waller, N. G. (1998). Adult attachment patterns: A test of the typographical model. In J. A. Simpson & W. S. Rholes (Eds.), *Attachment theory and close relationships* (pp. 77–114). New York: Guilford Press.

Friedman, S. (1992). Constructing solutions (stories) in brief family therapy. In S. H. Budman, M. F. Hoyt, & S. Friedman (Eds.), *The first session in brief therapy* (pp. 282–305). New York: Guilford Press.

Friedman, S., & Langer, M. T. (1991). *Expanding therapeutic possibilities.* Lexington, MA: Lexington Books.

Frijda, N. H. (1986). *The emotions.* Cambridge, England: Cambridge University Press.

Gendlin, E. T. (1996). *Focusing oriented psychotherapy.* New York: Guilford Press.

Gottman, J. M. (1979). *Marital interaction: Experimental investigations.* New York: Academic Press.

Gottman, J. M. (1991). Predicting the longitudinal course of marriages. *Journal of Marital and Family Therapy, 17,* 3–7.

Gottman, J. M. (1994). An agenda for marital therapy. In S. M. Johnson & L. S. Greenberg (Eds.), *The heart of the matter: Perspectives on emotion in marital therapy* (pp. 256–296). New York: Brunner-Mazel.

Gottman, J. M. (1999). *The seven principles for making marriage work.* New York: Crown Publishers.

Green, R., & Werner, P. D. (1996). Intrusiveness and closeness-caregiving: Rethinking the concept of family enmeshment. *Family Process, 35,* 115–136.

Greenberg, L. S., Ford, C., Alden, L., & Johnson, S. M. (1993). Change processes in emotionally focused therapy. *Journal of Consulting and Clinical Psychology, 61,* 78–84.

Greenberg, L. S., & Safran, J. D. (1987). *Emotion in psychotherapy: Affect and cognition in the process of change.* New York: Guilford Press.

Greenberg, L. S., James, P., & Conry, R. (1988). Reviewed change processes in emotionally focused couples therapy. *Family Psychology, 2,* 4–23.

Greenberg, L. S., & Johnson, S. (1985). Emotionally focused therapy: An affective systemic approach. In N. S. Jacobson & A. S. Gurman (Eds.), *Handbook of clinical and marital therapy.* New York: Guilford Press.

Greenberg, L. S., & Johnson, S. M. (1988). *Emotionally focused therapy for couples.* New York: Guilford Press.

Greenberg, L. S., Korman, L. M., & Paivio, S. C. (2002). Emotion in humanistic psychotherapy. In D. Cain & J. Seeman (Eds.), *Humanistic psychotherapies: Handbook of research and practice* (pp. 499–530). Washington, DC: APA Press.

Greenberg, L., Rice, L., & Elliott, H. (1993). *Facilitating emotional change: The moment-by-moment process.* New York: Guilford Press.

Gross, J. L. & Levenson, R. W. (1993). Emotional suppression. Journal of Personality and Social Psychology, 64, 970–986.

Guerney, B. G. (1994). The role of emotion in relationship enhancement marital/family therapy. In S. M. Johnson & L. S. Greenberg (Eds.), *The heart of the matter: Perspectives on emotion in marital therapy* (pp. 124–150). New York: Brunner-Mazel.

Guidano, V. F. (1991). Affective change events in a cognitive therapy system approach. In J. D. Safran & L. S. Greenberg (Eds.), *Emotion, psychotherapy, and change* (pp. 50–82). New York: Guilford Press.

Haddock, S., Schindler Zimmerman, T., & MacPhee, D. (2000). The power equity guide: Attending to gender in family therapy. *Journal of Marital and Family Therapy, 26*, 153–170.

Hazan, C., & Shaver, P. (1987). Conceptualizing romantic love as an attachment process. *Journal of Personality and Social Psychology, 52*, 511–524.

Hazan, C., & Shaver, P. (1994). Attachment as an organizational framework for research on close relationships: Target article. *Psychological Inquiry, 5*, 1–22.

Hazan, C., & Zeifman, D. (1999). Pair bonds as attachments: Evaluating the evidence. In J. Cassidy & P. Shaver (Eds.), *Handbook of attachment* (pp. 336–354). New York: Guilford Press.

Herman, J. L. (1992). *Trauma and recovery*. New York: Basic Books.

Hesse, E. (1999). The adult attachment interview. In J. Cassidy & P. Shaver (Eds.), *Handbook of attachment* (pp. 395–433). New York: Guilford Press.

Hetherington, M. E., & Kelly, J. (2001). *For better or for worse: Divorce reconsidered*. New York: Norton.

Hofer, M. A. (1984). Relationships as regulators: A psychobiologic perspective on bereavement. *Psychosomatic Medicine, 46*, 183–197.

Hoffman, L. (1981). *Foundations of family therapy*. New York: Basic Books.

Holmes, J. (1996). *Attachment, intimacy and autonomy: Using attachment theory in adult psychotherapy*. Northdale, NJ: Jason Aronson.

Huston, T. L., Caughlin, J. P., Houts, R. M., Smith, S. E., & George, L. J. (2001). The connubial crucible: Newlywed years as predictors of marital delight, distress and divorce. *Journal of Personality and Social Psychology, 80,* 237–252.

Izard, C. E. (1977) *Human emotions.* New York: Plenum Press.

Izard, C. E. (1992). Basic emotions, relations among emotions and emotion-cognition relations. *Psychological Review, 99,* 561–64

Izard, C., & Youngstrom E. A. (1996). The activation and regulation of fear. In D. A. Hope (Ed.), *Perspectives on anxiety, panic and fear: current theory and research in motivation* (pp.1–59). Lincoln: University of Nebraska Press.

Jacobson, N. S., Christensen, A., Prince, S., Cordova, J., & Eldridge, K. (2000). Integrative behavioral couples therapy. *Journal of Consulting and Clinical Psychology, 68,* 351–355.

Jacobson, N. S., & Addis, M. E. (1993). Research on couples and couples therapy: What do we know? Where are we going? *Journal of Consulting and Clinical Psychology, 61,* 85–93.

Jacobson, N. S., Follette, W. C., & Pagel, M. (1986). Predicting who will benefit from behavioral marital therapy. *Journal of Consulting and Clinical Psychology, 54,* 4, 518–522.

Jacobson, N. S., Holtzworth-Munroe, A., & Schmaling, K. B. (1989). Marital therapy and spouse involvement in the treatment of depression, agoraphobia, and alcoholism. *Journal of Consulting and Clinical Psychology, 57,* 5–10.

Jacobson, N. S., & Margolin, G. (1979). *Marital therapy: Strategies based on social learning and behavior exchange principles.* New York: Brunner-Mazel.

James, P. (1991). Effects of a communication training component added to an emotionally focused couples therapy. *Journal of Marital and Family Therapy, 17,* 263–276.

Johnson, M. D., & Bradbury, T. N. (1999). Marital satisfaction and topographical assessment of marital interaction: A longitudinal analysis of newlywed couples. *Personal Relationships, 6,* 19–40.

Johnson, S. M. (1993). *Healing broken bonds.* A marital therapy training video. Ottawa Couple & Family Institute, #201, 1869 Carling Ave., Ottawa, Canada, K2A 1E6.

Johnson, S. M. (1998). Listening to the music: Emotion as a natural part of systems theory. *Journal of Systemic Therapies, 17,* 1–17. Guilford Press.

Johnson, S. M. (2003). The Revolution in couple therapy: A practitioner-scientist perspective. *Journal of Marital and Family Therapy, 29,* 365–384.

Johnson, S. M. (2003b) Attachment theory: A guide for couples therapy. In S. M. Johnson & V. Whiffen (Eds.), *Attachment processes in couple and family therapy* (pp. 103–123). New York: Guilford Press.

Johnson, S. M. (2003c). Introduction to attachment: A therapist's guide to primary relationships and their renewal. In S. M. Johnson & V. Whiffen (Eds.), *Attachment processes in couple and family therapy* (pp. 3–17). New York: Guilford Press.

Johnson, S. M. (2003d) Emotionally Focused Therapy: Empiricism and art. In T. L. Sexton, G. Weeks, & M. Robbins (Eds.), Handbook of family therapy (pp. 263–280). New York: Brunner-Routledge.

Johnson, S. M. (2004). Attachment theory: A guide for healing couple relationships. In J. Simpson & S. Rholes (Eds.), *Adult attachment: New directions and emerging issues*. New York: Guilford Press.

Johnson, S. M., Bradley, B., Furrow, J., Lee, A., Palmer, G., & Tilley, D. (in press). *The emotionally focused couples therapy workbook*. New York Brunner-Routledge.

Johnson, S. M., & Boisvert, C. (2002). Treating couples and families from the humanistic perspective: More than symptoms—more than solutions. In D. Cain & J. Seeman (Eds.), *Humanistic psychotherapies* (pp. 309–338). Washington, DC: APA Press.

Johnson, S. M., & Greenberg, L. S. (1985). The differential effects of experiential and problem solving interventions in resolving marital conflicts. *Journal of Consulting and Clinical Psychology, 53*, 175–184.

Johnson, S. M., & Greenberg, L. S. (1988). Relating process to outcome in marital therapy. *Journal of Marital and Family Therapy, 14*, 175–184.

Johnson, S. M., & Greenberg, L. S. (1992). Emotionally focused therapy: Restructuring attachment. In S. H. Budman, M. Hoyt, and S. Friedman (Eds.), *The first session in brief therapy* (pp. 204–224). New York: Guilford Press.

Johnson, S. M., & Greenberg, L. S. (Eds.) (1994). *The heart of the matter: Perspectives on emotion in marital therapy*. New York: Brunner-Mazel.

Johnson, S. M., & Denton, W. (2002). Emotionally focused couples therapy: Creating secure connections. In A. S.

Gurman and N. Jacobson (Eds.), *Clinical handbook of marital therapy*, 3rd edition (pp. 221–250).

Johnson, S. M., Hunsley, J., Greenberg, L. S., & Schlinder, D. (1999). Emotionally focused couples therapy: Status and challenges. *Clinical Psychology Science and Practice, 6*, 67–79.

Johnson, S. M., & Lee, A. (2000). Emotionally focused family therapy: Restructuring attachment. In C. E. Bailey (Ed.), *Children in therapy: Using the family as a resource* (pp. 112–136). New York: Guilford Press.

Johnson, S. M., Maddeaux, C., & Blouin, J. (1998). Emotionally focused family therapy for bulimia: Changing attachment patterns. *Psychotherapy, 35*, 238–247.

Johnson, S. M., & Talitman, E. (1996). Predictors of success in emotionally focused couple therapy. *Journal of Marital and Family Therapy, 23*, 135–152.

Johnson, S. M., & Whiffen, V. (2003). *Attachment processes in couple and family therapy.* New York: Guilford Press.

Jordan, J. V., Kaplan, A. G., Miller, J. B., Stiver, I. P., & Surrey, J. L. (1991). *Women's growth in connection: Writings from the Stone Centre.* New York: Guilford Press.

Kempler, W. (1981). *Experiential psychotherapy within families.* New York: Brunner-Mazel.

Kerner, K., & Jacobson, N. S. (1994). Emotion and behavioral couple therapy. In S. M. Johnson & L. S. Greenberg (Eds.), *The heart of the matter: Perspectives on emotion in marital therapy* (pp. 207–226). New York: Brunner-Mazel.

Kiecolt-Glaser, J. K., Fisher, L. D., Ogrocki, P., Stout, J. C., Speicher, C. E., & Glaser, R. (1987). Marital quality; marital disruption, and immune function. *Psychosomatic Medicine, 49*, 13–34.

Kiecolt-Glaser, J. K., & Newton, T. L. (2001). Marriage & Health: His and hers. *Psychological Bulletin, 127*, 472–503.

Kobak, R., & Duemmler, S. (1994). Attachment and conversation: Towards a discourse analysis of adolescent and adult security. In K. Bartholomew & D. Perlman (Eds.), *Attachment processes in adulthood* (pp. 121–150). London, PA: Jessica Kingsley.

Kobak, R., Ruckdeschel, K., & Hazan, C. (1994). From symptom to signal: An attachment view of emotion in marital therapy. In S. M. Johnson & L. S. Greenberg (Eds.), *The heart of the matter: Perspectives on emotion in marital therapy* (pp. 46–74). New York: Brunner-Mazel.

Kowal, J., Johnson, S. M. & Lee, A. (2003). Chronic illness in couples: A case for emotionally focused therapy. *Journal of Marital and Family Therapy, 29,* 299–310.

Krause, I. (1993). Family therapy and anthropology: A case for emotions. *Journal of Family Therapy, 15,* 35–56.

Lazarus, R. S., & Lazarus, B. N. (1994). *Passion and reason.* New York: Oxford University Press.

Lebow, J. (1997). The integrative revolution in couple and family therapy. *Family Process, 36,* 1–17.

Lewis, J. M., Beavers, W. R., Gossett, J. T., & Phillips, V. A. (1976). *No single thread: Psychological health in families.* New York: Brunner-Mazel.

Lewis, M., & Haviland-Jones, J. M. (2000). *Handbook of emotions,* 2nd edition. New York: Guilford Press.

Liddle, H., Dakof, G., & Diamond, G. (1991). Multidimensional family therapy with adolescent substance abuse. In E. Kaufman & P. Kaufman (Eds.), *Family therapy with drug and alcohol abuse* (pp. 120–178). Boston: Allyn & Bacon.

Lussier, Y., Sabourin, S., & Turgeon, C. (1997) Coping strategies as moderators of the relationship between attachment and marital adjustment. *Journal of Social and Personal Relationships, 14,* 777–791.

McFarlane, A. C., & van der Kolk, B. (1996). Trauma and its challenge to society. In B. A. van der Kolk, A. C. Mcfarlane, & L. Weisaeth (Eds.), *Traumatic stress* (pp. 211–215). New York: Guilford Press.

Mackay, S. K. (1996). Nurturance: A neglected dimension in family therapy with adolescents. *Journal of Marital and Family Therapy, 22,* 489–508.

Mahoney, M. J. (1991). *Human change processes: The scientific foundations of psychotherapy.* New York: Basic Books.

Mahoney, M. (1998). Essential themes in the training of psychotherapists. *Psychotherapy in Private Practice, 17,* 43–59.

Main, M., & Goldwyn, R. (in press). Interview-based adult attachment classifications: Related to infant-mother and infant-father attachment developmental psychology.

Makinen, J. (2004). *Treating attachment injuries: Process and outcome.* Doctoral dissertation in clinical psychology, University of Ottawa, Ontario, Canada.

Merkel, W. T., & Searight, H. R. (1992). Why families are not like swamps, solar systems or thermostats: Some limits of systems theory as applied to family therapy. *Contemporary Family Therapy, 14,* 33–50.

Mikulincer, M. (1995). Attachment style and the mental representation of self. *Journal of Personality and Social Psychology, 69,* 1203–1215.

Mikulincer, M. (1997) Adult attachment style and information processing: Individual differences in curiosity and cognitive closure. *Journal of Personality and Social Psychology, 72,* 1217–1230.

Mikulincer, M. (1998). Attachment working models and the sense of trust: An exploration of interaction goals and affect regulation. *Journal of Personality and Social Psychology, 74,* 1209–1224.

Mikulincer, M., Florian, V., & Wesler, A. (1993). Attachment styles, coping strategies and post traumatic psychological distress. *Journal of Personality and Social Psychology, 64,* 817–826.

Millon, T. (1994). Personality disorders and the 5 factor model of personality. In P. Costa & A. Widiger (Eds.), *Personality disorders* (pp 279–301). Washington, DC: APA Press.

Minuchin, S., & Fishman, H. C. (1981). *Family therapy techniques.* Cambridge, MA: Harvard University Press.

Minuchin, S., & Nichols, M. P. (1993). *Family healing.* New York: The Free Press.

Moretti, M. M., & Holland, R. (2003). The journey of adolescence: Transitions in self within the context of attachment relationships. In S. M. Johnson & V. Whiffen (Eds.), *Attachment processes in couple and family therapy* (pp. 234–257). New York: Guilford Press.

Nichols, M. (1987) *The self in the system.* New York. Brunner-Mazel.

O'Hanlon, B., & Wilk, J. (1987). *Shifting contexts: The generation of effective psychotherapy.* New York: Guilford Press.

Pennebaker, J. W. (1990). *Opening up: The healing power of confiding in others.* New York: Avon Books.

Pierce, R. A. (1994). Helping couples make authentic emotional contact. In S. M. Johnson & L. S. Greenberg, *The heart of the matter: Perspectives on emotion in marital therapy* (pp. 207–226). (pp. 75–107). New York: Brunner-Mazel.

Plutchik, R. (2000). Emotions in the practice of psychotherapy. Washington, DC: APA Press.

Putnam, R. D. (2000). Bowling alone: The collapse and revival of American community. New York: Simon & Schuster.

Roberts, L. J., & Krokoff, L. J. (1990). A time-series analysis of withdrawal, hostility, and displeasure in satisfied and dissatisfied marriages. *Journal of Marriage and the Family*, *52*, 95–105.

Roberts, L. J., & Greenberg, D. R. (2002). Observational "windows" to intimacy processes in marriage. In P. Noller & J. A. Feeney (Eds.), *Understanding marriage: Developments in the study of marital interaction* (pp. 118–149). New York: Cambridge University Press.

Roberts, T. W. (1992). Sexual attraction and romantic love: Forgotten variables in marital therapy. *Journal of Marital and Family Therapy*, *18*, 357–364.

Rogers, C. (1951). *Client-centered therapy*. Boston: Houghton-Mifflin.

Rogers, C. (1961). *On becoming a person*. Boston: Houghton-Mifflin.

Rogers, C. (1975). Empathy: An unappreciated way of being. *The Counseling Psychologist*, *5*, 2–10.

Ruvolo, A. P., & Jobson Brennen, C. (1997). What's love got to do with it? Close relationships and perceived growth. *Personality and Social Psychology Bulletin*, *23*, 814–823.

Sable, P. (2000). *Attachment and adult psychotherapy*. Northdale, NJ: Jason Aronson.

Salovey, P., Hsee, C., & Mayer, J. D. (1993). Emotional intelligence and the self regulation of affect. In D. Wegner & J. W. Pennebaker (Eds.), *Handbook of mental control*. Englewood Cliffs, NJ: Prentice Hall.

Schore, A. (1994). *Affect regulation and the organization of self*. Hillsdale, NJ: Erlbaum.

Shaver, P., & Clarke, C. L. (1994). The psychodynamics of adult romantic attachment. In J. Masling & R. Borstein (Eds.), *Empirical perspectives on object relations theory* (pp. 105–156). Washington, DC: American Psychological Association.

Shaver, P., Hazan, C., & Bradshaw, D. (1988). Love as attachment: The integration of three behavioral systems. In R. J. Pope (Ed.), *On love and loving* (pp. 68–99).

Shaver, P. R., & Mikulincer, M.(2002). Attachment-related psychodynamics. *Attachment and Human Development*, *4*,133–161.

Siegel, D. J. (1999) *The developing mind: How relationships and the brain interact to shape who we are.* New York: Guilford Press.

Siegel, D., & Hartzell, M. (2003). *Parenting from the inside out.* New York: Penguin Putnam.

Simpson, J. A., Rholes, W. S., & Nelligan, J. S. (1992). Support seeking and support giving within couples in an anxiety provoking situation: The role of attachment styles. *Journal of Personality and Social Psychology, 62,* 434–446.

Snyder, D. K., & Wills, R. M. (1989). Behavioral versus insight oriented marital therapy: Effects on individual and interspousal functioning. *Journal of Consulting and Clinical Psychology, 57,* 39–46.

Spanier, G. (1976). Measuring dyadic adjustment. *Journal of Marriage and Family, 13,* 113–126.

Stern, D. N. (1985). *The interpersonal world of the infant.* New York: Basic Books.

Sternberg, R. J., & Barnes, M. L. (1988). The psychology of love. New Haven, CT: Yale University Press.

Taylor, S. E. (2002). *The tending instinct.* New York: Times Books: Holt & Co.

Taylor, S. E., Cousino Klein, L., Lewis, B. P., Gruenewald, T., Regan, A., Gurung, R., & Updegraff, J. A. (2000). Biobehavioral responses to stress in females: Tend and befriend, not fight and flight. *Psychological Review, 107,* 411–429.

Tomkins, S. (1991). *Affect, imagery and consciousness.* New York: Springer.

Twenge, J. M. (2000). The age of anxiety? Birth cohort change in anxiety and neuroticism. *Journal of Personality and Social Psychology, 79,* 1007–1021.

Uchino, B. J., Cacioppo, J., & Kiecolt-Glaser, J. (1996). The relationship between social support and psychological processes. *Psychological Bulletin, 119,* 488–531.

Vanaerschot, G. (2001). Empathic resonance as a source of experiencing enhancing interventions. In A. Bohart & L. S. Greenberg (Eds.), *Empathy reconsidered* (pp. 141–166). Washington, D.C.: APA Press.

Van der Kolk, B. A., McFarlane, A. C., & Weisaeth, L. (Eds.), *Traumatic stress.* New York: Guilford Press.

van Ijzendoorn, M. H., & Sagi, A. (1999). Cross cultural patterns of attachment: Universal and contextual dimensions. In J. Cassidy & P. Shaver (Eds.), *Handbook of attachment: Theory, research and clinical applications* (pp. 713–734). New York: Guilford Press.

Vatcher, C. A. & Bogo, M. (2001). The feminist/emotionally focused practice model: An integrated approach for couples therapy. *Journal of Marital and Family Therapy, 27*, 69–84.

Walker, J., Johnson, S., Manion, I., & Cloutier, P. (1995). An emotionally focused marital intervention for couples with chronically ill children. Submitted to *Journal of Consulting and Clinical Psychology*.

Warner, M. S. (1997) Does empathy cure? A theoretical consideration of empathy, processing and personal narrative. In A. Bohart & L. S. Greenberg (Eds.), *Empathy reconsidered* (pp. 125–140). Washington, DC: APA Press.

Watson, J. C. (2002). Revisioning empathy. In D. Cain & J. Seeman (Eds.), *Humanistic psychotherapies: Handbook of research and practice* (pp. 445–472). Washington, DC: APA Press.

Watzlawick, P., Weakland, J. H., & Fisch, R. (1974). *Change: Principles of problem formation and problem resolution.* New York: Norton.

Whiffen, V., & Johnson, S. M. (1998). An attachment theory framework for the treatment of childbearing depression. *Clinical Psychology: Science and Practice, 5*, 478–492.

Whisman, M. A. (1999). Martial dissatisfaction and psychiatric disorders: Results from the National Co-morbidity Study. *Journal of Abnormal Psychology, 108*, 701–706.

White, M. (1993). Deconstruction and therapy. In S. Gilligan, and R. Price (Eds.), *Therapeutic conversations* (pp. 22–61). New York: Norton.

White, M., & Epston, D. (1990). *Narrative means to therapeutic ends.* New York: Norton.

Wile, D. (1981). *Couples therapy: A non-traditional approach.* New York: Wiley.

Wile, D (2002). Collaborative couple therapy. In A. S. Gurman & N. S. Jacobson (Eds.), *Clinical handbook of couple therapy* (pp. 281–307). New York: Guilford Press.

Wile, D. B. (1994). The ego-analytic approach to emotion in couples therapy. In S. M. Johnson, and L. S. Greenberg, *The heart of the matter: Perspectives on emotion in marital therapy* (pp. 27–45). New York: Brunner-Mazel.

Worthington, E., & DiBlasio, F. A. (1990). Promoting mutual forgiveness within the fractured relationship. *Psychotherapy*, *27*, 2219–2223.

Yalom, I. D. (1980). *Existential psychotherapy*. New York: Basic Books.

Zimmerman, J. L., & Dickerson, V. C. (1993). Bringing forth the restraining influence of pattern in couples therapy. In S. Gilligan & R. Price (Eds.), *Therapeutic conversations* (pp. 197–214). New York: Norton.

ADDITIONAL READINGS

BOOKS

1. Johnson, S. M. (2004). *The practice of emotionally focused couple therapy: Creating connection*, 2nd edition. New York: Brunner-Routledge.
2. Johnson, S. M. & Whiffen, V. (2003). *Attachment processes in couples and families*. New York: Guilford Press. (Chapters 6, 14, 15, and 16 refer to EFT specifically.)
3. Johnson, S. M. (2002). *Emotionally focused couple therapy with trauma survivors: Strengthening attachment bonds*. New York: Guilford Press.
4. Johnson, S. M. & Greenberg, L. S. (1994). *The heart of the matter: Perspectives on emotion in marital therapy*. New York: Brunner-Mazel.
5. Greenberg, L. S. & Johnson, S. M. (1988). *Emotionally focused therapy for couples*. New York: Guilford Press.

RECENT CHAPTERS

1. Bradley, B. & Johnson, S. M. (in press). Emotionally focused couples therapy: An integrative contemporary approach. In M. Haraway (Ed.), *Handbook of couple therapy*. New York: Wiley.

2. Bradley, B. & Johnson, S. M. (in press). Task analysis of couple and family change events. In D. Sprenkle & F. Piercy (Eds.), *Research methods in family therapy*, 2nd edition. New York: Guilford Press.

3. Johnson, S. M. (in press). An emotionally focused approach to infidelity. In F. Piercy (Ed.), *Handbook on treating infidelity*. Binghamton, NY: Haworth Press.

4. Woolley, S. & Johnson, S. M. (in press). Emotionally focused interventions. In J. Lebow (Ed.), *Handbook of clinical family therapy*. New York: Wiley.

5. Johnson, S. M. (in press). Emotion and the repair of close relationships. In W. Pinsof & T. Patterson (Eds.), *Family psychology: The art of the science*. New York: Oxford University Press.

6. Johnson, S. M. (2004, in press). Attachment theory: A guide for healing couple relationships. In J. Simpson & S. Rholes (Eds.), *Adult attachment: New directions and emerging issues* (pp. 367–387). New York: Guilford Press.

7. Johnson, S. M. (2003). Introduction to attachment: A therapist's guide to primary relationships and their renewal. In S. M. Johnson & V. Whiffen (Eds.), *Attachment processes in couples and families* (pp. 3–17). New York: Guilford Press.

8. Johnson, S. M. (2003). Attachment theory: A guide for couple therapy. In S. M. Johnson & V. Whiffen (Eds.), *Attachment processes in couples and families*, pp. 103–123. New York: Guilford Press.

9. Johnson, S. M. (2004). *Facing the dragon together: Emotionally focused couples therapy with trauma survivors*. In D. Catherall (Ed.), *Stress, trauma and the family*. Washington, DC: APA Press.

10. Johnson, S. M. (2003). Emotionally focused couples therapy: Empiricism and art. In T. Sexton, G. Weeks, & M. Robbins (Eds.), *The handbook of family therapy*. New York: Brunner-Routledge.

11. Johnson, S. M. (2002). Marital problems. In D. Sprenkle (Ed.), *Effectiveness research in marriage and family therapy* (pp. 163–190). Alexandria, VA: American Association for Marriage and Family Therapy.

12. Johnson, S. M. & Makinen, J. (2003). Creating a safe haven and a secure base: Couples therapy as a vital element in the

treatment of post-traumatic stress disorder. In D. Snyder & M. Whisman (Eds.), *Treating difficult couples* (pp. 308–329). New York: Guilford Press.

13. Johnson, S. M. & Denton, W. (2002). Emotionally focused couples therapy: Creating connection. In A. S. Gurman (Ed.), *The clinical handbook of couple therapy*, 3rd edition (pp. 221–250). New York: Guilford Press.

14. Johnson, S. M. (2003). An antidote to post-traumatic stress disorder: The creation of secure attachment. In L. Atkinson & S. Goldberg (Eds.), *Attachment issues in psychopathology and intervention* (pp. 207–228). Mahwah, NJ: Erlbaum.

15. Johnson, S. M. & Best, M. (2002). A systematic approach to restructuring adult attachment: The EFT model of couples therapy. In P. Erdman & T. Caffery (Eds.), *Attachment and family systems: Conceptual, empirical and therapeutic relatedness* (pp. 165–192). New York: Springer.

16. Johnson, S. M. & Lee, A. (2000). Emotionally focused family therapy: Children in therapy. In Everett Bailey (Ed.), *Working with children in family therapy* (pp. 112–116). New York: Guilford Press.

17. Johnson, S. M. & Boisvert, C. (2002). Humanistic couples and family therapy. In D. Kane (Ed.), *Humanistic psychotherapies* (pp. 309–337). Washington, DC: APA Press.

18. Johnson, S. M. & Sims, A. (2000). Creating secure bonds in couples therapy. In T. Levy (Ed.), *Handbook of attachment interventions* (pp. 167–191). New York: Academic Press.

19. Johnson, S. M. (2004). An antidote to post-traumatic stress disorder: The creation of secure attachment. In L. Atkinson & S. Goldberg (Eds.), *Attachment issues in psychopathology and intervention* (pp. 207–228). Mahwah, NJ: Erlbaum.

20. Johnson, S. M. (2000). Emotionally focused couples therapy: Creating a secure bond. In F. M. Dattilio (Ed.), *Comparative treatments in relationship dysfunction* (pp. 163–185). New York: Springer.

21. Johnson, S. M. (1999). Emotionally focused therapy: Straight to the heart. In J. Donovan (Ed.), *Short term couple therapy* (pp. 11–42). New York: Guilford Press.

22. Johnson, S. M. (1998). Emotionally focused interventions: Using the power of emotion. In F. Dattilio (Ed.), *Case studies in couple and family therapy: Systemic and cognitive perspectives* (pp. 450–472). New York: Guilford Press.

23. Johnson, S. M. & Greenberg, L. S. (1995). The emotionally focused approach to problems in adult attachment. In N. S. Jacobson & A. S. Gurman (Eds.), *The clinical handbook of marital therapy*, 2nd edition. New York: Guilford Press.

RECENT ARTICLES

1. Johnson, S. M. (in press). Broken bonds: An emotionally focused approach to infidelity. *Journal of Couple & Family Relationship Therapy*.
2. Knowal, J., Johnson, S., & Lee, A. (2003). Chronic illness in couples: A case for emotionally focused therapy. *Journal of Marital and Family Therapy, 29,* 299–310.
3. Johnson, S. M. (2003). The revolution in couple therapy: A practitioner-scientist perspective. *Journal of Marital and Family Therapy, 29,* 365–384.
4. Clothier, P., Manion, I., Gordon-Walker, J., & Johnson, S. M. (2002). Emotionally focused interventions for couples with chronically ill children: A two-year follow-up. *Journal of Marital and Family Therapy, 28,* 391–399.
5. Dessaulles, A., Johnson, S. M., & Denton, W. (2003). The treatment of clinical depression in the context of marital distress. *American Journal of Family Therapy, 31,* 345–353.
6. Johnson, S. M. (2003). Let us keep emotion at the forefront: A reply to Roberts and Koval. *Journal of Couple and Relationship Therapy, 2,* 15–20. Haworth Press.
7. Palmer, G. & Johnson, S. M. (2002). Becoming an emotionally focused therapist. *Journal of Couple and Relationship Therapy, 1,* No. 3, 1–20. Haworth Press.
8. Johnson, S. M., Makinen, J., & Millikin, J. (2001). Attachment injuries in couples relationships: A new perspective on impasses in couple therapy. *Journal of Marital and Family Therapy, 27,* 145–156.
9. Johnson, S. M. & Lebow, J. (2000). The coming of age of couple therapy: A decade review. *Journal of Marital and Family Therapy, 26,* 9–24.
10. Schwartz, R. & S. M. Johnson. (2000). Does family therapy have emotional intelligence? *Family Process, 39,* 29–34.
11. Johnson, S. M. & Whiffen, V. (1999). Made to measure: Attachment styles in couples therapy. *Clinical Psychology:*

Science & Practice, 6, 366–381. Special edition on individual differences and couples therapy.

12. Johnson, S., Hunsley, J., Greenberg, L., & Schindler, D. (1999). Emotionally focused couples therapy: Status & challenges. *Clinical Psychology: Science & Practice, 6*, 67–79.

13. Johnson, S. (1998). The use of emotion in couples and family therapy. Special edition of the *Journal of Systemic Therapies, 17*, 1–17. New York: Guilford Press.

14. Johnson, S. (1998). Listening to music: Emotion as a natural part of systems theory. Special edition of the *Journal of Systemic Therapies, 17*, 1–17. New York: Guilford Press.

15. Johnson, S., and Williams Keeler, L. (1998). Creating healing relationships for couples dealing with trauma. *Journal of Marital and Family Therapy, 24*, 25–40.

16. Johnson, S., Maddeux C., & Blouin J. (1998). Emotionally focused family therapy for bulimia: Changing attachment patterns. *Psychotherapy: Theory, Research and Practice, 35*, 238–247.

17. Whiffen, V. & Johnson, S. M. (1998). An attachment theory framework for the treatment of childbearing depression. *Clinical Psychology, Science & Practice, 5*, 478–492.

18. Johnson, S. (1997). The biology of love. *Family Therapy Networker*, Sept. 1997, 36–41.

EMPIRICAL SUPPORT FOR THE EFFECTIVENESS OF EFT

1. Johnson, S. M. (2003). The revolution in couples therapy: A practitioner-scientist perspective. *Journal of Marital and Family Therapy, 29*, 365–385.

2. Dessaulles, A., Johnson, S. M., & Denton, W. (2003). Emotion focused therapy for couples in the treatment of depression: A pilot study. *American Journal of Family Therapy, 31*, 345–353.

3. Johnson, S., Hunsley, J., Greenberg, L. & Schindler, D. (1999). Emotionally focused couples therapy: Status & challenges (a meta-analysis). *Clinical Psychology: Science and Practice, 6*, 67–79.

4. Denton, W., et al. (2000). A rationalized trial of emotionally focused therapy for couples. *Journal of Marital and Family Therapy, 26*, pp. 65–78.

5. Clothier, P., Manion, I., Gordon-Walker, J., & Johnson, S. M.
    (2002). An emotionally focused intervention for couples
    with chronically ill children: A two-year follow-up. *Journal
    of Marital and Family Therapy, 28*, 391–398.
6. Johnson, S., Maddeaux, C., & Blouin, J. (1998). Emotionally
    focused family therapy for bulimia: Changing attachment
    patterns. *Psychotherapy: Theory, Research and Practice, 35*,
    238–247.
7. Baucom, D., Shoham, V., Mueser, K., Daiuto, A., & Stickle,
    T. (1998). Empirically supported couple and family
    interventions for marital distress and adult mental health
    problems. *Journal of Consulting and Clinical Psychology, 58*,
    53–88.
8. Talitman, E. & Johnson, S. (1997). Predictors of outcome in
    emotionally focused marital therapy. *Journal of Marital and
    Family Therapy, 23*, 135–152.
9. Gordon-Walker, J., Johnson, S., Manion, I., & Cloutier, P.
    (1996). An emotionally focused marital intervention for
    couples with chronically ill children. *Journal of Consulting
    and Clinical Psychology, 64*, 1029–1036.
10. Dandeneau, M. & Johnson, S. (1994). Facilitating intimacy:
    A comparative outcome study of emotionally focused and
    cognitive interventions. *Journal of Marital and Family
    Therapy, 20*, 17–33.
11. James, P. (1991). Effects of a communication training
    component added to an emotionally focused couples therapy.
    Journal of Marital and Family Therapy, 17, 263–276.
12. Desaulles, A., Johnson, S. M., & Denton, W. (2003).
    Emotionally focused therapy for couples in the treatment of
    depression: A pilot study. *American Journal of Family
    Therapy, 31*, 345–353.
13. Goldman, A. & Greenberg, L. (1989). A comparison of
    systemic and emotionally focused outcome studies. *Journal
    of Marital amd Family Therapy, 15*, 21–28.
14. Johnson, S. & Greenberg, L. (1985). The differential
    effectiveness of experiential and problem solving
    interventions in resolving marital conflict. *Journal of
    Consulting and Clinical Psychology, 53*, 175–184.
15. Johnson, S. & Greenberg, L. (1985). Emotionally focused
    couples therapy: An outcome study. *Journal of Marital and
    Family Therapy, 11*, 313–317.

RECENT ARTICLES ON EFT BY OTHER AUTHORS

1. Bradley, B. & Furrow, J. L. (2004) Toward a mini-theory of the blamer softening event: Tracking the moment by moment process. *Journal of Marital and Family Therapy, 30*, 233–246.

2. Chapters in *Attachment processes in couple and family therapy* (2003). S. Johnson & V. Whiffen (Eds.). Guilford Press: Bradley & Palmer (pp. 281–299). Attachment in later life: Implications for intervention with older adults; Whiffen, V. (pp. 321–341). Adult attachment and childbearing depression; Josephson, G. (pp. 300–320) Using an attachment-based intervention for same sex couples.

3. Dankoski, Mary, D. (2001). Pulling on the heart strings: An emotionally focused approach to family life cycle transitions. *Journal of Marital and Family Therapy, 27*, 177–189.

4. Denton, W., et al. (2000). A randomized trial of emotion-focused therapy for couples at a training clinic. *Journal of Marital and Family Therapy, 26*, 65–78.

5. Jencius, M. (2003). This thing called love (interview with Susan Johnson). *The Family Journal: Counseling and Therapy for Couples and Families, 11*, No. X, 1–8. Sage Publications.

6. Vatcher, C. & Bogo, M. (2001). The feminist/emotionally focused therapy practice model: An integrated approach for couple therapy. *Journal of Marital and Family Therapy, 27*, 69–84.

7. Protinsky, H., et al. (2001). Using eye movement desensitization and reprocessing to enhance treatment of couples. *Journal of Marital and Family Therapy, 27*, 157–165. (Includes a discussion of EFT.)

8. Bradley, B. (2001). An intimate look into emotionally focused therapy: An interview with Susan M. Johnson. *Marriage and Family—A Christian Journal, 4*, 117–124.

9. Keiley, M. (2001). Affect regulation and attachment focused treatment of a husband with OCD and his wife. *Journal of Couple and Relationship Therapy, 1*, 25–44.

10. Schwartz, R. & Johnson, S. M. (2000). Commentary: Does couple and family therapy have emotional intelligence? *Family Process, 39*, 29–34.

INDEX